GYPSY WITCH SPELL BOOK

CHARLES GODFREY LELAND

INNER LIGHT PUBLICATIONS

GYPSY WITCH SPELL BOOK

Originally Titled

Gypsy Sorcery and Fortune Telling

By Charles Godfrey Leland

ISBN 1 60611 062 4
EAN 978 1 60611 062 1

Science/New Age/Occult Technology

Timothy Green Beckley, Editor Director
Carol Rodriguez, Publisher's Assistant
Tim Swartz; Sean Casteel Assistant Editors

Free catalog from Inner Light Publications
Box 753, New Brunswick, NJ 08903

Visit our website at:
www.conspiracyjournal .com

CONTENTS

Gypsy Witch Spell Book

(1891)

Charles Godfrey Leland

Charles Godfrey Leland:
Trailblazer of Modern Maqickal Methods
By Dragonstar

THERE are a handful of people whose research over the years into the world of the esoteric has enriched our knowledge of the mysteries of this world and the next. One of these researchers, Charles Godfrey Leland, contributed so much to our present day understanding of magick and the people who practice it, that it is both mystifying and heartbreaking that little is remembered or attributed to this amazing man.

In the article "Charles Godfrey Leland: A Biography," Raven Grimassi writes that today, most people think that Gerald Gardner, who wrote about Wicca/Witchcraft in the mid-twentieth century, was the founder of modem Wicca/Witchcraft movement. However, according to Grimassi, over half a century earlier Charles Godfrey Leland wrote on many of the same topics later popularized by Gardner. For example, the theme of witches meeting at the time of the full moon, being nude, calling their ways The Old Religion, celebrating with ritual cakes and wine, and worshipping a god and goddess all appear in Leland's writings on Italian Witchcraft circa 1896.

In chapter four of his book ***Gypsy Sorcery & Fortune Telling,*** published in 1891, Leland makes the earliest connection between Wicca and modern Witchcraft:

> "...as for the English word witch, Anglo-Saxon Wicca, comes from a root implying wisdom..." Leland's footnote here reads: "Witch. Mediaeval English wicche, both masculine and feminine, a wizard, a witch. Anglo-Saxon wicca, masculine, wicce feminine. Wicca is a corruption of witga, commonly used as a short form of witega, a

prophet, seer, magician, or sorcerer. Anglo-Saxon witan, to see, allied to witan, to know..."

EARLY INVOLVEMENT IN ANCIENT MAGICKAL PRACTICES

Apparently, Leland's involvement in the world of magickal practices started almost from the very start of his life. Charles Godfrey Leland was born in Philadelphia, Pennsylvania on August 15, 1824. Immediately after his birth his nurse took the baby to the attic and performed a ritual, laying a Bible, a key, and knife on his breast, lighted candles, money and salt at his head. The nurse performed her ritual to ensure the child had a long life as a "scholar and a wizard." Her ritual was more successful than anyone would have guessed. If anything, Charles Leland was a product of his time. An adventurer, warrior, journalist and one who took delight in the arts. He lived to pursue the occult and, at times, he embellished his work to suit his concepts of what the world should be in his mind.

According to Leland's niece, Elizabeth Robins Pennell, who in 1906 published a two-volume biography about her uncle, Leland's mother claimed to have an ancestress who married into "sorcery." Leland writes in his memoirs: "my mother's opinion was that this was a very strong case of atavism, and that the mysterious ancestor had through the ages cropped out in me."

Leland traveled throughout Europe in 1869, and eventually settled in London. During this time he made a study of the Gypsy culture and over the course of time he won the confidence of a man named Matty Cooper, king of the Gypsies in England. Cooper personally taught Leland to speak Romany, the language of the Gypsies. It took many years before Leland was totally accepted by the Gypsies as one of their own. After extensive study of their mysteries, Leland went on to author two groundbreaking books about the Gypsies, establishing himself as an authority on the subject among the scholars of his time.

Charles Leland was certainly a product of his generation. The middle to late 19th century was exploding in new revelations about religion, spirituality and Mankind's place in the universe. The old viewpoints on organized religion were being severely challenged by not only new thoughts and ideas on science, but also by paranormal interests in the form of the newly emerging Spiritualism.

Men like Charles Leland were free to study the old pagan traditions of magical thought and practices and apply them to the modern emergence of spiritism and other forms of mystical beliefs. It is debatable if Leland would have been able to pursue his interest in the esoteric if he had been born at any other time in modern history.

Leland studied witchcraft and magick with the impersonal curiosity of the scholar. He did, however, carry amulets such as his "Black Stone of Voodoos" and small rocks he had found with holes in them. But, his actual practice of witchcraft was more than likely a state of mind rather than an actual physical act. He never indicated in his writings that he was a participant and, in fact, was almost totally silent concerning witchcraft in his Memoirs.

Leland believed that witchcraft was the "first stage" of shamanism, which he also believed to be the first and universal religion of the Paleolithic period. He considered voodoo to be a direct offshoot of this prehistoric and evil religion. "An immense amount of it [witchcraft-shamanism] in its vilest conceivable forms," he wrote, "still exists among negroes as Voodoo." Sorcery was, according to Leland's mind, the original religion. Magick, witchcraft and shamanism were the basis for Mankind's religious traditions and those traditions continue within modern society. It was Leland's desire to convince everyone that the romantic world of magick and mystery still existed as it always had.

We can thank Charles Leland for his efforts, for without him, this modern world would be a much duller place. Our society would be devoid of the rich myths and traditions that were necessary to enable Mankind's mind to grow and blossom out of the harsh, primitive beginnings that are now lost in antiquity.

Preface

THIS work contains a collection of the customs, usages, and ceremonies current among gypsies, as regards fortune-telling, witch-doctoring, love-philtering, and other sorcery, illustrated by many anecdotes and instances, taken either from works as yet very little known to the English reader or from personal experiences. Within a very few years, since Ethnology and Archæology have received a great inspiration, and much enlarged their scope through Folk-lore, everything relating to such subjects is studied with far greater interest and to much greater profit than was the case when they were cultivated in a languid, half-believing, half-sceptical spirit which was in reality rather one of mere romance than reason. Now that we seek with resolution to find the whole truth, be it based on materialism, spiritualism, or their identity, we are amazed to find that the realm of marvel and mystery, of wonder and poetry, connected with what we vaguely call "magic," far from being explained away or exploded, enlarges before us as we proceed, and that not into a mere cloudland, gorgeous land, but into a country of reality in which men of science who would once have disdained the mere thought thereof are beginning to stray. Hypnotism has really revealed far greater wonders than were ever established by the fascinatores of old or by mesmerists of more modern times. Memory, the basis of thought according to PLATO, which was once held to be a determined quantity, has been proved, (the word is not too bold), by recent physiology, to be practically infinite, and its perfect development to be identical with that of intellect, so that we now see plainly before us the power to perform much which was once regarded as miraculous. Not less evident is it that men of science or practical inventors, such as DARWIN, WALLACE, HUXLEY, TYNDALE, GALTON, JOULE, LOCKYER, and EDISON, have been or are all working in common with theosophists, spiritualists, Folk-lorists, and many more, not diversely but all towards a grand solution of the Unknown.

Therefore there is nothing whatever in the past relating to the influences which have swayed man, however strange, eccentric, superstitious, or even repulsive they may seem, which is not of great and constantly increasing value. And if we of the present time begin already to see this, how much more important will these facts be to the men of the future, who, by virtue of more widely extended knowledge and comparison, will be better able than we are to draw wise conclusions undreamed of now. But the chief conclusion for us is to collect as much as we can, while it is yet extant, of all the strange lore of the olden time, instead of wasting time in forming idle theories about it.

In a paper read before the Congrès des Traditions populaires in Paris, 1889, on the relations of gypsies to Folk-lore, I set forth my belief that these people have always been the humble priests of what is really the practical religion of all peasants and poor people; that is their magical ceremonies and medicine. Very few have any conception of the degree to which gypsies have been the colporteurs of what in Italy is called "the old faith," or witchcraft.

As regards the illustrative matter given, I am much indebted to DR. WLISLOCKI, who has probably had far more intimate personal experience of gypsies than any other learned man who ever lived, through our mutual friend, Dr. ANTHON HERRMANN, editor of the *Ethnologische Mitteilungen*, Budapest, who is also himself an accomplished Romany scholar and collector, and who has kindly taken a warm interest in this book, and greatly aided it. To these I may add Dr. FRIEDRICH S. KRAUSS, of Vienna, whose various works on the superstitions and Folk-lore of the South Slavonians—kindly presented by him to me—contain a vast mine of material, nearly all that of which he treats being common property between peasants and the Romany, as other sources abundantly indicate. With this there is also much which I collected personally among gypsies and fortune-tellers, and similar characters, it being true as regards this work and its main object, that there is much cognate or allied information which is quite as valuable as gypsy-lore itself, as all such subjects mutually explain one of the others.

Gypsies, as I have said, have done more than any race or class on the face of the earth to disseminate among the multitude a belief in fortune-telling, magical or sympathetic cures, amulets and such small sorceries as now find a place in Folk-lore. Their women have all pretended to possess occult power since prehistoric times. By the exercise of their wits they have actually acquired a certain art of reading character or even thought, which, however it be allied to deceit, is in a way true in itself, and well worth careful examination. MATTHEW ARNOLD has dwelt on it with rare skill in his poem of

"The Gypsy Scholar." Even deceit and imposture never held its own as a system for ages without some ground-work of truth, and that which upheld the structure of gypsy sorcery has never been very carefully examined. I trust that I have done this in a rational and philosophic spirit, and have also illustrated my remarks in a manner which will prove attractive to the general reader.

There are many good reasons for believing that the greatest portion of gypsy magic was brought by the Romany from the East or India. This is specially true as regards those now dwelling in Eastern Europe. And it is certainly interesting to observe that among these people there is still extant, on a very extended scale indeed, a Shamanism which seems to have come from the same Tartar-Altaic source which was found of yore among the Accadian-Babylonians, Etruscan races, and Indian hill-tribes. This, the religion of the drum and the demon as a disease-or devil doctoring-will be found fully illustrated in many curious ways in these pages. I believe that in describing it I have also shown how many fragments of this primitive religion, or cult, still exist, under very different names, in the most enlightened centres of civilization. And I respectfully submit to my reader, or critic, that I have in no instance, either in this or any other case, wandered from my real subject, and that the entire work forms a carefully considered and consistent whole. To perfect my title, I should perhaps have added a line or two to the effect that I have illustrated many of the gypsy sorceries by instances of Folk-lore drawn from other sources; but I believe that it is nowhere inappropriate, considering the subject as a whole. For those who would lay stress on omissions in my book, I would say that I have never intended or pretended to exhaust gypsy superstitions. I have not even given all that may be found in the works Of WLISLOCKI alone. I have, according to the limits of the book, cited so much as to fully illustrate the main subject already described, and this will be of more interest to the student of history than the details of gypsy chiromancy or more spells and charms than are necessary to explain the leading ideas.

What is wanted in the present state of Folk-lore, I here repeat, is collection from original sources, and material, that is from people and not merely from books. The critics we have—like the poor—always with us, and a century hence we shall doubtless have far better ones than those in whom we now rejoice—or sorrow. But material abides no time, and an immense quantity of it which is world-old perishes every day. For with general culture and intelligence we are killing all kinds of old faiths, with wonderful celerity. The time is near at hand when it will all be incredibly valuable, and then men will wish sorrowfully enough that there had been more collectors to accumulate and fewer critics to detract from their labours and to discourage them, For the collector must form his theory, or system great or small, good or bad, such as it is, in order to gather his facts; and then the theory is shattered by the critic and the collection made to appear ridiculous. And so collection ends.

There is another very curious reflection which has been ever present to my mind while writing this work, and which the reader will do well carefully to think out for himself. It is that the very first efforts of the human mind towards the supernatural were gloomy, strange, and wild; they were of witchcraft and sorcery, dead bodies, defilement, deviltry, and dirt. Men soon came to believe in the virtue of the repetition of certain rhymes or spells in connection with dead men's bones, hands, and other horrors or "relics." To this day this old religion exists exactly as it did of yore, wherever men are ignorant, stupid, criminal, or corresponding to their prehistoric ancestors. I myself have seen a dead man's hand for sale in Venice. According to DR. BLOCK, says a writer in *The St. James's Gazette*, January 16, 1889, the corpse-candle superstition is still firmly enshrined among the tenets of thieves all over Europe. In reality, according to The Standard, we know little about the strange thoughts which agitate the minds of the criminal classes. Their creeds are legends. Most of them are the children and grandchildren of thieves who have been brought up from their youth in the densest ignorance, and who, constantly at war with society, seek the aid of those powers of darkness in the dread efficacy of which they have an unshaken confidence.

"Fetishism of the rudest type, or what the mythologists have learned to call 'animism' is part and parcel of the robber's creed. A 'habit and repute' thief has always in his pocket, or somewhere about his person, a bit of coal, or chalk, or a 'lucky stone,' or an amulet of some sort on which he relies for safety in his hour of peril. Omens he firmly trusts in. Divination is regularly practised by him, as the occasional quarrels over the Bible and key, and the sieve and shears, testify. The supposed power of witches and wizards make many of them live in terror, and pay blackmail, and although they will lie almost without a motive, the ingenuity with which the most depraved criminal will try to evade 'kissing the book,' performing this rite with his thumb instead, is a curious instance of what may be termed perverted religious instincts. As for the fear of the evil eye, it is affirmed that most of the foreign thieves of London dread more being brought before a particular magistrate who has the reputation of being endowed with that fatal gift than of being summarily sentenced by any other whose judicial glare is less severe."

This is all true, but it tells only a small part of the truth. Not only is Fetish or Shamanism the real religion of criminals, but of vast numbers who are not suspected of it. There is not a town in England or in Europe in which witchcraft (its beginning) is not extensively practised, although this is done with a secrecy the success of which is of itself almost a miracle. We may erect churches and print books, but wherever the prehistoric man exists—and he is still to be found everywhere by millions—he will cling to the old witchcraft of his remote ancestors. Until you change his very nature, the only form in which he can realize supernaturalism will be by means of superstition, and the grossest superstition at that. Research and reflection have taught me that this sorcery is far more widely and deeply extended than any cultivated person dreams—instead of yielding to the progress of culture it seems to actually advance with it. Count ANGELO DE GUBERNATIS once remarked to one of the most distinguished English statesmen that there was in the country in Tuscany ten times as much heathenism as Christianity. The same remark was made to me by a fortune-teller in Florence. She explained what she meant. It was the vecchia religione—"the old religion"—not Christianity, but the dark and strange sorceries of the stregha, or witch, the compounding of magical medicine over which spells are muttered, the making love-philters, the cursing enemies, the removing the influence of other witches, and the manufacture of amulets in a manner prohibited by the Church.

It would seem as if, by some strange process, while advanced scientists are occupied in eliminating magic from religion, the coarser mind is actually busy in reducing it to religion alone. It has been educated sufficiently to perceive an analogy between dead man's hands and "relics" as working miracles, and as sorcery is more entertaining than religion, and has, moreover, the charm of secrecy, the prehistoric man, who is still with us, prefers the former. Because certain forms of this sorcery are no longer found among the educated classes we think that superstition no longer exists; but though we no longer burn witches or believe in fairies, it is a fact that of a kind and fashion proportionate to our advanced culture, it is, with a very few exceptions, as prevalent as ever. Very few persons indeed have ever given this subject the attention which it merits, for it is simply idle to speculate on the possibility of cultivating or sympathizing with the lowest orders without really understanding it in all its higher forms. And I venture to say that, as regards a literal and truthful knowledge of its forms and practices, this work will prove to be a contribution to the subject not without value.

I have, in fact, done my best to set forth in it a very singular truth which is of great importance to every one who takes any real interest in social science, or the advance of intelligence. It is that while almost everybody who contributes to general literature, be it books of travel or articles in journals, has ever and anon something clever to say about superstition among the lower orders at home or abroad, be it in remote country places or in the mountains of Italy, with the usual cry of "Would it be believed—in the nineteenth century?" &c.; it still remains true that the amount of belief in magic—call it by what name we will—in the world is just as great as ever it was. And here I would quote with approbation a passage from "***The Conditions for the Survival of Archaic Customs***," by G. L. Gomme, in *The Archæological Review* of January, 1890:

> "If Folk-lore has done nothing else up to this date it has demonstrated that civilization, under many of its phases, while elevating the governing class of a nation, and thereby no doubt elevating the nation, does not always reach the lowest or even the lower strata of the population. As Sir Arthur Mitchell puts it, 'There is always a going up of some and a going down of others,' and it is more than probable that just as the going up of the few is in one certain direction, along certain well-ascertained lines of improvement or development, so the going down of the many is in an equally well-ascertained line of degradation or backwardness The upward march is always towards political improvement, carrying with it social development; the downward march is always towards social degradation, carrying with it political backwardness. It seems difficult indeed to believe that monarchs like Alfred, Eadward, William, and Edward, could have had within their Christianized kingdom groups of people whose status was still that of savagery; it seems difficult to believe that Raleigh and Spenser actually beheld specimens of the Irish savage; it seems impossible to read Kemble and Green and Freeman and yet to understand that they are speaking only of the advanced guard of the English nation, not of the backward races within the boundary of its island home. The student of archaic custom has, however, to meet these difficulties, and it seems necessary, therefore, to try and arrive at some idea as to what the period of savagery in these islands really means."

Which is a question that very few can answer. There is to be found in almost every cheap book, or "penny dreadful" and newspaper shop in Great Britain and America, for sale at a very low price a ***Book of Fate***—or something equivalent to it, for the name of these works is legion—and one publisher advertises that he has nearly thirty of them, or at least such books with different titles. In my copy there are twenty-five pages of incantations, charms, and spells, every one of them every whit as "superstitious" as any of the gypsy ceremonies set forth in this volume. I am convinced, from much inquiry, that next to the Bible and the Almanac there is no one book which is so much disseminated among the million as the fortune-teller, in some form or other. 1 That is to say, there are, numerically, many millions more of believers in such small sorcery now in Great Britain than there were centuries ago, for, be it remembered, the superstitions of the masses were always petty ones, like those of the fate-books; it was only the aristocracy who consulted Cornelius Agrippa, and could afford la haute magic. We may call it by other names, but fry, boil, roast, powder or perfume it as we will, the old faith in the supernatural and in occult means of getting at it still exists in one form or another—the parable or moral of most frequent occurrence in it being that of the Mote and the Beam, of the real and full meaning of which I can only reply in the ever-recurring refrain of the Edda: Understand ye this—or what?

---

[1] I was once myself made to contribute, involuntarily, to this kind of literature. Forty years ago I published a Folk-lore book entitled "The Poetry and Mystery of Dreams," in which the explanations of dreams, as given by ASTRAMPSYCHIUS, ARTEMIDORUS, and other ancient oneirologists, were illustrated by passages from many poets and popular ballads, showing how widely the ancient symbolism had extended. A few years ago I found that some ingenious literary hack had taken my work (without credit), and, omitting what would not be understood by servant girls, had made of it a common sixpenny dream-book.

CHAPTER I

The Origin of Witchcraft, Shamanism, And Sorcery – Vindictive And Mischievous Magic

AS their peculiar perfume is the chief association with spices, so sorcery is allied in every memory to gypsies. And as it has not escaped many poets that there is something more strangely sweet and mysterious in the scent of cloves than in that of flowers, so the attribute of inherited magic power adds to the romance of these picturesque wanderers. Both the spices and the Romany come from the far East—the fatherland of divination and enchantment. The latter have been traced with tolerable accuracy, If we admit their affinity with the Indian Dom and Domar, back to the threshold of history, or well-nigh into prehistoric times, and in all ages they, or their women, have been engaged, as if by elvish instinct, in selling enchant. merits, peddling prophecies and palmistry, and dealing with the devil generally ill a small retail way. As it was of old so it is to-day—

Ki shan i Romani—
Adoi san' i chov'hani.

Wherever gypsies go,
There the witches are, we know.

It is no great problem ill ethnology or anthropology as to how gypsies became fortune-tellers. We may find a very curious illustration of it in the wren. This is apparently as humble, modest, prosaic little fowl as exists, and as far from mystery and wickedness as an old hen. But the ornithologists of the olden time, and the myth-makers, and the gypsies who lurked and lived in the forest, knew better. They saw how this bright-eyed, strange little creature in her elvish way slipped in and out of hollow trees and wood shade into sunlight, and anon was gone, no man knew whither, and so they knew that it was an uncanny creature, and told wonderful tales of its deeds in human form, and to-day it is called by gypsies in Germany, as in England, the witch-bird, or more briefly, chorihani, "the witch." Just so the gypsies themselves, with their glittering Indian eyes, slipping like the wren in and out of the shadow of the Unknown, and anon away and invisible, won for themselves the name which now they wear. Wherever Shamanism, or the sorcery which is based on exorcising or commanding spirits, exists, its professors from leading strange lives, or from solitude or wandering, become strange and wild-looking. When men have this appearance people associate with it mysterious power. This is the case in Tartary, Africa, among the Eskimo, Lapps, or Red Indians, with all of whom the sorcerer, voodoo or medaolin, has the eye of the "fascinator," glittering and cold as that of a serpent. So the gypsies, from the mere fact of being wanderers and out-of-doors livers in wild places, became wild-looking, and when asked if they did not associate with the devils who dwell in the desert places, admitted the soft impeachment, and being further questioned as to whether their friends the devils, fairies, elves, and goblins had not taught them how to tell the future, they pleaded guilty, and finding that it paid well, went to work in their small way to improve their "science," and particularly their pecuniary resources. It was an easy calling; it required no property or properties, neither capital nor capitol, shiners nor shrines, wherein to work the oracle. And as I believe that a company of children left entirely to themselves would form and grow up with a language which in a very few years would be spoken fluently, 1 so I am certain that the shades of night, and fear, pain, and lightning and mystery would produce in the same time conceptions of dreaded beings, resulting first in demonology and then in the fancied art of driving devils away. For out of my own childish experiences and memories I retain with absolute accuracy material enough to declare that without any aid from other people the youthful mind forms for itself strange and seemingly supernatural phenomena. A tree or bush waving in the night breeze by moonlight is perhaps mistaken for a great man, the mere repetition of the sight or of its memory make it a personal reality. Once when I was a child powerful doses of quinine caused a peculiar throb in my ear which I for some time believed was the sound of somebody continually walking upstairs. Very young children sometimes imagine invisible playmates or companions talk with them, and actually believe that the unseen talk to them in return. I myself knew a small boy who had, as he sincerely believed, such a companion, whom he called Bill, and when he could not understand his lessons he consulted the mysterious William, who explained them to him. There are children who, by the voluntary or involuntary exercise of visual perception or volitional eye-memory, 2 reproduce or create images which they imagine to be real, and this faculty is much commoner than is supposed. In fact I believe that where it exists in most remarkable degrees the adults to whom the children describe their visions dismiss them as "fancies" or falsehoods. Even in the very extraordinary cases recorded by Professor HALE, in which little children formed for themselves spontaneously a language in which they conversed fluently, neither their parents nor anybody else appears to have taken the least interest in the matter. However, the fact being that babes can form for themselves supernatural conceptions and embryo mythologies, and as they always do attribute to strange or terrible-looking persons power which the latter do not possess, it is easy, without going further, to understand why a wild Indian gypsy, with eyes like a demon when excited, and unearthly-looking at his calmest, should have been supposed to be a sorcerer by credulous child-like villagers. All of this I believe might have taken place, or really did take place, in the very dawn of man's existence as a rational creature—that as soon as "the frontal convolution of the brain which monkeys do not possess," had begun with the "genial tubercule," essential to language, to develop itself, then also certain other convolutions and tubercules, not as yet discovered, but which ad interim I will call "the ghost-making," began to act. "Genial," they certainly were not—little joy and much sorrow has man got out of his spectro-facient apparatus—perhaps if it and talk are correlative he might as well, many a time, have been better off if he were dumb.

So out of the earliest time, in the very two o'clock of a misty morning in history, man came forth believing in non-existent terrors and evils as soon as he could talk, and talking about them as fast as he formed them. Long before the conception of anything good or beneficent, or of a Heavenly Father or benevolent angels came to him, he was scared with nightmares and spirits of death and darkness, hell, hunger, torture, and terror. We all know how difficult it is for many people when some one dies out of a household to get over the involuntary feeling that we shall unexpectedly meet the departed in the usual haunts. In almost every family there is a record how some one has "heard a voice they cannot hear," or the dead speaking in the familiar tones. Hence the belief in ghosts, as soon as men began to care for death at all, or to miss those who had gone. So first of all came terrors and spectres, or revenants, and from setting out food for the latter. which was the most obvious and childlike manner to please them, grew sacrifices to evil spirits, and finally the whole system of sacrifice in all its elaboration.

It may therefore be concluded that as soon as man began to think and speak and fear the mysterious, he also began to appease ghosts and bugbears by sacrifices. Then there sprung up at once—quite as early—the magus, or the cleverer man, who had the wit to do the sacrificing and eat the meats sacrificed, and explain that he had arranged it all privately with the dead and the devils. He knew all about them, and he could drive them away. This was the Shaman. He seems to have had a Tartar-Mongol-mongrel-Turanian origin, somewhere in Central Asia, and to have spread with his magic drum, and songs, and stinking smoke, exorcising his fiends all over the face of the earth, even as his descendant, General Booth, with his "devil-drivers" is doing at the present day. But the earliest authentic records of Shamanism are to be found in the Accadian, proto-Chaldæan and Babylon records. According to it all diseases whatever, as well as all disasters, were directly the work of evil spirits, which were to be driven away by songs of exorcism, burning of perfumes or evil-smelling drugs, and performing ceremonies, many of which, with scraps of the exorcisms are found in familiar use here and there at the present day. Most important of all in it was the extraordinary influence of the Shaman himself on his patient, for he made the one acted on sleep or wake, freed him from many apparently dire disorders in a minute, among others of epilepsies which were believed to be caused by devils dwelling in man—the nearest and latest explanation of which magic power is given in that very remarkable book, "***Psycho-Therapeutics, or Treatment by Sleep and Suggestion***," by C. LLOYD TUCKEY, M.D. (London: Bailliere and Co., 1889), which I commend to all persons interested in ethnology as casting light on some of the most interesting and perplexing problems of humanity, and especially of "magic."

It would seem, at least among the Laplanders, Finns, Eskimo, and Red Indians, that the first stage of Shamanism was a very horrible witchcraft, practised chiefly by women, in which attempts were made to conciliate the evil spirits; the means employed embracing everything which could revolt and startle barbarous men. Thus fragments of dead bodies and poison, and unheard-of terrors and crimes formed its basis. I think it very probable that this was the primitive religion among savages everywhere. An immense amount of it in its vilest conceivable forms still exists among negroes as Voodoo.

After a time this primitive witchcraft or voodooism had its reformers—probably brave and shrewd men, who conjectured that the powers of evil might be "exploited" to advantage. There is great confusion and little knowledge as yet as regards primitive man, but till we know better we may roughly assume that witch-voodooism was the religion of the people of the paleolithic period, if they could talk at all, since language is denied to the men of the Neanderthal, Canstadt, Egnisheim, and Podhava type. All that we can declare with some certainty is that we find the advanced Shamanism the religion of the early Turanian races, among whose descendants, and other people allied to them, it exists to this day. The grandest incident in the history of humanity is the appearance of the Man of Cromagnon. He it was who founded what M. DE QUATREFAGES calls "a magnificent race," probably one which speedily developed a high civilization, and a refined religion. But the old Shamanism with its amulets, exorcisms, and smoke, its noises, more or less musical, of drums and enchanted bells, and its main belief that all the ills of life came from the action of evil spirits, was deeply based among the inferior races and the inferior scions of the Cromagnon stock clung to it in forms more or less modified. just as the earlier witchcraft, or the worship and conciliation of evil, overlapped in many places the newer Shamanism, so the latter overlapped the beautiful Nature-worship of the early Aryans, the stately monotheism of the Shemites, and the other more advanced or ingenious developments of the idea of a creative cause. There are, in fact, even among us now, minds to whom Shamanism or even witchcraft is deeply or innately adapted by nature, and there are hundred of millions who, while professing a higher and purer doctrine, cling to its forms or essentials, believing that because the apparatus is called by a different name it is in no respect whatever the same thing. Finally there are men who, with no logical belief whatever in any kind of supernaturalism, study it, and love it, and are moved by it, owing to its endless associations, with poetry, art, and all the legends of infancy or youth. HEINE was not in his reasoning moments anything more or less than a strict Deist or Monotheist, but all the dreams and spectres, fairies and goblins, whether of the Middle Ages or the Talmud, were inexpressibly dear to him, and they move like myriad motes through the sunshine of his poetry and prose, often causing long rays when there were bars at the window—like that on which the saint hung his cloak. It is probable or certain that Shamanism (or that into which it has very naturally developed) will influence all mankind, until science, by absorbing man's love of the marvellous in stupendous discoveries shall so put to shame the old thaumaturgy, or wonder-working, that the latter will seem poor and childish. In all the "Arabian Nights" there is nothing more marvellous than the new idea that voices and sounds may be laid aside like real books, and made to speak and sing again years afterwards. And in all of that vast repertory of occult lore, "Isis Unveiled," there is nothing so wonderful as the simple truth that every child may be educated to possess an infinitely developed memory of words, sights, sounds, and ideas, allied to incredible quickness of perception and practice of the constructive faculties. These, with the vast fields of adjusting improved social relations and reforms—all of which in a certain way opens dazzling vistas of a certain kind of enchantment or brilliant hope—will go fast and far to change the old romance to a radically different state of feeling and association.

It is coming—let it come! Doubtless there was an awful romance of darkness about the old witchcraft which caused its worshippers to declare that the new lights of Shamanism could never dissipate it. just so many millions of educated people at present cannot be brought to understand that all things to which they are used are not based on immutable laws of nature, and must needs be eternal. They will find it hard to comprehend that there can ever be any kind of poetry, art, or sentiment, utterly different from that to which they and their ancestors have been accustomed. Yet it is clear and plain before them, this New Era, looking them directly in the face, about to usher in a reformation compared to which all the reformations and revolutions and new religions which the world has ever seen were as nothing; and the children are born who will see more than the beginning of it.

In the next chapter I will examine the Shamanic spells and charms still used among certain gypsies. For, be it observed, all the gypsy magic and sorcery here described is purely Shamanic—that is to say, of the most primitive Tartar type—and it is the more interesting as having preserved—from prehistoric times many of the most marked characteristics of the world's first magic or religion. It treats every disease, disorder, trouble, or affliction as the work of an evil spirit; it attempts to banish these influences by the aid of ceremonies, many of which, by the disgusting and singular nature of the ingredients employed, show the lingering influences of the black witchcraft which preceded Shamanism; and it invokes favourable supernatural agencies, such as the spirits of the air and Mashmurdalo', the giant of the forests. In addition to this there will be found to be clearly and unmistakably associated with all their usages, symbols and things nearly connected with much which is to be found in Greek, Roman, and Indian mythology or symbolism. Now whether this was drawn from "classic" sources, or whether all came from some ancient and obscure origin, cannot now be accurately determined. But it certainly cannot be denied that Folk-lore of this kind casts a great deal of light on the early history of mankind, and the gradual unfolding or evolution of religion and of mind, and that, if intelligently studied, this of the gypsies is as important as any chapter in the grand work.

The gypsies came, historically speaking, very recently from India. It has not been so carefully observed as it might that all Indians are not of the religion of Brahma, much less of Buddha or of Mahommed, and that among the lower castes, the primæval Altaic Shamanism, with even earlier witchcraft, still holds its own. Witchcraft, or Voodoo, or Obi, relies greatly on poisoning for its magic, and the first gypsies were said to poison unscrupulously. Even to this day there is but one word with them as with many Hindoos for both medicine and poison—id est drab. How exactly this form of witchcraft and Shamanism exists today in India appears from the following extract from The St. James's Gazette, September 8, 1888:

THE HINDOO PRIEST

In India, the jadoo-wallah, or exorcist, thrives apace; and no wonder, for is not the lower-caste Hindoo community bhut, or demon-ridden? Every village, graveyard, burning-ghat, has its special bhut or bhuts; and the jadoo-wallah is the earthly mediator between their bhutships and the common folk. The exorcist is usually the spiritual adviser to the population of a low-caste village, and is known as a gooroo, or priest: that is to say, he professes to hold commune with the spirits of defunct Hindoos which have qualified for their unique position in the other world—by their iniquity in this one, perhaps. Every Hindoo has a guardian bhut that requires propitiating, and the gooroo is the medium.

Amongst the Jaiswars and other low-caste Hindoos, caste is regulated by carnal pice, and a man is distinguished amongst them by a regulated monetary scale. One person may be a 14-anna caste man while another may only be a 12-anna caste man. Does the 12-anna caste man wish to supersede the 14-anna caste man, then he consults the gooroo, who will, in consideration of a certain contribution, promote him to a higher-caste grade. A moneyed man having qualms about his future state should join the Jaiswars, where at least he would have an opportunity of utilizing his spare cash for the good of his soul. The average gooroo will be only too glad to procure him everlasting glory for a matter of a few rupees.

The gooroo, then, serves as regulator of the lower-caste Hindoo, system. But it is our intention to exhibit him in his peculiar position of exorcist-general to the people. This will perhaps be best explained by an account of the case of one Kaloo. Kaloo was a grass-cutter, and had been offended by Kasi, a brother grass-cutter. Kasi, it appears, had stolen Kaloo's quilt one night during his temporary absence at a neighbouring liquor-shop. Kaloo, on his return, finding his quilt gone, raised the hue-and-cry; and Mooloo, the village policeman, traced the robbery to Kasi's hut. Yet, in spite of this damning proof, the village panchayet, or bench of magistrates, decided that, as Kaloo could not swear to the exact colour of his lost quilt—Kaloo was colour-blind—it could not possibly be his. Anyhow, Kaloo kept Kasi in view and hit upon a plan to do him a grievous bodily injury. Scraping together a few rupees, he went to the village gooroo and promised that worthy a reward if he would only exorcise the bhuts and get them to "make Kasi's liver bad." The gooroo, in consideration of five rupees cash, promised compliance. So that night we find the gooroo busy with sandal-wood and pig's blood propitiating the neighbouring bhuts. Needless to say that Kasi had in a very short space of time all the symptoms of liver complaint. Whether the bhuts gave Kasi a bad liver or the gooroo gave him a few doses of poison is a question. Anyhow, Kasi soon died. Another case in point is that of Akuti. Akuti was a retired courtesan who had long plied a profitable trade in the city. We find her, however, at her native village of Ramghur, the wife of one Balu. Balu soon got tired of his Akuti, and longed for the contents of her strong box wherein she kept her rupees, bracelets, nose-rings, and other valuables. This was a rather awkward matter for Balu, for Akuti was still in the prime of life. Balu accordingly visits the gooroo and wants Akuti's liver made bad. "Nothing easier," says the gooroo: "five rupees." Balu has reckoned without his host, however: for the gooroo, as general spiritual adviser to the Ramghur community, visits Akuti and tells her of Balu's little scheme. Naturally Balu's liver is soon in a decline, for Akuti's ten rupees were put in the opposite side of the gooroo's scales.

Knaves of the gooroo genus flourish in India, and when their disposition is vicious the damage they can do is appalling. That these priests exist and do such things as I have illustrated is beyond question. Ask any native of India his views on the bhut question, and he will tell you that there are such things, and, further, that the gooroo is the only one able to lay them, so to speak. According to the low-caste Hindoo, the bhut is a spiteful creature which requires constant supplies of liquor and pork; otherwise it will wreak its vengeance on the forgetful votary who neglects the supply. A strange idea, too, is this of pork being pleasing to the bhuts; but when it is remembered that the Jaiswars, Chamars, and other low-caste Hindoos are inordinately fond of that meat themselves, they are right in supposing pig to be the favourite dish of the bhuts, who, after all, are but the departed spirits of their own people. Naturally bhai (brother) Kaloo, or bahin (sister, English gypsy pen) Muti, the quondam grass-cutter and courtesan of Ramghur village, who in this life liked nothing better than a piece of bacon and a dram of spirits, will, in their state of bhuthood hanker after those things still. Acting on these notions of the people, the gooroo lives and thrives exceedingly.

Yet of all this there is nothing "Hindoo," nothing of the Vedas. It is all pre-Aryan, devil-worshipping, poisoning, and Turanian; and it is exactly like voodooing in Philadelphia or any other city in America. It is the old faith which came before all, which existed through and under Brahminism, Buddhism, and Mahommedanism, and which, as is well known, has cropped out again and flourishes vigorously under British toleration. And this is the faith which forms the basis of European gypsy sorcery, as it did of yore that of the Chaldæan and Etrurian, which still survive in the witchcraft of the Tuscan Romagna. Every gypsy who came to Europe a few centuries ago set up as a gooroo, and did his sorceries after the same antique fashion. Even to-day it is much the same, but with far less crime. But the bhut or malignant spirit is, under other names, still believed, in, still doctored by gypsies with herbs and smoke, and "be rhymed like an Irish rat," and conjured into holes bored in trees, and wafted away into running streams, and naively implored to "go where he is wanted," to where he was nursed, and to no longer bother honest folk who are tired of him. And for all this the confiding villager must pay the gypsy wise-woman "so much monies"—as it was in the beginning and is now in good faith among millions in Europe who are in a much better class of society. And from this point of view I venture to say that there is not a charm or spell set down in this work or extant which will not be deeply interesting to every sincere student of the history of culture. Let me, however, say in this beginning once for all that I have only given specimens sufficient to illustrate my views, for my prescribed limits quite forbid the introduction of all the gypsy cures, spells, &c., which I have collected.

Vide an extremely interesting paper on "The Origin of Languages and the Antiquity of Speaking Man," by Horatio Hale. ["Proceedings of the American Association for the Advancement of Science," vol. xxv.] As I had, owing to studies for many years of baby-talk and jargons, long ago arrived at Mr. Hale's conclusions, I was astonished to learn that they have been so recently formed by anybody.

Vide "Practical Education," by C. G. Leland (London: Whittaker and Co., 1888), in which this faculty is fully discussed, pp. 184-213.

K.W.

CHAPTER II

Charms And Conjurations To Cure The Disorders Of Grown People Hungarian Gypsy Magic

THOUGH not liable to many disorders, the gypsies in Eastern Europe, from their wandering, out-of-doors life, and camping by marshes and pools where there is malaria, suffer a great deal from fevers, which in their simple system of medicine are divided into the shilale—i.e., chills or cold—and the tate shilalyi, "hot-cold," or fever and ague. For the former, the following remedy is applied: Three lungs and three livers, of frogs are dried and powdered and drunk in spirits, after which the sick man or woman says:

"C(uckerdya pal m're per
C(áven save miseçe!
C(uckerdya pal m're per
Den miseçeske drom odry prejiál!

"Frogs in my belly
Devour what is bad
Frogs in my belly
Show the evil the way out!"

By "the evil" is understood evil spirits. According to the old Shamanic belief, which was the primæval religion of all mankind, every disease is caused by an evil spirit which enters the body and can only be driven out by magic. We have abundant traces of this left in our highest civilization and religion among people who gravely attribute every evil to the devil instead of the unavoidable antagonisms of nature. Nothing is more apparent in the New Testament than that all diseases were anciently regarded as coming from devils, or evil occult, spiritual influences, their negative or cure being holiness in some form. This the Jews, if they did not learn it from the Assyrians in the first place, had certainly studied deeply in Babylon, where it formed the great national cult. "It was the devil put it into my head," says the criminal; and there is not a point of this old sorcery which is not earnestly and seriously advocated by the Roman Catholic Church and the preachers of the Salvation Army. Among the American Red Indians the idea of evil spirits is carried to logical extremes. If a pen drops from our fingers, or a penny rolls from our grasp, the former of course falls on our new white dress, while the latter nine times out of ten goes directly to the nearest grating, or crack or rat-hole. I aver that it is literally true, if I ever search for a letter or paper it is almost always at the bottom of the rest, while ink-wipers and pens seem to be endowed with more than mere instinct or reason—they manifest genius in concealing themselves. The Indians having observed this have come to the conclusion that it is all the work of certain busy little mischievous goblins, in which I, to a certain extent, agree with them, holding, however, that the dwelling-place of these devilkins, is in our own brain. What are our dreams but the action of our other mind, or a second Me in my brain? Certainly it is with no will or effort, or act of mine, that I go through a diabolical torturing nightmare, or a dreadful dream, whose elaborate and subtle construction betrays very often more ingenuity than I in my waking hours possess. I have had philosophical and literary dreams, the outlines of which I have often remembered waking, which far transcended anything of the kind which I could ever hope to write. The maker of all this is not I or my will, and he is never about, or on hand, when I am self-conscious. But in the inadvertent moments of oblivion, while writing, or while performing any act, this other I, or I's, (for there may be a multitude of them for aught I know) step in and tease—even as they do in dreams. Now the distinction between this of subjective demons acting objectively, and objective or outside spirits, is really too fine to be seen even by a Darwinian-Carpenterian-Häeckelite, and therefore one need not be amazed that PIEL SABADIS or TOMAQUAH, of the Passamaquoddy tribe, or OBEAH GUMBO of New Orleans, should, with these experiences, jump at ghosts and "gobblers," is not to be wondered at; still less that they should do something to conciliate or compel these haunting terrors, or "buggs," as they were once called—whence bogeys. It is a fact that if one's ink-wipers get into the habit of hiding all we have to do is to deliberately destroy them and get others, or at least watch them carefully, and they will soon be cured of wandering. On the other hand, sacrifices to conciliate and please naturally occur, and the more expensive these are the better are they supposed to be. And as human beings were of old the most valuable property, they were as naturally supposed to be most acceptable to the gods, or, by the monotheists, to God. A West Indian voodoo on being reproached for human sacrifices to the serpent, and for eating the bodies slain, replied, "Do you believe that the Son of God was sacrificed to save man, and do you not eat what your priests say is His very body?" So difficult is it to draw distinctions between that which is spiritual and the mockeries which appear to be such!

The scape-goat, or sufferer, who is martyred that many may escape—or in other words, the unfortunate minority—is a natural result of sacrifice. There is a curious trace of it in Hungarian Gypsy Shamanism. On Easter Monday they make a wooden box or receptacle which is called the bìcáben, pronounced like the English gypsy word bitchapen and meaning the same, that is—a sending, a thing sent or gift. In this, at the bottom, are two sticks across, "as in a cradle," and on these are laid herbs and other fetish stuff which every one touches with the finger; then the whole is enveloped in a winding of white and red wool, and carried by the oldest person of the tribe from tent to tent; after which it is borne to the next running stream and left there, after every one has spat upon it. By doing this they think that all the diseases and disorders which would have befallen them during the coming year are conjured into the box. But woe to him who shall find the box and open it, instead of throwing it at once into the stream! All the diseases exorcised by the gypsy band will fall upon him and his in full measure.

It would be an interesting question to know how many good people there are, let us say in London, who, if they had all opportunity to work off all their colds, gouts, scarlet-fevers, tooth- head- and stomach-aches, with the consequent doctors' bills, or all suffering and expenses, on some other family by means of secret sorcery, would or would not "try it on"? It is curious to observe the resemblance of the gypsy ceremony., with its box full of mischief, and the Jewish goat; not forgetting the red wool handed down from heathen sacrifice and sorcery of old. In the Bible white wool is the symbol of purification (Isaiah i. 18). The feet of the statues of the gods were enveloped in wool—Dü laneos habent pedes—to signify that they are slow to avenge, if sure. It is altogether an interesting object, this gypsy casket, and one would like to know what all the channels were through which the magic ran ere it carne to them.

Another cure against the fever is to go to a running stream and cast pieces of wood nine times backwards into the running water, repeating the rhymes:

"Shilályi prejiá,
Páñori me tut 'dáv!
Náñi me tut kámáv
Andakode prejiá,

Odoy tut cuciden,
Odoy tut ferinen,
Odoy tut may kámen
Mashurdalo sastyár!"

Fever go away from me,
I give it, water, unto thee
Unto me thou art not dear,
Therefore go away from here
To where they nursed thee,
Where they shelter thee,
Where they love thee,
Mashurdalo—help!"

This is a very remarkable invocation which takes us into true heathenism. Mâshurdálo, or, correctly speaking, Mâshmurdálo (it would be Mâsmérdo in English gypsy), means meat-killer. He is a sylvan giant—he has his hold by wodo and woldc as outlawes wont to do, in faraway forests and lonely rocky places, where he lurks to catch beast and men in order to devour them. It is needless to say to those who are aware that the taste of white people's flesh is like that of very superior chicken, and a negro's something much better than grouse, that Mâshmurdálo prefers, like a simple, unsophisticated savage as he is, men to animals.

Like the German peasant who remarked, "It's all meat, anyhow," when he found a mouse in his soup, Mâshmurdálo is not particular. He is the guardian of great treasures; like most men in the "advance business" he knows where the "money" is to be found—unlike them he is remarkably stupid, and can be easily cheated of his valuables. But if anybody does this Morgante a service he is very grateful, and aids his benefactor either with a loan or with his enormous strength. In many respects he bears a remarkable resemblance to two giants in the American Algonkin mythology, especially to At-was-kenni ges—the Spirit of the Forest—who is equally powerful, good-natured, and stupid, and to the Chenoo, who is a cannibal giant and yet grateful to friends, and also to several Hindoo gods. The gypsies have here evidently fused several Oriental beings into one., This is a process which occurs in the decline of mythologies as in languages. In the infancy of a speech, as in its old age, many words expressing different ideas, but which sound somewhat alike, become a single term. In English gypsy I have found as many as eight or ten Hindi words thus concentrated into one.

Another cure for a fever. The sufferer goes in the forest and finds a young tree. When the first rays of the rising sun fall on it the patient shakes it with all his might and exclaims:

> "Shilályi, shilályi prejia
> Káthe tu beshá, káthe tu beshá!
>
> "Fever, fever, go away!
> Here shalt thou stay. Here shalt thou stay!"

It is here plain that the shaking the sapling is intended to transfer the shakes, as the chill and shuddering of the fever is called in America, to the tree.

"Then the fever passes into the tree." Perhaps it was in this way that the aspen learned to tremble. But among the gypsies in the south of Hungary, among whom the vaccination or inoculation of trees is greatly the fashion, a hole is bored into the wood, into which the patient spits thrice, repeats the spell, and then stops the hole with a plug. The boring of holes in trees or transferring illness to them is also practised without formulas of speech. Thus, if while a man is lying down or sitting in the spring he hears the song of the cuckoo he believes that he will be ill all the time for a year to come, especially with fevers, unless he goes. nine times to a tree, bores a hole in it, and spits into it three times. Then he is safe. In German mythology "the cuckoo is a bird which brings bad luck" (FRIEDRICH), and the inhabitants of Haiterbach were so persuaded of this that they introduced a prayer against it into their church service, whence they got the name of cuckoos (WOLF, "***Zeitschrift für Deutsche Myth***," Vol. i. p. 440). It announces to men the infidelity of wives, and tells listeners how many years they have to live.

It is possible that this is a relic of an old form of sacrifice, or proof that the idea occurs to all men of thus making a casket of a tree. The occasional discovery of stone axe-heads in very old trees in America renders this probable. And where the wood grows up and encloses the object it would very rarely happen that it would ever be discovered. It should be added to the previous instance that when they have closed the hole, the Transylvanian gypsies eat some of the bark of the next tree.

Another cure for fever is effected by going in the morning before sunrise to the bank of a stream, and digging a hole with some object—for instance, a knife—which has never been used. Into this hole the patient makes water, then fills up the hole, saying:

"Shilályi ác(kathe
Náává kiyá mánge!
Sutyárá andré c(ik!
Ává kiyá mánge
Káná káthe ná hin páñi!"

"Fever stay here!
Do not come to me!
Dry up in dust,
Come unto me
When no water is here."

Dr. WLISLOCKI translates this last line, "When there is no more water in the river," which is certainly what is meant. "While water runs or grass grows," &c. is a formula common to ail countries. Another cure for fever is this: the patient must take a kreutzer, an egg, and a handful of salt, and before sunrise go with them to a cross-road, throw them away backwards, and repeat:

"Káná ádálá kiyá mánge áven
Âvâ tu kiyâ mánge shilályi."

"When these things again I see,
Fever then return to me."

Or literally, "When these things to me come." For the next three days the invalid must not touch money, eggs, or salt. There is an old MS. collection of English charms and ceremonies, professedly of "black witchcraft," in which we are told that if a girl will walk stark-naked by the light of the full moon round a field or a house, and cast behind her at every step a handful of salt, she will get the lover whom she desires. Salt, says MORESINUS, was sacred to the infernal deities, and it was a symbol of the soul, or of life, because it preserved the body while in it (PITISCUS, "Leg. Ant. Rom." ii. p. 675). The devil never eats salt. Once there was in Germany a peasant who had a witch for a wife, and the devil invited them to supper. But all the dishes were without any seasoning, and the peasant, despite all nudges and hints to hold his tongue kept crying for salt. And when it was brought and he said, "Thank God, here is salt at last!" the whole Spuck, or ghastly scene, vanished (HORST, "***Dæmonomagie***," Frankfurt, 1818, vol. ii. p. 213). For a great deal of further information and symbolism on and of salt, including all the views of the ancient Rabbis and modern rationalists on the subject of Lot's wife, the reader may consult "***Symbolik und Mythologie der Natur***," by J. B. FRIEDRICH, Wurzburg, 1859: "Salt is put into love-philtres and charms to ensure the duration of an attachment; in some Eastern countries it is carried in a little bag as an amulet to preserve health."

Another cure for fever. The patient must drink, from a new jug, water from three brooks, and after every drink throw into the running stream a handful of salt. Then he must make water into the first and say:

"Káthe hin t'ro sherro!"

"Here is thy head!"

At the second he repeats the sacred ceremony and murmurs

"Káthe hin t'ro perá!"

"Here is thy belly!"

And again at the third he exclaims:

"Te kathehin t're punrá.
Já átunci ándre páñi!"

"And here are thy feet.
Go now into the water!"

But while passing from one stream to another he must not look back once, for then he might behold the dread demon of the fever which follows him, neither must he open his mouth, except while uttering the charm, for then the fever would at once enter his body again through the portal thus left unclosed. This walking on in apprehension of beholding the ugly spectre will recall to the reader a passage in the "Ancient Mariner," of the man who walks in fear and dread,

"Nor turns around his head,
For well he knows a frightful fiend
Doth close behind him tread."

The wise wives among the gypsies in Hungary have many kinds of miraculous salves for sale to cure different disorders. These they declare are made from the fat of dogs, bears, wolves, frogs, and the like. As in all fetish remedies they are said to be of strange or revolting materials, like those used by Canidia of yore, the witches of Shakespeare and Ben Jonson, and of Burns in Tam O'Shanter.

When a man has been "struck by a spirit" there results a sore swelling or boil, which is cured by a sorceress as follows: The patient is put into a tent by himself, and is given divers drinks by his attendant then she rubs the sufferer with a salve, the secret of which is known only to her, while she chants:

"Prejiá, prejiá, prejiá,
Kiyá miseçeske, ác odoy;
Trianda sapa the çaven tut,
Trianda jiuklá tut c(ingeren,
Trianda káçná tut c(unáven!"

"Begone, begone, begone
To the Evil One; stay there.
May thirty snakes devour thee,
Thirty dogs tear thee,
Thirty cocks swallow thee!"

After this she slaughters a black hen, splits it open, and lays it on the boil. Then the sufferer must drink water from three springs or rivulets, and throw wood nine times into the fire daily until he is well. But black hens cost money, according to WLISLOCKI; albeit the gypsies, like the children of the Mist in "Waverley," are believed to be acquainted with a far more economical and direct method of obtaining such commodities. Therefore this expensive and high-class cure is not often resorted to, and when it is the sorceress generally substitutes something cheaper than poultry. It may be here observed that the black hen occurs frequently in mediæval witch-lore and legend as a demon-symbol (WOLF, "***Niederländische Sagen***," pp. 647, 650). Thus the bones of sorcerors turn into black hens and chickens, and it is well if your black hen dies, for if she had not you would have perished in her place. Black hens were walled up in castles as sacrifices to the devil, that the walls might long endure; hence the same fowl occurs in the arms of the family of Henneberg (NORK, "***Mythologie der Volksagen***," p. 381). The lore on this subject is very extensive.

The following remedy against headache is in general use among Transylvanian gypsies. The patient's head is rubbed, and then washed, with vinegar or hot water while the following charm is repeated:

"Oh duk ándro m'ro shero
The o dád miseçesero,
Adá dikhel ákáná,
Man tu máy dostá, márdyás,
Miro shero tu márdyás!
Tu ná ac(tu ándre me.
Já tu, já tu, já kere.
Káy tu miseç c(uc(ides,
Odoy, odoy sikoves!
Ko jál pro m'ro ushályin,
Adáleske e duk hin!"

Oh, pain in my head,
The father of all evil,
Look upon thee now!
Thou hast greatly pained me,
Thou tormentest my head,
Remain not in me!
Go thou, go thou, go home,
Whence thou, Evil One, didst suck,
Thither, thither hasten!
Who treads upon my shadow,
To him be the pain!"

It will be seen that the principle of treading on the tail of the coat practised in Ireland is much outdone by the gypsies who give a headache to any one who so much as treads on their shadows. And it is not difficult to understand that, as with children, the rubbing the head, the bathing it with warm water or vinegar, and, finally, the singing a soothing song, may all conduce to a cure. The readers of "Helen's Babies" will remember the cures habitually wrought on Budge by singing to him, "Charley boy one day." Gypsies are in many respects mere children, or little Budges. There can be no doubt that where faith is very strong, and imagination is lively, cures which seem to border on the miraculous are often effected—and this is, indeed, the basis of all miracle as applied to relieving bodily afflictions. All of this may be, if not as yet fully explained by physiology, at least shown to probably rest on a material basis. But no sound system of cure can be founded on it, because there is never any certainty, especially for difficult and serious disorders, that they can ever be healed twice in succession. The "faith" exacted is sometimes a purely hereditary gift, at other times merely a form of blind ignorance and credulity. It may vividly influence all the body, and it may fail to act altogether. But the "Faith Healer" and "Christian Scientist," or "Metaphysical Doctor," push boldly on, and when they here and there heal a patient once, it is published to the four winds as a proof of invariable infallibility. And as everybody believes that he has "faith," so he hopes to be cured. In popular custom for a man to say he believes in anything, and to be sure that he really has nothing against it, constitutes as much "faith" as most men understand. A man may be utterly destitute of any moral principle and yet live in a constant state of "faith" and pious conviction. Here the capacity for cure by means of charms is complete.

In connection with these charms for the head we may find not less interesting those in reference to the hair, as given by the same authority, Dr. von WLISLOCKI. The greatest pains are taken to ensure even for the new-born child what is called a full head, because every one who dies bald is turned into a fish, and must remain in this form till he has collected as many hairs as would make an ordinary wig. But this lasts a long time, since he can find but a single hair every month or moon. The moon is in many ways connected in gypsy faith with the hair. He who sleeps bare-headed in its light will lose his hair, or else it will become white. To have a heavy growth a man must scoop up with his left hand water from a running brook, against the current, and pour it on his head.

Immediately after the first bathing of a newly-born child, and its anointing, its forehead and neck are marked with a semicircle—perhaps meant to indicate the moon—made with a salve called barcali, intended to promote the growth of the hair. A brew, or mess, is made from beans and the blood of a cow. Hairs are taken from the heads of the father and mother, which hairs are burnt to a powder and mixed with the brew. It is remarkable that the beans are only used for a boy, their object being to insure for him great virile or sexual power. "The bean," says FRIEDRICH ("Sym. d. N."), "is an erotic symbol, or one signifying sexual pleasure." Hence it was forbidden to the Egyptian priests, the Pythagoreans, the priests of Jupiter in Rome, and to the Jewish high priests on certain festivals. But if the child is a girl, the seeds of the pumpkin or sunflower are substituted for beans, because the latter would make her barren.

It is an old belief, and one widely spread, that if the witches or the devil can get a lock of anybody's hair, they can work him evil. The gypsies have the following articles of faith as regards hairs:

> *Should birds find any, and build them into their nests, the man who lost them will suffer from headaches until, during the wane of the moon, he rubs his head with the yolk of eggs and washes it clean in running water.*

It would be very curious if this method of cleaning the hair and giving it a soft gloss, so much in vogue among English ladies, should have originated in sorcery. Beyond this, the sufferer must mix some of his hairs with food and give them to a white dog to eat.

> *If hairs which have fallen or been cut away are found by a snake and carried into its hole, the man from whom they came will continue to lose more until those in the snake's nest are quite decayed.*

> *If you see human hairs in the road do not tread on them, since, in that case, if they came from a lunatic, you, too, will go mad.*

According to MARCELLUS BURDIGALENSIS, if you pick up some hairs in the road just before entering a city gate, tie one to your own head, and, throwing the rest away, walk on without looking behind you, you can cure a headache. I have found nearly the same charm for the same purpose in Florence, but accompanied by the incantation which is wanting in MARCELLUS. Also his cure for headache with ivy from the head of a statue, which is still used in Tuscany with the incantation which the Roman omits.

Finding a hair hanging to your coat, carefully burn it, since you may by so doing escape injury by witchcraft. And we may remark in confirmation of this, that when you see a long hair on a man's coat it is an almost certain sign that he has been among the witches, or is bewitched; as the Countess thought when she found one clinging to the button of her lover, Von Adelstein, as set forth in "***Meister Karl's Sketch-book***."

But to bewitch your enemy get some of his combed-out hair, steep it in your own water, and then throw it on his garments. Then he will have no rest by night or day. I have observed that in all the Tuscan charms intended to torment a foe, the objects employed are like this of a disgusting nature.

If a wife will hold her husband to her in love, she must take of her own hair and bind it to his. This must be done three times by full moonlight.

Or if a maid will win the love of a young man, she must take of her own hair, mix it with earth from his footsteps—"und mischt diese mit dem Speichel einer läufigen Hundinn auf"—burn the whole to powder, and so manage that the victim shall eat it—which, it is needless to say, it is not likely that he will do, knowing what it is. Earth from the footsteps of any one is regarded as a very powerful means of bewitching him in Italian and ancient sorcery.

If a man bind the combings of his hair to the mane of a strange horse it will be wild and shy till the hairs are removed.

For easy childbirth red hair is sewed in a small bag and carried on the belly next the skin during pregnancy. Red hair indicates good luck, and is called bálá kámeskro, or sun-hairs, which indicates its Indian origin.

If any one dreams much of the dead, let him sew some of his hair into an old shoe, and give it to any beggar. Thereby he will prevent evil spirits from annoying him.

If a child suffers from sleeplessness, some of its mother's hair should be sewed into its wrappings, and others pulverized, mixed with a decoction of elderberries, be given it to drink. In German Folk-lore, as I shall show more fully anon, the elder often occurs as a plant specially identified with sorcery. In gypsy it is called yakori bengeskro, or the devil's eye, from its berries.

Nails cut on Friday should be burned, and the ashes mingled with the fodder of cattle, who are thus ensured against being stolen or attacked by wild beasts. If children are dwarfish, the same ashes in their food will make them grow. If a child suffers from pains in the stomach, a bit of nail must be clipped from its every finger; this is mixed with the dried dung of a foal, and the patient exposed to the smoke while it is burned.

A child's first tooth must, when it falls out, be thrown into a hollow tree. Those which come out in the seventh year are carefully kept, and whenever the child suffers from toothache, one is thrown into a stream.

Teeth which have been buried for many years, serve to make a singular fetish. They are mingled with the bones of a tree-frog, and the whole then sewed up in a little bag. If a man has anything for sale, and will draw or rub this bag over it, he will have many offers or customers for the articles thus enchanted. The bones are prepared by putting the frog into a glass or earthen receptacle full of small holes. This is buried in an ant-hill. The ants enter the holes and eat away all the flesh, leaving the bones which after a few weeks are removed.

To bear healthy and strong children women wear a string of bears' claws and children's teeth. Dr. von WLISLOCKI cites, apropos of this, a passage from JACOBUS RUEFF, "***Von Empfengnussen***": "Etlich schwanger wyber pflägend einen bären klauen von einem bären tapen yngefaszet am hals zuo tragen" (Some women when with child are accustomed to wear mounted bears' claws on their necks). In like manner boars' teeth, which much resemble them, are still very commonly worn in Austria and Italy and almost over all Europe and the East. It is but a few days since I here, in Florence, met with a young English lady who had bought a very large one mounted in silver as a brooch, but who was utterly unaware that there was any meaning attached to it. I have a very ancient bear's tooth and whistle in silver, meant for a teething child. It came from Munich.

Pain in the eyes is cured with a wash made of spring or well water and saffron. During the application the following is recited

"Oh dukh ándrál yákhá
Já ándré páñi
Já andrál páñi
Andre safráne
André pçuv.
Já andrál pçuv
Kiyá Pçuvusheske—
Odoy hin cerçá,
Odoy ja te ça."

Oh, pain from the eyes
Go into the water,
Go out of the water
Into the saffron,

Go out of the saffron
Into the earth.
To the Earth-Spirit.
There's thy home.
There go and eat."

This incantation casts light upon the earliest Shamanic remedies. When it was discovered that certain herbs really possessed curative qualities, this was attributed to inherent magic virtues. The increase of their power by combining them with water, or mingling them, was due to mystic affinities by which a spirit passed from one to another. The Spirit of Earth went into saffron, that of saffron into water. The magician thus, by a song sent the pain into its medical affinity, and so on back to the source whence it came. From early times saffron, as one of the earliest flowers of spring, owing to its colour, was consecrated to magic and love. Eos, the goddess of the Aurora, was called krokotieplos, the one with the saffron garment. Therefore the public women wore a yellow robe. Even in Christian symbolism it meant love, as PORTALIS declares: "In the Christian religion the colours saffron and orange were the symbols of God embracing the heart and illuminating the souls of the faithful" ("***Des Couleurs Symboliques***," Paris, 1837, p. 240). So we can trace the chain from the prehistoric barbarous Shamanism, preserved by the gypsies, to the Greek, and from the Greek to the mediæval form still existent.

The same sympathetic process of transmission may be traced in the remedy for the erysipelas. The blood of a bullfinch is put into a new vessel with scraped elder-bark, and then laid on a cloth with which the eyes are bound up overnight. Meanwhile the patient repeats:

"Duy yákhá hin mánge
Duy punrá hin mánge
Dukh ándrál yákhá
Já ándre punrá
Já ándrál punrá,
Já ándre pçuv,
Já ándrál pçuv
Andro meriben!"

"I have two eyes,
I have two feet,
Pain from my eyes
Go into my feet!
Go from my feet,

Go into the earth
Go from the earth
Into death!"

We have here in the elder-bark associations of magic which are ancient and widely spread, and which still exist; for at the present day country people in New England attribute to it curative virtues which it really does not possess. From the earliest times among the Northern races the Lady Elder, as we may learn from the Edda, or FIN MAGNUSEN ("***Priscæ veterum Borealium Mythologiæ Lexicon***," pp. 21, 239), and NYERUP ("***Worterbuch der Scandinavischen Mythologie***"), had an unearthly, ghostly reputation. Growing in lonely, gloomy places its form and the smell of its flowers seemed repulsive, so that it was associated with death, and some derived its name from Frau Holle, the sorceress and goddess of death. But SCHWENKI ("***Mythologie der Slaven***") with more probability traces it from hohl, i.e., hollow, and as spirits were believed to dwell in all hollow trees, they were always in its joints. The ancient Lithuanians, he informs us, worshipped their god Puschkeit, who was a form of Pluto, in fear and trembling at dusk, and left their offerings under the elder-tree. Everybody has seen the little puppets made of a piece of elder-pith with half a bullet under them, so that they always stand upright, and jump up when thrown down. Among the Slovaks these seem to have had some magical application. Perhaps their priests persuaded them that these jumping Jacks were miraculous, for they called them Pikuljk, a name derived from Peklo, the under-world. They still believe in a Pikuljk, who is a servant of the Evil One. He does all kinds of favours for men, but ends by getting their souls. The ancestors of the Poles were accustomed to bury all their sins and sorrows under elder-trees, thinking that they thereby gave to the lower world what properly belonged to it. This corresponds accurately to the gypsy incantation which passes the disease on from the elder bark into the earth, and from earth unto death. Frau Ellhorn, or Ellen, was the old German name for this plant. "Frau, perhaps, as appropriate to the female elf who dwelt in it" (FRIEDRICH, "***Symbolik***," p. 293). When it was necessary to cut one down, the peasant always knelt first before it and prayed: "Lady Ellhorn, give me of thy wood, and I will give thee of mine when it shall grow in the forest." GRIMM ("***Deutsche Mythologie***," cxvi.) cites from a MS. Of 1727 the following: "Paga nismo ortum debet superstitio, sambucam non esse exscindendum nisi prius rogata permissione his verbis: Mater Sambuci permitte mihi tuæ cædere sylvam!" On the other hand, Elder had certain protective and healing virtues. Hung before a stable door it warded off witchcraft, and he who planted it conciliated evil spirits.

And if a twig of it were planted on a grave and it grew, that was a sign that the soul of the deceased was happy, which is the probable reason why the very old Jewish cemetery in Prague was planted full of elders. In a very curious and rare work, entitled "***Blockesberge Berichtung***" (Leipzig, 1669), by JOHN PRÆTORIUS, devoted to "the Witch-ride and Sorcery-Sabbath," the author tells us that witches make great use of nine special herbs—"nam in herbis, verbis et lapidibus magna vis est." Among these is Elder, of which the peasants make wreaths, which, if they wear on Walpurgis night, they can see the sorceresses as they sweep through the air on their brooms, dragons, goats, and other strange steeds to the Infernal Dance. Or when they anderswo herumvagiren—"go vagabonding anywhere else." "Yea, and I know one fellow who sware unto men, that by means of this herb he once saw certain witches churning butter busily, and that on a roof, but I mistrust that this was a sell (Schnake), and that the true name of this knave was Butyrolambius" ("***Blocksberg***," p. 475). The same author informs us that Hollunder (or Elder) is so called from hohl, or hollow, or else is an anagram of Unholden, unholy spirits, and some people call it Allhuren, from its connection with witches and debauchery, even as CORDUS writes:

"When elder blossoms bloom upon the bush,
Then women's hearts to sensual pleasure rush."

He closes his comments on this subject with the dry remark that if the people of Leipzig wear, as is their wont, garlands of elder with the object of preventing breaches of the seventh commandment among them, it has in this instance, at least, utterly failed to produce the expected effect. "Quasi! creadt Judæus Apella!"

It should be mentioned that in the gypsy spell the next morning the cloth with the elder-bark must be thrown into the next running water. To cure toothache the Transylvanian gypsies wind a barley-straw round a stone, which is thrown into a running stream, while saying:

"Oh dukh ándre m're dándá,
Tu ná báres cingerá!
Ná ává kiyá mánge,
Mire muy ná hin kere!
Tut ñikáná me kámáv,
Ac(tu mánge pál pác(á;

Káná e pǫus yárpakri
Avel tele páñori!"

"Oh, pain in my teeth,
Trouble me not so greatly!
Do not come to me,
My mouth is not thy house.
I love thee not all,
Stay thou away from me;
When this straw is in the brook
Go away into the water!"

Straw was anciently a symbol of emptiness, unfruitfulness, and death, and it is evidently used in this sense by the gypsies, or derived by them from some tradition connected with it. A feigned or fruitless marriage is indicated in Germany by the terms Strohwittwer and Strohwittwe. From the earliest times in France the breaking a straw signified that a compact was broken with a man because there was nothing in him. Thus in 922 the barons of Charles the Simple, in dethroning him, broke the straws which they held (CHARLOTTE DE LA TOUR, "***Symbols of Flowers***").

Still, straws have something in them. She who will lay straws on the table in the full moonlight by an open window, especially on Saturday night, and will repeat:

"Straw, draw, crow craw,
By my life I give thee law"

Then the straws will become fairies and dance to the cawing of a crow who will come and sit on the]edge of the window. And so witches were wont to make a man of straw, as did Mother Gookin, in Hawthorne's tale, and unto these they gave life, whence the saying of a man of straw and straw bail, albeit this latter is deemed by some to be related to the breaking of straws and of dependence, as told in the tale of Charles the Simple. Straw-lore is extensive and curious. As in elder-stalks, small fairies make their homes in its tubes. To strew chopped straw before the house of a bride was such an insult to her character, in Germany, and so common that laws were passed against it. I possess a work printed about 1650, entitled "***De Injuriis quæ haud raro Novis Nuptis inferri solent. I. Per sparsionem dissectorum culmorum frugum. Germ. Dusch das Werckerling Streuen***," &c. An immense amount of learned quotation and reference by its author indicates that this custom which was influenced by superstition, was very extensively written on in its time. It was allied to the binding of knots and other magic ceremonies to prevent the consummation of marriages.

There is a very curious principle involved in curing certain disorders or afflictions by means of spells or verses. A certain word is repeated many times in a mysterious manner, so that it strikes the imagination of the sufferer. There is found in the Slavonian countries a woolly caterpillar called Wolos, whose bite, or rather touch, is much dreaded. I have myself, when a boy, been stung by such a creature in the United States. As I remember, it was like the sting of a bee. The following (Malo Russian) spell against it was given me by Prof. DRAGOMANOFF in Geneva. It is supposed that a certain kind of disorder, or cutaneous eruption, is caused by the Wolos:

"Wolosni—Wolosnicéh!
Holy Wolos.
Once a man drove over empty roads
With empty oxen,
To an empty field,
To harvest empty corn,
And gather it in empty ricks. p. 33
He gathered the empty sheaves,
Laid them in empty Wagons,
Drove over empty roads,
Unto an empty threshing-floor.
The empty labourers threshed it,
And bore it to the empty Mill.
The empty baker (woman)
Mixed it in an empty trough,
And baked it in an empty oven.
The empty people ate the empty bread.
So may the Wolos swallow this disorder
From the empty ——- (here the name of the patient.)

What is here understood by "empty" is that the swelling is taken away, subtracted, or emptied, by virtue of the repetition of the word, as if one should say, "Be thou void. Depart! depart! depart! Avoid me!"

There is a very curious incantation also apparently of Indian-gypsy origin, since it refers to the spirits of the water who cause diseases.

In this instance they are supposed to be exorcised by Saint Paphnutius, who is a later Slavonian-Christian addition to the old Shamanic spell. In the Accadian-Chaldæan formulas these spirits are seven; here they are seventy.

The formula in question is against the fever:

"In the name of God and his Son and the Holy Ghost. Amen!

"Seventy fair maids went up out of the ocean.

"They met the Saint Paphnutius, who asked:

"'Whence come ye, oh Maidens?'

"They answered, 'From the ocean-sea.

"'We go into the world to break the bones of men.

"'To give them the fever. (To make hot and cold).'"

Then the holy Paphnutius began to beat them, and gave them every one seventy-seven days:

"They began to pray, 'O holy Paphnutius!

"'Forgive us, (and) whoever shall bear with him (thy) name, or write it, him we will leave in peace.

"'We will depart from him

"'Over the streams, over the seas.

"'Over the reeds (canes) and marshes.

"'O holy Paphnutius, sua misericordia, of thy mercy,

"'Have pity on thy slave, even on the sick man ——— (the name is here uttered).

"'Free him from fever!'"

It is remarkable that, as a certain mysterious worm, caterpillar, or small lizard (accounts differ) among the Algonkin Indians is supposed to become at will a dragon, or sorcerer, or spirit, to be invoked or called on so the Wolos worm is also invoked, sometimes as a saint or sorcerer, and sometimes as a spirit who scatters disease. The following gypsy-Slavonian incantation over an invalid has much in common with the old Chaldæan spells.

> "Wolosni, Wolosnicéh!
> Thou holy Wolos!
> God calls thee unto his dwelling,
> Unto his seat.
> Thou shalt not remain here,
> To break the yellow bones.
> To drink the red blood,
> To dry up the white body.
> Go forth as the bright sun
> Goes forth over the mountains,
> Out from the seventy-seven veins,
> Out from the seventy limbs (parts of the body).
> Before I shall recognize thee,
> Before I did not name thee (call on thee).
> But now I know who thou art;
> I began to pray to the mother of God,
> And the mother of God began to aid me.
> Go as the wind goes over the meadows or the shore (or banks),
> As the waves roll over the waters,
> So may the Wolos go from ———
> The man who is born,
> Who is consecrated with prayer."

The Shamanic worship of water as a spirit is extremely ancient, and is distinctly recognized as such by the formulas of the Church in which water is called "this creature." The water spirits play a leading part in the gypsy mythology. The following gypsy-Slav charm, to consecrate a swarm of bees, was also given to me by Prof. DRAGOMANOFF, who had learned it from a peasant:

> "One goes to the water and makes his prayer and greets the water thus:
>
> "Hail to thee, Water!
> Thou Water, Oliana!
> Created by God,
> And thou, oh Earth, Titiana!

And ye the near springs, brooks and rivulets,
Thou Water, Oliana,
Thou goest over the earth,
Over the neighbouring fountains and streams,
Down unto the sea,
Thou dost purify the sea,
The sand, the rocks, and the roots—
I pray thee grant me
Of the water of this lake,
To aid me,
To sprinkle my bees.
I will speak a word,
And God will give me help,
The all-holy Mother of God,
The mother of Christ,
Will aid me,
And the holy Father
The holy Zosimos, Sabbateus and the holy Friday Parascabeah!

"When this is said take the water and bear it home without looking back. Then the bees are to be sprinkled therewith."

The following Malo-Russian formula from the same authority, though repointed and gilt with Greek Christianity, is old heathen, and especially interesting since Prof. DRAGOMANOFF traces it to a Finnic Shaman source:

CHARM AGAINST THE BITE OF A SERPENT

"The holy Virgin sent a man
Unto Mount Sion,
Upon this mountain
Is the city of Babylon,
And in the city of Babylon
Lives Queen Volga.p. 36
Oh Queen Volga,
Why dost thou not teach
This servant of God
(Here the name of the one bitten by a serpent is mentioned)
So that he may not be bitten
By serpents?"

> (The reply of Queen Volga) "Not only will I teach my descendants But I also will prostrate myself Before the Lord God."

"Volga is the name of a legendary heathen princess of Kief, who was baptized and sainted by the Russian Church. The feminine form, Olga, or Volga, corresponds to the masculine name Oleg, or Olg, the earliest legendary character of Kief. His surname was Viechtchig—the sage or sorcerer" (i.e., wizard, and from a cognate root). "In popular songs he is called Volga, or Volkh, which is related to Volkv, a sorcerer. The Russian annals speak of the Volkv of Finland, who are represented as Shamans." Niya Predania i Raikazi ("***Traditions and Popular Tales of Lesser Russia***," by M. DRAGOMANOFF, Kief, 1876) in Russian.

I have in the chapter on curing the disorders of children spoken of Lilith, or Herodias, who steals the newborn infants. She and her twelve daughters are also types of the different kinds of fever for which the gypsies have so many cures of the same character, precisely as those which were used by the old Bogomiles. The characteristic point is that this female spirit is everywhere regarded as the cause of catalepsy or fits. Hence the invocation to St. Sisinie is used in driving them away. This invocation written, is carried as an amulet or fetish. I give the translation of one of these from the Roumanian, in which the Holy Virgin is taken as the healer. It is against cramp in the night:

SPELL AGAINST NIGHT-CRAMP

"There is a mighty hill, and on this hill is a golden apple-tree,

"Under the golden apple-tree is a golden stool.

"On the stool—who sits there?

"There sits the Mother of God with Saint Maria; with the boxes in her right hand, with the cup in her left.

"She looks up and sees naught, she looks down and sees my Lord and Lady Disease.

"Lords and Ladies Cramp, Lord and Lady Vampire—Lord Wehrwolf and his wives.

"They are going to ——— (the sufferer), to drink his blood and put in him a foul heart.

"The Mother of God, when she saw them, went down to them, spoke to them, and asked them, 'Whither go ye, Lord and Lady Disease,—Lords and Ladies Cramp, &c.?'

"'We go to ——— to drink his blood, to change his heart to a foul one.'

"'No, ye shall return; give him his blood back, restore him his own heart, and leave him immediately.'

"Cramps of the night, cramps of the midnight, cramps of the day, cramps wherever they are. From water, from the wind, go out from the brain, from the light of he face, from the hearing of the ears, from his heart, from his hands and feet, from the soles of his feet.

"Go and hide where black cocks never crow, 1 where men never go, where no beast roars.

"Hide yourself there, stop there, and never show yourself more!

"May ——— remain pure and glad, as he was made by God, and was fated by the Mother of God!

"The spell is mine—the cure is God's."

In reference to the name Herodias (here identified with Lilith, the Hebrew mother of all devils and goblins); it was a great puzzle to the writers on witchcraft why the Italian witches always said they had two queens whom they worshipped—Diana and Herodias. The latter seems to have specially presided at the witch-dance. In this we can see an evident connection with the Herodias of the New Testament.

I add to this a few more very curious old Slavonian spells from Dr. Gaster's work, as they admirably illustrate one of the principal and most interesting subjects connected with the gypsy witchcraft; that is to say, its relation to early Shamanism and the forms in which its incantations were expressed. In all of these it may be taken for granted, from a great number of closely-allied examples, that the Christianity in them is recent and that they all go back to the earliest heathen times. The following formula, dating from 1423, against snakebites bears the title:

PRAYER OF ST. PAUL AGAINST SNAKES

"In the name of the Father, the Son, and the Holy Ghost. I once was a persecutor, but am now a true follower; and I went from my dwelling-place in Sicily, and they set light to a trunk, and a snake came therefrom and bit my right hand and hung from it. But I had in me the power of God, and I shook it off into the burning fire and it was destroyed, and I suffered no ill from the bite. I laid myself down to sleep; then the mighty angel said: 'Saul, Paul, stand up and receive this writing'; and I found in it the following words:

"'I exorcise you, sixty and a half kinds of beasts that creep on the earth, in the name of God, the Creator of Heaven and Earth, and in the name of the immovable throne.

"'Serpent of Evil, I exorcise thee in the name of the burning river which rises under the footstool of the Saviour, and in the name of His incorporeal angels!

"'Thou snake of the tribe of basilisks, thou foul-headed snake, twelve-headed snake, variegated snake, dragon-like snake, that art on the right side of hell, whomsoever thou bitest thou shalt have no power to harm, and thou must go away with all the twenty-four kinds. If a man has this prayer and this curse of the true, holy apostle, and a snake bites him, then it will die on the spot, and the man that is bitten shall remain unharmed, to the honour of the Father, the Son, and the Holy Ghost, now and for all time. Amen.'"

It is not improbable that we have in PAUL and the Serpent and the formula for curing its bite (which is a common symbol for all disease) a souvenir of Esculapius, the all-healer, and his serpent. The following is "a prayer against the toothache, to be carried about with one," i.e., as an amulet prayer:

SPELL FOR THE TOOTHACHE

"Saint Peter sat on a stone and wept. Christ came to him and said, 'Peter, why weepest thou?' Peter answered, 'Lord, my teeth pain me.' The Lord thereupon ordered the worm in Peter's tooth to come out of it and never more go in again. Scarcely had the worm come out when the pain ceased. Then spoke Peter, 'I pray you, O Lord, that when these words be written out and a man carries them he shall have no toothache.' And the Lord answered, "'Tis well, Peter; so may it be!'"

It will hardly be urged that this Slavonian charm of Eastern origin could have been originated independently in England. The following, which is there found in the north, is, as Gaster remarks, "in the same: wording":

"Peter was sitting on a marble stone,
And Jesus passed by.
Peter said, 'My Lord, my God,
How my tooth doth ache!'
Jesus said, Peter art whole
And whosoever keeps these words for My sake
Shall never have the toothache.'

The next specimen is a—

CHARM AGAINST NOSE-BLEEDING

"Zachariah was slain in the Lord's temple, and his blood turned into stone. Then stop, O blood, for the Lord's servant, ———. I exorcise thee, blood, that thou stoppest in the name of the Saviour, and by fear of the priests when they perform the liturgy at the altar."

Those who sell these charms are almost universally supposed to be mere quacks and humbugs. If this were the case, why do they so very carefully learn and preserve these incantations, transmitting them "as a rich legacy unto their issue." But they really do believe in them, and will give great prices for them. Prof. DRAGOMANOFF told me that once in Malo-Russia it became generally known that he had made a MS. collection of such spells. A peasant who was desirous of becoming a sorcerer, but who had very few incantations of his own, went whenever he could by stealth into the Professor's library and surreptitiously copied his incantations. And when Prof. DRAGOMANOFF returned the next year to that neighbourhood, he found the peasant doing a very good business as a conjuring doctor, or faith-healer. I have a lady correspondent in the United States who has been initiated into Voodoo and studied Indian-negro witchcraft under two eminent teachers, one a woman, the other a man. The latter, who was at the very head of the profession, sought the lady's acquaintance because he had heard that she possessed some very valuable spells. In the fourth or highest degree, this Indian-Voodoo deals exclusively with the spirits of the forest and stream.

M. Kounavine, as set forth by Dr. A. Elysseeff (***Gypsy-Lore Journal***, July, 1890), gives a Russian gypsy incantation by which the fire is invoked to cure illness. It is as follows:

> "Great Fire, my defender and protector, son of the celestial fire, equal of the sun who cleanses the earth of foulness, deliver this man from the evil sickness that torments him night and day!"
> The fire is also invoked to punish, or as an ordeal, e.g.:
>
> "Fire, who punishest the evil-doer, who hatest falsehood, who scorchest the impure, thou destroyest offenders; thy flame devoureth the earth. Devour ——— if he says what is not true, if he thinks a lie, and if he acts deceitfully."

These are pronounced by the gypsy sorcerer facing the burning hearth. There is another in which fire is addressed as Jandra:

> "Jandra, bearer of thunderbolts, great Periani (compare Parjana, an epithet of Indra, Slavonic Perun), bearer of lightning, slay with thy thunderbolt and burn with thy celestial fire him who dares to violate his oath."

CHAPTER III

Gypsy Conjurations and Exorcisms—The Cure of Children-- Hungarian Gypsy Spells—A Curious Old Italian "Secret"— The Magic Virture of Garlic—A Florentine Incantation Learned From A Witch—Lilith, The Child Stealer, and Queen of The Witches

IN all the schools of Shamanic sorcery, from those of the Assyrian Accadian to the widely-spread varieties of the present day, the Exorcism forms the principal element. An exorcism is a formula, the properties or power of which is that when properly pronounced, especially if this be done with certain fumigations and ceremonies, it will drive away devils, diseases, and disasters of every description; nay, according to very high, and that by no means too ancient, authority, it is efficacious in banishing bugs, mice, or locusts, and it is equal to Persian powder as a fuge for fleas, but is, unfortunately, too expensive to be used for that purpose save by the very wealthy. It has been vigorously applied against the grape disease, the Colorado beetle, the army worm, and the blizzard in the United States, but, I believe, without effect, owing possibly to differences of climate or other antagonistic influences.

Closely allied to the Exorcism is the Benediction, which soon grew out of it as a cure. The former being meant to repel and drive away evil, the latter very naturally suggested itself, by a law of moral polarity, as a means of attracting good fortune, blessings, health, and peace. As the one was violently curative, the other was preventive. The benediction would keep the devils and all their works away from a man or his home—in fact, if stables be only well blessed once a year, no mishaps can come to any of the animals who inhabit them; and I myself have known a number of donkeys to receive a benediction in Rome, the owner being assured that it would keep them safe from all the ills which donkeys inherit. And in the year 1880, in one of the principal churches of Philadelphia, blessed candles were sold to a

congregation under guarantee that the purchase of one would preserve its possessor for one year against all disorders of the throat, on which occasion a sermon was preached, in the which seven instances were given in which people had thus been cured.
Between blessing and banning it soon became evident that many formulas of words could be used to bring about mysterious results. It is probable that the Exorcism in its original was simply the angry, elevated tone of voice which animals as well as men instinctively employ to repel an enemy or express a terror. For this unusual language would be chosen, remembered, and repeated. With every new utterance this outcry or curse would be more seriously pronounced or enlarged till it became an Ernulphian formula. The next step would be to give it metric form, and its probable development is very interesting. It does not seem to have occurred to many investigators that in early ages all things whatever which were remembered and repeated were droned and intoned, or sing-sung, until they fell of themselves into a kind of metre. In all schools at the present day, where boys are required to repeat aloud and all together the most prosaic lessons, they end by chanting them in rude rhythm. All monotone, be it that of a running brook, falls into cadence and metre. All of the sagas, or legends, of the Algonkin-Wabanaki were till within even fifty years chants or songs, and if they are now rapidly losing that character it is because they are no longer recited with the interest and accuracy which was once observed in the narrators. But it was simply because all things often repeated were thus intoned that the exorcisms became metrical.

It is remarkable that among the Aryan races it assumed what is called the staff-rhyme, like that which SHAKESPEARE, and BEN JONSON, and BYRON, and many more employ, as it would seem, instinctively, whenever witches speak or spells or charms are uttered. It will not escape the reader that, in the Hungarian gypsy incantations in this work, the same measure is used as that which occurs in the Norse sagas, or in the scenes of Macbeth. It is also common in Italy. This is intelligible—that its short, bold, deeply-marked movement has in itself something mysterious and terrible. If that woefully-abused word "weird" has any real application to anything, it is to the staff-rhyme.

I believe that when a man, and particularly a woman, does not know what else to say, he or she writes "lurid," or "weird," and I lately met with a book of travels in which I found the latter applied seventy-six times to all kinds of conundrums, until I concluded that, like the coachman's definition of an idea in HEINE'S "***Reisebilder***," it meant simply "any d——d nonsense that a man gets into his head." But if weird really and only means that which is connected with fate or destiny, from the Anglo-Saxon Weordan, to become, German, Werden, then it is applicable enough to rhymes setting forth the future and spoken by the "weird sisters," who are so-called not because they are awful or nightmarish, or pokerish, or mystical, or bug-a-boorish, but simply because they predict the future or destiny of men." The Athenians as well as Gentiles excelled in these songs of sorcery, hence we are told (VARRO, "Q. de Fascin") that in Achaia, when they learned that a certain woman who used them was an Athenian they stoned her to death, declaring that the immortal gods bestowed on man the power of healing with stones, herbs, and animals, not with words" ("De Rem. Superstit. Cognoscendis"). Truly, doctors never agree.

It was in 1886 that I learned from a girl in Florence two exorcisms or invocations which she was accustomed to repeat before telling fortunes by cards. This girl, who was of the Tuscan Romagna and who looked Etruscan with a touch of gypsy blood, was a repertory of popular superstitions, especially witch-lore, and a maker and wearer of fetishes, always carrying a small bag full of them. Bon sang ne peut mentir.

The two formulas were as follows. I omit a portion from each:

"Venti cinque carte siete!
Venti cinque diavoli diventerete,
Diventerete, anderete
Nel' corpo, nel' sangue nell' anima,
Nell' sentimenti del corpo;
Del mio amante non posso vivere,
Non passa stare ne bere,
Ne mangiare ne . . .
Ne con uomini ne con donne non passa favellare,
Finche a la porta di casa mia
Non viene picchiare!"

"Ye are twenty-five cards.
Become twenty-five devils
Enter into the body, into the blood, into the soul .
Into the feelings of the body
Of my lover, from whom I cannot live.
For I cannot stand (exist), or drink,
Or eat . . .

Nor can I converse with men or women
Till at the door of my house
He shall come to knock."

The second incantation was the same, but beginning with these words:

"I put five fingers on the wall,
I conjure five devils,
Five monks and five friars,
That they may enter the body
Into the blood, into the soul," &c.

If the reader will take Le Normant's "Magie Chaldaienne," and carefully compare these Italian spells with those of ancient Nineveh, he will not only find a close general resemblance, but all the several details or actual identity of words. And it is not a little curious that the same formulas which were repeated—

"Once on a time when Babylon was young"—

should still be current in Italy. So it passed through the ages--races came and went--and among the people the old sorcery was handed across and adown, so that it still lives. But in a few years more the Folk-lorist will be its only repository.

This chapter is devoted to conjuring diseases of children by gypsies. It bears a great likeness to one in the very devout work of PETER PIPERNUS, "***De Pueris affectis morbis magicis***" ("Of Boys who have been Bewitched into Disease"), only that PIPERNUS uses Catholic incantations, which he also employs "pro ligatis in matrimonio," "pro incubo magico," "de dolóribus stomachi magicis," &c., for to him, as he declares, all disease is of magic origin.

The magic of the gypsies is not all deceit, though they deceive with it. They put faith themselves in their incantations, and practise them on their own account. "And they believe that there are women, and sometimes men, who possess supernatural power, partly inherited and partly acquired." The last of seven daughters born in succession, without a boy's coming into the series, is wonderfully gifted, for she can see hidden treasure or spirits, or enjoy second sight of many things invisible to men. And the same holds good for the ninth in a series of boys, who may become a seer of the same sort. Such a girl, *i.e.*, a seventh daughter, being a fortune in herself, never lacks lovers. In 1883 the young Vojvode, or leader, of the Kukaya gypsy tribe, named DANKU NICULAI, offered the old gypsy woman, PALE BOSHE, one hundred ducats if she would persuade her seventh daughter to marry him. In the United States of America there are many women who advertise in the newspapers that they also are seventh daughters of seventh daughters at that, and who make a good thing of it as fortunetellers; but they have a far more speedy, economical, and effective way of becoming the last note in an octave, than by awaiting the slow processes of being begotten or born, inasmuch as they boldly declare themselves to be sevenths, which I am assured answers every purpose, as nobody ever asks to see their certificates of baptism any more than of marriage.

Most of these witch-wives—also known in Hungary as *cohalyi*, or "wise women," or *gule romni*, "sweet" or "charming women"—are trained up from infancy by their mothers in medicine and magic. A great part of this education consists in getting by heart the incantations or formulas of which specimens will be given anon, and which, in common with their fairy tales, show intrinsic evidence of having been drawn at no very distant period from India, and probably in common with the lower or Shamanic religion of India from Turanian sources. But there is among the Hungarian gypsies a class of female magicians who stand far above their sisters of the hidden spell in power. These are the *lace romni*, or "good women," who draw their power directly from the *Nivasi* or *Pchuvusi*, the spirits of water and earth, or of flood and fell. For the Hungarian gypsies have a beautiful mythology of their own which at first sight would seem to be a composition of the Rosicrucian as set forth by Paracelsus and the Comte de GABALIS, with the exquisite Indo-Teutonic fairy tales of the Middle Ages. In fact, in some of the incantations used we find the *Urme*, or fairies, directly appealed to for help.

With the gypsies, as among the early Accadians, diseases are supposed to be caused by evil supernatural influences. This is more naturally the case among people who lead very simple lives, and with whom sickness is not almost a natural or normal condition, as it is with ladies and gentlemen, or the inhabitants of cities, who have "always something the matter with them." Nomadic life is conducive to longevity. "Our grandfathers died on the gallows—we die from losing our teeth," said an old gypsy to Doctor von WLISLOCKI, when asked what his age was. Therefore among all people who use charms and spells those which are devoted to cure occupy the principal position. However, the Hungarian Romany have many medicines, more or less mysterious, which they also apply in connection with the "healing rhymes." And as in the struggle for life the weakest go first to the wall, the remedies for the diseases of children are predominant.

When a mother begins to suffer the pangs of childbirth, a fire is made before her tent, which is kept up till the infant is baptized, in order to drive away evil spirits. Certain women feed this fire, and while fanning it (fans being used for bellows) murmur the following rhyme:

"Oh yakh, oh yakh pçabuva,
Pçabuva,
Te čavéstár tu trada,
Tu trada,
Pçávushen te Nivashen
Tire tçuva the traden!
Lače Urmen ávená,
Čaves báçtáles dena,
Káthe hin yov báçtáles,
Andre lime báçtáles!
Motura te ráná,
Te átunci but' ráná,
Matura te ráná,
Te átunci, but' rana,
Me dav' andre yákherá!
Oh yákh, oh yákh pçabuva,
Rovel čavo: áshuna!"

It may here be remarked that the pronunciation of all these words is the same as in German, with the following additions . Č = *teh* in English, or to *ch* in church. C = *ch* in German as in *Buch.* J = *azs*, or the English *j*, in James; *ñ*, as in Spanish, or *nj* in German, while *sh* and *y* are pronounced as in English. Á is like *ah.* The literal translation is

"Oh Fire, oh Fire, burn!
Burn!
And from the child (do) thou drive away
Drive away!
Pçuvuse and Nivashi
And drive away thy smoke (pl.)
(Let) good fairies come (and)
Give luck to the child,
Here it is lucky (or fortunate)
In the world fortunate

Brooms and twigs (fuel)
Arid then more twigs,
And then yet more twigs
I put (give) to the fire.
Oh fire, oh fire—burn!
The child weeps: listen!"

In South Hungary the gypsy women on similar occasions sing the following charm:

"Eitrá Pçuvushá, efta Nivásha
André mal avená
Pçabuven, pçabuven, oh yákhá!
Dáyákri punro dindálen,
Te gule čaves mudáren
Pçabuven, pçabuven, oh yákhá;
Ferinen o čaves te daya!"

"Seven Pçuvushe, seven Nivasi
Come into the field,
Burn, burn, oh fire
They bite the mother's foot,
They destroy the sweet child;
Fire, fire, oh burn!
Protect the child and the mother!"

When the birth is very difficult, the mother's relations come to help, and one of them lets an egg fall, *zwischen den Beinen derselben.* On this occasion the gypsy women in Southern Hungary sing:

"Anro, ánro in obles,
Te e pera in obles:
Ava čavo sástávestes!
Devlá, devlá, tut akharel!"

The egg, the egg is round,
And the belly is round,
Come child in good health
God, God calls thee!"

If a woman dies in child-bed two eggs are placed under her arms and the following couplet is muttered:

"Kana anro kirnes hin,
Kathe nañi tçudá him!"

"When this egg is (shall be) decayed,
Here (will be) is no milk!"

When the after-pains begin it is the custom with some of the gypsy tribes in the Siebenburgen to smoke the sufferer with decayed willow-wood which is burned for the purpose while the women in attendance sing:

"Sik te sik o tçu urál,
Te urál o čon urál!
Kana len hádjináven
Sasčipená tut' áven;
Káná o tçu ná urál--
Tute nañi the dukhal,
Tute náñi the dukhál."

"Fast and fast the smoke flies,
And flies, the moon flies,
When they find (themselves)
Health (yet) will come to thee,
When the smoke no (longer) flies
Thou wilt feel pain no more!"

There is a strange, mysterious affinity between gypsies and the moon. A wonderful legend, which they certainly brought from India since in it Mekran is mentioned as the place where its incident occurred, details that there, owing to the misrepresentations of a sorcerer, the gypsy leader, CHEN, was made to, marry his sister GUIN, or KAN, which brought the curse of wandering upon his people. Hence the Romany are called Chen-Guin. It is very evident that here we have CHON and KAN, or KAM, the Moon and Sun, which is confirmed by another gypsy legend which declares that the Sun, because he once violated or still seeks to seduce his sister, the Moon, continually follows her, being destined to wander for ever. And as the name Chen-Kan, or Zingan, or Zigeuner, is known all over the East, and, as this legend shows, is of Indian origin, it is hardly worth while to believe with MIKLOSICH that it is derived from an obscure Greek heretical sect of Christians--the more so as it is most difficult to believe that the Romany were originally either Greeks or Christians or Christian heretics.

When a gypsy woman is with child she will not, if she can help it, leave her tent by full moonshine. A child born at this time it I's believed will make a happy marriage. So it is said of birth in the Western World:

"Full moon, high sea,
Great man thou shalt be;
Red dawning, cloudy sky,
Bloody death shalt thou die.

"Pray to the Moon when she is round,
Luck with you will then abound,
What you seek for shall be found
On the sea or solid ground."

Moon-worship is very ancient; it is alluded to as a forbidden thing in the Book of Job. From early times witches and other women worked their spells when stark-naked by the light of the full moon, which is evidently derived from the ancient worship of that planet and the shameless orgies connected with it. Dr. WLISLOCKI simply remarks on this subject that the moon has, in the gypsy incantation, "eine Phallische Bedeutung." In ancient symbolism the horns of the moon were regarded as synonymous with the horns of the ox-hence their connection with agriculture, productiveness, and fertility, or the generative principle, and from this comes the beneficent influence not only of the horns, but of horse-shoes, boars' tusks, crabs' claws, and pieces of coral resembling them.

The great love of gypsy mothers for their children, says WLISLOCKI, induces their friends to seek remedies for the most trifling disorders. At a later period, mother and child are left to Mother Nature--or the *vis medicatrix Naturæ*. What is greatly dreaded is the *Berufen*, or being called on, "enchanted," in English "overlooked," or subjected to the evil eye. An universal remedy for this is the following:

A jar is filled with water from a stream, and it must be taken *with*, not against, the current as it runs. In it are placed seven coals, seven handfuls of meal, and seven cloves of garlic, all of which is put on the fire. When the water begins to boil it is stirred with a three-forked twig, while the wise woman repeats:--

"Misec̓ yakhá tut dikhen,
Te yon káthe mudáren
Te átunci eftá coká

Te çaven miseçe yakhá;
Miseç' yakhá tut dikhen,
Te yon káthe mudáren
But práhestár e yakhá
Atunci kores th'ávená;
Miseç' yakhá tut dikhen
Te yon káthe mudáren
Pçábuvená pçábuvená
Andre develeskero yakhá!"

"Evil eyes look on thee,
May they here extinguished be
And then seven ravens
Pluck out the evil eyes
Evil eyes (now) look on thee.
May they soon extinguished be!
Much dust in the eyes,
Thence may they become blind,
Evil eyes now look on thee;
May they soon extinguished be!
May they burn, may they burn
In the fire of God!"

Dr. WLISLOCKI remarks that the "seven ravens" are probably represented by the seven coals, while the three-pointed twig, the meal and the garlic, symbolize lightning. He does not observe that the stick may be the triçula or trident of Siva--whence probably the gipsy word *trushul*, a cross; but the connection is very obvious. It is remarkable that the gypsies assert that lightning leaves behind it a smell like that of garlic. As garlic forms an important ingredient in magic charms, the following from "The Symbolism of Nature" ("**Die Symbolik und Mythologie der Natur**"), by J. B. FRIEDRICH, will be found interesting:

"We find in many forms spread far and wide the belief that garlic possesses the magic power of protection against poison and sorcery. This comes, according to Pliny, from the fact that when it is hung up in the open air for a time, it turns black, when it is supposed to attract evil into itself--and, consequently, to withdraw it from the wearer. The ancients believed that the herb which Mercury gave to Ulysses to protect him from the enchantment of Circe, and which Homer calls *moly*, was the *alium nigrum*, or garlic, the poison of the witch being a narcotic. Among the modern Greeks and Turks, garlic is regarded as the most powerful charm against evil spirits, magic, and misfortune. For this reason they carry it with them, and hang it up in their houses as a protection against storms and bad weather. So their sailors carry with them a sack of it to avert shipwreck. If any one utters a word of praise with the intention of fascinating or of doing harm, they cry aloud 'Garlic!' or utter it three times rapidly. In ***AULUS PERSIUS FLACCUS*** (*Satyr. V.*) to bite garlic averts magic and the evils which the gods send to those who are wanting in reverence for them. According to a popular belief the mere pronunciation of 'Garlic!' protects one from poison."

It appears to be generally held among them and the Poles that this word prevents children from "*beschreien werden*," that is, from being banned, or overlooked, or evil-eyed. And among the Poles garlic is laid under children's pillows to protect them from devils and witches. (BRATRANECK, "*Beiträge zur Æsthetik der Pflanzenweit*," p. 56). The belief in garlic as something sacred appears to have been very widely spread, since the Druids attributed magic virtues to it; hence the reverence for the nearly allied leek, which is attached to King David and so much honoured by the Welsh.

> "Tell him I'll knock his leek about his pate
> Upon Saint David's Day."—SHAKESPEARE.

The magic virtues of garlic were naturally enough also attributed to onions and leeks, and in a curious Italian work, entitled "Il Libro del Comando," attributed (falsely) to Cornelius Agrippa, I find the following:

> "*Segreto magico d'indovinare, colle cipole, la salute d'una persona lontana.* A magic secret to divine with onions the health of a person far distant. Gather onions on the Eve of Christmas and put them on an altar, and under every onion write the name of the persons as to whom one desires to be informed, *ancorche non scrivano*, even if they do not write.
>
> "The onion (planted) which sprouts the first will clearly announce that the person whose name it bears is well.
>
> "And in the same manner we can learn the name of the husband or wife whom we should choose, and this divination is in use in many cantons of Germany."

Very much allied to this is the following love charm from an English gypsy:

"Take an onion, a tulip, or any root of the kind (*i.e.* a bulbous root?), and plant it in a clean pot never used before; and while you plant it repeat the name of the one whom you love, and every day, morning and evening, say over it

"As this root grows
And as this blossom blows,
May her heart be
Turned unto me!"

"And it will come to pass that every day the one whom you love will be more and more inclined to you, till you get your heart's desire."

A similar divination is practised by sowing cress or lettuce seed in the form of names in gardens. If it grows well the one who plants it will win the love of the person indicated.

As regards the use of coals in incantations, MARCELLUS BURDIGALENSIS, a Latin physician of the third century, who has left us a collection of Latin and Gaelic charms, recommends for a cure for toothache: "Salis granum, panis micam, carbonem mortuum in phœnicio alligabis," *i.e.*, to carry a grain of salt, a crumb of bread, and a coal, in a red bag.

When the witch-brew of coals, garlic, and meal is made, and boiled down to a dry residuum, it is put into a small three-cornered bag, and hung about the child's neck, on which occasion the appropriate rhyme is repeated nine times. "And it is of special importance that the bag shall be made of a piece of linen, which must be stolen, found, or begged."

To learn whether a child has been overlooked, or evil-eyed, or enchanted, the "wise woman" takes it in her arms, and goes to the next running stream. There she holds the face of the babe as nearly as she can to the water, and repeats:--

"Páñi, páñi sikova,
Dikh the upré, dikh télé!
Buti páñi sikovel
Buti pál yákh the dikhel
Te ákáná mudárel."

"Water, water, hasten!
Look up, look down
Much water hastens
(May) as much come into the eye
Which looked evil on thee,
And may it now perish."

If the running brook makes a louder sound than usual then it is supposed to say that the child is enchanted, but if it runs on as before then something else is the matter, and to ascertain what it is other charms and ceremonies are had recourse to. This incantation indicates, like many others, a constant dwelling in lonely places, by wood and stream, as gypsies wont to do, and sweet familiarity with Nature, until one hears sermons in stones, books in the running brooks, and voices in the wind.

Civilized people who read about Red Indian sorcerers and gypsy witches very promptly conclude that they are mere humbugs or lunatics—they do not realize how these people, who pass half their lives in wild places watching waving grass and falling waters, and listening to the brook until its cadence speaks in real song, believe in their inspirations, and feel that there is the same mystical feeling and presence in all things that live and move and murmur as well as in themselves. Now we have against this the life of the clubs and family, of receptions and business, factories and stock markets, newspapers and "culture." Absolutely no one who lives in "the movement" can understand this sweet old sorcery. But nature is eternal, and while grass grows and rivers run man is ever likely to fall again into the eternal enchantments. And truly until he does he will have no new poetry, no fresh art, and must go on copying old ideas and having wretchedly worn-out exhibitions in which there is not one original idea.

If it appears that the child is overlooked, or "berufen," many means are resorted to, "one good if another fails," but we have here to do only with those which are connected with incantations. A favourite one is the following: Three twigs are cut, each one from a different tree, and put into a pipkin which has been filled with water dipped or drawn *with*, not against, the current of a stream. Three handfuls of meal are then put in and boiled down to a *Brei*, or pudding. A horse hair is then wound round a needle, which is stuck not by the point but by the head into the inner bottom of a tube, which is filled with water, and placed upon this is the pipkin with the pudding. Then the "overlooked," or evil-seen child is held over the tub while the following rhyme is chanted

> "Páñi, páñi lunjárá,
> Páñi, páñi isbiná;
> Te náshválipen çucá
> Náshválipen mudárá,
> Mudára te ákáná,
> Káthe beshá ñikáná,
> Sár práytiña sutyárel,
> Káthe ándre piri, ándre piri,
> Nivasheshe les dávás!"

> "Water, water, spread
> Water, water, stretch
> And sickness disappear,
> Sickness be destroyed,
> Be destroyed now.
> Romain not here at all
> Who ever has overlooked this child
> As this leaf in the pot (maybe)
> Be given to the Nivashi!"

This is repeated nine times, when the water in the tub, with the pipkin and its contents, are all thrown into the stream from which the water was drawn. This is a widely-spread charm, and it is extremely ancient. The pipkin placed across the tub or trough—*trog*—here signifies a bridge, and WLISLOCKI tells us that no Transylvanian tent-gypsy will cross a bridge without first spitting thrice over the rails into the water. The bridge plays an important part in the mythology and Folklore of many races. The ancient Persians had their holy mountain, Albordi, or Garotman, the abode of gods and blessed souls, to which they passed by the bridge Cin-vat, or Chinevad, whence the creed: "I believe in the resurrection of the dead; that all bodies shall live renewed again, and I believe that by the bridge Cin-vat all good deeds will be rewarded, and all evil deeds punished." The punishment is apparent from the parallel of the bridge Al Sirat, borrowed by the Mahommedans from the Persians, over which the good souls passed to reward, and from which the wicked tumbled down into hell.

When I first met EMERSON in 1849 I happened to remark that a bridge in a landscape was like a vase in a room, the point on which an eye trained to the picturesque involuntarily rested. Nearly thirty years after, when we were both living at Shepherd's Hotel in Cairo, he reminded me of this one day when by the Nile we were looking at a bridge. As a bridge must cross a stream, or a torrent which is generally beautiful by itself, and as the cross or span has the effect of defining and framing the picture, as a circlet or tiara sets off a beautiful head, it is not remarkable that in all ages men have made such objects subjects of legend and song. Hence the oft-repeated Devil's Bridge, so-called because it seemed to simple peasants impossible for mere mortals to build, although bridges are habitually and more naturally connected with salvation and saints. He who in early ages built a bridge, did a great deed in times when roads were rare; hence the great priest was called the Pontifex.

Another spell for the purpose of averting the effects of the evil eye is as follows: The mother of the overlooked child fills her mouth with salt water, and lets it drop or trickle on the limbs of the infant, and when this has been done, repeats:

"Miseç yákhá tut dikhen
Sár páñori--
Mudaren!
Náshvalipen prejia:
Andral t'ro shero
Andral t're kolyin,
Andral t're per
Andral t're punrá
Andral t're vástá
Kathe prejánen,--
Andre yákhá yon jánen!"

"False (evil) eyes see thee,
Like this water
May they perish
Sickness depart
From thy head,
From thy breast,
From thy belly,
From thy feet
From thy hands,
May they go hence
Into the evil eyes!"

It may be observed that meal forms an ingredient in several of these sorceries. It is a very ancient essential to sacrifices, and is offered to the spirits of the stream to appease them, as it was often given for the same purpose to the wind. The old Germans, says PRÆTORIUS, imagined the storm-wind as a starving, ravenous being, and sought to appease it by throwing meal to it. So it happened once even of later years near Bamberg when a mighty wind was raging one night that an old woman took her meal-bag and threw its contents out of the window, saying:

"Lege dich, lieber Wind,
Bringe diss deinem Kind!"

"Dear Wind, be not so wild,
Take that unto thy child!"

"In which thing," adds the highly Protestant PRÆTORIUS ("***Anthropodemus Plutonicus***," p. 429), "she was like the Papists who would fain appease the *Donnerwetter*, or thunderstorms, with the sound of baptized bells, as though they were raging round like famished lions, or grim wolves, or a soldier foraging, seeking what they may devour." The Wind here represents the Wild Hunter, or the Storm, the leader of the *Wüthende Heer*, or "raging army," who, under different names, is the hero of so many German legends.

That the voice of the wind should seem like that of wild beasts roaring for food would occur naturally enough to any one who was familiar with both.

When a child refuses the breast the gypsies believe that a Pçuvus-wife, or a female spirit of the earth has secretly sucked it. In such a case they place between the mother's breasts onions, and repeat these words:

"Pçuvushi, Pçuvushi,
Ac tu náshvályi
Tito tçud ač yakhá,
Andre pçuv tu pçábuvá!
Thávdá, thávdá miro tçud,
Thávdá, thávdá, parno tçud,
Thávdá, thávdá, sár kámáv,--
Mre čáveske bokhale!"

"Earth-spirit! Earth-spirit
Be thou ill.
Let thy milk be fire

Burn in the earth!
Flow, flow, my milk!
Flow, flow, white milk!
Flow, flow, as I desire
To my hungry child!"

The same is applied when the milk holds back or will not flow, as it is then supposed that a Pçuvus-wife has secretly suckled her own child at the mother's breast. It is an old belief that elves put their own offspring in the place of infants, whom they sometimes steal. This subject of elf-changelings is extensively treated by all the writers on witchcraft. There is even a Latin treatise, or thesis, devoted to defining the legal and social status, rights, &c., of such beings. It is entitled, "***De Infantibus Supposititiis, vulgo Wechsel-Bälgen***," Dresden, 1678. "Such infants," says the author (JOHN VALENTINE MERBITZ), "are called Cambiones, Vagiones (*à continuo vagitu*), Germanis Küllkräpfe, Wechselkinder, Wechselbälge, all of which indicates, in German belief, children which have nothing human about them except the skin."

When the child is subject to convulsive weeping or spasms, and loses its sleep, the mother takes a straw from the child's sleeping-place and puts into her mouth. Then, while she is fumigated with dried cow-dung, into, which the hair of the father and mother have been mingled, she chants:

"Bala, bálá pçubuven,
Čik te bálá pçubuven,
Čik te bálá pçubuven,
Pçábuvel náshvályipen!"

"Hair, hair, burn!
Dirt and hair burn
Dirt and hair burn
Illness be burned!"

This bears manifest mark of Hindoo origin, and I have no doubt that the same ceremony in every detail is practised in India at the present day. In Southern Hungary convulsive weeping in children is cured as follows: In the evening, when the fire burns before the tent, the mother takes her child in her arms and carries it three times around the fire, putting on it a pipkin full of water, into which she puts three coals. With this water she washes the head of her child, and pours some of it on a black dog. Then she goes to the next stream or brook, and lets fall into it a red twist, saying:

> "Lává Nivâshi ádá bolditori te láhá m're čaveskro rovipen! Káná sástavestes ánáv me tute pçábáyá te yándrá."

"Nivashi take this twist, and with it the weeping of my child. When it is well I will bring thee apples and eggs."

When a child "bumps" its head the swelling is pressed with the blade of a knife, and the following spell is muttered thrice, seven, or nine times, according to the gravity of the injury:--

"Ač tu, ač in, ač kovles,
The may sik tu mudarés!
Andre pcuv tu jiá,
Dikav tut me ñikáná!
Shuri, shuri áná,
Do pal pçuv!"

"Be thou, be thou, be thou weak (*i.e.*, soft)
And very soon perish!
Go thou into the earth,
May I see thee never more
Bring knives, knives,
Give (*i.e.*, put) into the earth."

Then the knife is stuck three, seven, or nine times into the earth. If the child or a grown person has a bleeding at the nose, some of the blood is covered with earth, and the following verse repeated

"Pçuvush, dáv tute
Pcuvush, lává mánge,
De tre cáveske
Hin may táte!
Sik lava!"

"Pcuvus, I give to thee,
Pcuvus, oh take from me,
Give it to thy child,
It is very warm,
Take it quickly!"

If the child has pains in the stomach, the hair of a black dog is burned to powder and kneaded with the mother's milk and some of the feces of the child into a paste. This prescription occurs in the magical medical formulas Of MARCEI.LUS BURDIGALENIS, the court-physician at Rome in the fourth century: "Cape mel atticum et stercus infantis quod primum demittit, statim ex lacte mulieris quæ puerum allactat permiscebis et sic inunges," &c. Most of the prescriptions of Marcellus were of ancient Etrurian origin, and I have found many of them still in use in the Romagna Toscana. This is put into a cloth and bound on the belly of the child. When it falls asleep a hole is bored in a tree and the paste put into it. The hole is then stopped up with a wooden plug, and while this is being done the following is repeated:

"Andrál por prejiá,
André selene beshá!
Beshá beshá tu káthe!
Penáv, penáv me tu te!"

"Depart from the belly
Live in the green! (tree)
Remain, remain thou here
I say, I say to thee!"

The black dog is in many countries associated with sorcery and diabolical influences, and "in European heathendom it was an emblem of the evil principle. The black demon Černobog was represented by the Slavs as a black dog. Among the Wallachians there is a horrible vampire-like creature called Priccolitsh, or Priculics, who appears as a man in fine healthy condition, but by night he becomes a dog, kills people by the mere touch, and devours them." The black dogs of Faust and of Cornelius Agrippa will occur to most readers.

Gypsies have always been regarded as sorcerers and child-stealers, and it is remarkable that Lilith, the mother of all witchcraft, did the same. At the present day the Slavonian gypsies have spells against such a spirit.

In the Chaldæan magic, as set forth by Lenormant, as I have already stated, the powers of evil are incarnate diseases, they are seven in number, and they are invoked by means of verses which bear an extraordinary resemblance to those which are still current in Italy as well as in other countries. According to some writers this is all mere chance coincidence, or due to concurrent causes and similar conditions in different countries.

That diseases, like hunger, or death, or the terrors of the night, may have been incarnated as evil spirits naturally by all mankind may be granted, but when we find them arranged in categories of numbers, in widely different countries, employing the same means of banishing them--that is, by short songs and drum-beating--when we find these incantations in the same general forms, often with the same words, our belief as to the identity of origin is confirmed at every step. We can admit that the Jews were in Babylon and wandered thence all over the world, but that any other religious or superstitious system should have done the same would be obstinately denied. And by an incredible inconsistency, scholars who admit the early migrations of whole races on a vast scale, from the remotest regions of the East to Western Europe, deny that legends and myths come with them or that they could have spread in like manner.

One of the attributes of the witch of the Middle Ages in which she has been confused with the Queen of the Fairies, and fairies in general, is that she steals newly-born children. This is a very ancient attribute of the female demon or sorceress or *strega*, and it is found among Jews at the present day who believe in the *Benemmerinnen*, or witches who haunt women in childbirth as well as in Lilith.

"The Jews banish this first wife of Adam by writing on the walls, '*Adam chava chuz Lilith,*' ('Keep away from here, Lilith!')" ("***Anthropodemus Plutonicus,***" by JOHN PRÆTORIUS, 1666). That it is very ancient is rendered probable because the famous Bogomile formula of incantation against the twelve fever-fits (*Tresevica*), or kinds of fever, turns entirely on the legend of six children stolen by the demon who is compelled to restore them. Here we have the very oldest form of witchcraft known, that is incarnate disease in numbers allied to child-stealing.

This spell of the Tresevica. is attributed, says Dr. GASTER, to Pope JEREMIA, the founder of Bogomilism (the great Oriental Slavonian heresy which spread over Europe in the Middle Ages and prepared the way for . "There is no doubt, therefore, that the spell is derived from the East, and I have else where proved its existence in that quarter as early as the eighth century. It may have been of Manichæan origin. It has been preserved up to the present day in all the lands of Eastern Europe and, with certain modifications, exists among Germans and Jews." Though attributed to Sisynios, the immediate follower Of MANES, as chief of the Manichæans, it seems to have been derived from an earlier Oriental tale which became the basis of all later formulæ. I give it here in the Roumanian form, which closely resembles the old one. Here, as in all the other variants, the demon is a feminine one. The following is the legend:

> "I, Sisveas, I came down from the Mount of Olives, saw the Archangel Gabriel as he met the Avestitza, wing of Satan, and seized her by the hair and asked her where she was going. And she answered that she was going to cheat the holy Virgin by her tricks, steal the new-born child, and drink its blood. The archangel asked her how she could get into houses so as to steal the children, and she answered that she changed herself into a fly or a cat or such forms. But whosoever knew her twelve and a half (nineteen) names and wrote them out she could not touch. She told him these names, and they were written down."

There is a Coptic as well as a Greek parallel to this. The fairy who steals the children is called Lilith, and is further identified with Herodias and her twelve daughters as personifications of different kinds of fever. This is extremely interesting, as it casts some light on a question which has greatly puzzled all writers on witchcraft as to how or why *Herodias* was so generally worshipped in company with Diana by witches as a goddess in Italy. This is mentioned by PIPERNUS, GRILLANDUS, MIRANDOLA, and HORST. The name is probably much older than that of the Herodias of the New Testament.

CHAPTER IV

South Slavonian And Other Gypsy Witch-Lore—The Words For A Witch—Vilas And The Spirits Of Earth And Air-Witches, Eggshells, And Egg-Lore-Egg Proverbs—Ova De Crucibus

THERE is current in the whole of the Southern Slavonian provinces a vast mass of legends and other lore relating to witches, which, in the opinion of Dr. FRIEDRICH S. KRAUSS, may also be regarded as Romany, since it is held in common with the gypsies. There can, indeed, be very little doubt that most of it was derived from, or disseminated by, them, since they have been the principal masters in magic and doctors in medicine in the Slavonic lands for many centuries. There are others deeply learned in this subject who share the same opinion, it being certain that the gypsies could hardly have a separate lore for themselves and one for magic practices on others, and I entertain no doubt that they are substantially the same; but to avoid possible error and confusion, I give what I have taken in this kind from Dr. KRAUSS and others by itself.

As the English word *witch*, Anglo-Saxon *Wicca*, comes from a root implying wisdom, so the pure Slavonian word *vjestica*, Bulgarian, *vjescirica* (masculine, *viestae*), meant originally the one knowing or well informed, and it has preserved the same power in allied languages, as *Veaa* (New Slovenish), knowledge, *Vedavica*, a fortune-teller by cards, *Viedma* (Russian), a witch, and *Vedwin, fatidicus*. In many places, especially in Dalmatia, witches are more gently or less plainly called *Krstaca*, the crossed, from *Krst*, a cross, *i.e.*, χριστός {Greek *xristós*}, or *Rogulja*, "horned," derived from association with the horns of devils. In Croatia the Italian Striga is used, while among the Slovenes and Kai-Kroats the term *copernica* (masculine, *coprnjak*). "But it enrages the witches so much to be called by this word that when they hear that any one has used it they come to his house by night and tear him in four pieces, which they cast afar into the four quarters of the earth, yea, and thereunto carry away all the swine, horses, and cattle, so intolerable is their wrath." Therefore men use the word *hmana zena*, or "common woman," *hmana* being the Slavonic pronunciation of the German word *gemein*, or common. In Dalmatia and far into Servia a witch is called *macisnica*, and magic, mačija, which is, evidently enough, the Italian *magia*. But there are witches and witches, and it appears that among the learned the *vjestica* differs from the *macionica*, and this from the *Zlokobnica* who, as the "evil-meeter," or one whom it is unlucky to encounter in the morning, is probably only one who has the evil eye. A quotation from a Servian authority, given by Dr. KRAUSS, is as follows:--

"I have often heard from old Hodzas and Kadijas, that every female Wallach, as soon as she is forty years old, abandons the 'God be with us!' and becomes a witch (*vjestica*), or at least a *zlokobnica* or *macionica*. A real witch has a mark of a cross under her nose, a *zlokobnica* has some hairs of a beard, and a *macionica* may be known by a forehead full of dark folds (frowns), with blood-spots in her face" ("*Niz srpskih pripoviedaka*. VUK. *vit. Vecevica. Pancevo*," p. 93. 1880.

Of the great number of South Slavonian terms for the verb to enchant or bewitch, it may suffice to say that the commencement, *carati, cari carani, carovnik*, &c., appear to have much more affinity to the gypsy *chor-ava*, to steal or swindle, and *chov-hani*, a witch, than to the Italian *ciarlatano*, and the French and English *charlatan*, from which Dr. KRAUSS derives them.

THE VILAS-SYLVANA ELEMENTARY SPIRITS.

Among the Slavonic and gypsy races all witchcraft, fairy- and Folk-lore rests mainly upon a belief in certain spirits of the wood and wold, of earth and water, which has much in common with that of the Rosicrucians and PARACELSUS, but much more with the gypsy mythology (as given by Wlislocki, "Vom Wandernden Zigeunervolke," pp. 49-309), which is apparently in a great measure of directly Indian origin.

"In the *Vile*," says Dr. KRAUSS, "also known as *Samovile*, *Samodivi*, and *Vilevrjaci*, we have near relations to the forest and field spirits, or the 'wood-' and 'moss-folk' of Middle Germany, France, and Bavaria; the 'wild people' of Eifel, Hesse, Salzburg, and the Tyrol; the wood-women and wood-men of Bohemia; the Tyrolese *Fanggen*, *Fänken*, *Nörkel*, and Happy Ladies; the Roumanish *Orken*, *Euguane*, and *Dialen*; the Danish *Ellekoner*, the Swedish *Skogsnufvaz*, and the Russian *Ljesje*;

while in certain respects they have affinity with the Teutonic *Valkyries*." Yet they differ on the whole from all of these, as from English fairies, in being more like divinities, who exert a constant and familiar influence for good or evil on human beings, and who are prayed to or exorcised on all occasions. They have, however, their *exact* parallel among the Red Indians of North America as among the Eskimo, and it is evident that they are originally derived from the old or primeval Shamanic faith, which once spread all over the earth. It is very true, as Dr. KRAUSS remarks, that in the West of Europe it is becoming almost impossible to trace this true origin of spirits now regarded as merely diabolical, or otherwise put into new *rôles*; but among the South Slavonians and gypsies we can still find them in very nearly their old form and playing the same parts. We can still find the Vila as set forth in old ballads, the incarnation of beauty and power, the benevolent friends of sufferers, the geniuses of heroes, the dwellers by rock and river and greenwood tree. But they are implacable in their wrath to all who deceive them, or who break a promise; nay, they inflict terrible punishment even on those who disturb their rings or the dances which they make by midsummer moonlight. Hence the proverb applied to any man who suddenly fell ill: "*Naiso je na vilinsko kolo*" ("He stepped on a fairy-ring"). From this arbitrary exercise of power we find the Vila represented at times as a spirit who punishes and torments.

Thus we are told that there was once a shepherd named STANKO, who played beautifully on the flute. One evening he was so absorbed in his own music that when the Ave Maria bell rung, instead of repeating the prayer he played it. As he ended he saw a Vila sitting on a hedge. And from that hour she never left him, By table, by his bed, at work or play, the white form and unearthly eyes of the spirit were close to him.

> "By a spell to him unknown,
> He could never be alone."

Witches and wizards were summoned to aid him, but to no avail; nay, it made matters worse, for the Vila now often beat him, and when, people asked him why it was, he replied that the Vila did so because he refused to wander out into the world with her. And yet again he would be discovered in the top of a tree, bound with bast; and so it went on for years, till he was finally found one morning drowned in a ditch. So in the Wolf Dietrich legend the hero refuses the love of *die rauhe Else*, and is made mad by the witch and runs wild. All of which is identical with what is told in an Algonkin tale (*vide* "The Algonkin Legends of New England").

There are three kinds of witches or spirits among the Southern Slavonians which correspond in every respect exactly to those in which the gypsies believe. The first of these are the *Zracne Vile*, or aerial spirits. These, like the spirits of the air of Scripture, are evily-disposed to human beings, playing them mischievous tricks or inflicting on them fatal injuries. They lead them astray by night, like Friar Rush and Robin Goodfellow, or the English gypsy *Mullo doods*, or bewilder and frighten them into madness. Of the second kind are the Earth spirits, *Pozemne Vile*, in gypsy *Pcûvushi* or *Pûvushi*. These are amiable, noble, and companionable beings, who often give sage counsel to men. Thirdly are the Water sprites, in Slavonic *Povodne Vile*, in gypsy *Nivashi*, who are to the highest degree vindictive at times, yet who behave kindly to men when they meet them on land. But woe to those who, while swimming, encounter them in streams or lakes, for then the goblins grasp and whirl them about until they perish. From this account by Dr. KRAUSS, it appears as if this Slavonic mythology were derived from the gypsy, firstly, because it is more imperfect than the latter, and secondly, because in it Vilas, or spirits, are confused with witches, while among the gypsies they are clearly separated and distinctly defined.

Dr. WLISLOCKI Says ("Vom Wand. Zigeunervolke," p. 253) that "gypsies are still a race given to Shamanism, but yet they reverence a highest being under the name of *devla* or *del*." This is, however, the case to-day with *all* believers in Shaman or Sorcery-religion, the difference between them and monotheists being that this highest god is little worshipped or even thought of, all *practical* devotion being paid to *spirits* who are really their saints. By close examination the Gypsy religion, like that of the country-folk in India, appears to be absolutely identical in spirit with that of American Indians. And I should say that the monk mentioned by PRÆTORIUS, who declared that though God and Christ should damn him, yet he could be saved by appealing to Saint Joseph, was not very far removed from being a Shamanist.

The Hungarian gypsies are divided into tribes, and one of these, the Kukaya, believes itself to be descended from the *Pçuvushi*, or earth-fairies, according to the following story, narrated by Dr. H. von WLISLOCKI in his paper on the genealogy and family relations of the Transylvanian Tent Gypsies:

> "Many thousand years ago there were as yet in the world very few *Pchuvushi.* These are beings of human form dwelling under the earth. There they have cities, but they very often come to the world above. They are ugly, and their men are covered with hair. (All of this indicates a prehistoric subterranean race like the Eskimo, fur-clad.) They carry off mortal girls for wives. Their life is hidden in the egg of a black hen."

This is the same as that of the *Orco* or Ogre in the Italian tale, "I Racconti delle Fate, Cesare da Causa," Florence, 1888. Whoever kills the hen and throws the egg into a running stream, kills the *pchuvush.*

> "Once a young Pchûvush woman came up to the world and sat in a fair green forest. She saw a very beautiful youth sleeping in the shade, and said: 'What happiness it must be to have such a husband. Mine is so ugly!' Her husband, who had stolen silently after her, heard this, and reflected 'What a good idea it would be to lend my wife to this young man till she shall have borne a family of beautiful children! Then I could sell them to my rich Pchuvûs friends.' So he said to his wife: 'You may live with this youth for ten. years if you will promise to give me either the boys or the girls which you may bear to him.' She agreed to this. Then the Pchûvûs began to sing:
>
> "'Kuku, kukáya
> Kames to adala?
> Kuku, kukaya.'

That is in English:

> "'Kuku, kukaya
> Do you want this (one) here
> Kuku, kukaya.'

Then the young man awoke, and as the goblin offered him much gold and silver with his wife, he took her and lived with her ten years, and every year she bore him a son. Then came the Pchuvush to get the children. But the wife said she had chosen to keep all the sons, and was very sorry but she had no girls to give him! So he went away sorrowfully, howling

> "'Kuku, kukáya!
> Ada kin jirklá!
> Kuku, kukaya!'

"That is to say:

> "'Kuku, kukaya
> These are dogs here!
> Kuku, kukaya!'

"Then the ten boys laughed and said to their father We will call ourselves Kukaya.' And so from them came the race."

Dr. WLISLOCKI points out that there are races which declare themselves to be descended from dogs, or, like the Romans, from wolves. It is a curious coincidence that the Eskimo are among the former.

In all parts of Eastern Europe, as in the West, many people are not only careful to burn the parings of their nails 1 and the combings of hair, for fear lest witches and imps should work sorcery with them to the injury of those from whom they came, but they also destroy the shells of eggs when they have eaten their contents. So A. WUTTKE tells us in his book, "***Der Deutsche Volks Aberglaube der Gegenwart***," 1869 "When one has eaten eggs the shells must be broken up or burned, or else the hens will lay no more, or evil witches will come over them." And in England, Spain, the Netherlands, or Portugal, there are many who believe or say that if the witches can get such shells from which people have eaten, unbroken, they can, by muttering spells, cause them to grow so large that they can use them as boats. Dom LEITAS GANET ("***Donna Branca ou à Conquista do Algarre***," Paris, 1826), however, assures us that is a very risky thing for the witches, because if they do not return home before midnight the shell-boat perishes, "whence it hath come to pass that many of these sorceresses have been miserably drowned."

However, an egg hung up in a house is a lucky amulet, hence the ostrich eggs and cocoanuts resembling them which are so common in the East. And it is to be observed that every gypsy in England declares that a *pivilioi*, or cocoanut, as a gift brings *bâk* or luck, I myself having had many given to me with this assurance. This is evidently and directly derived from India, in which country there are a mass of religious traditions referring to it.

"Once there was a gypsy girl who noticed that when anybody ate eggs they broke up the shells, and asking why this was done received for answer:

"'You must break the shell to bits for fear
Lest the witches should make it a boat, my dear.
For over the sea away from home,
Far by night the witches roam.'

"Then the girl said: 'I don't see why the poor witches should not have boats as well as other people.' And saying this she threw the shell of an egg which she had been eating as far as she could, and cried, '*Chovihani, lav tro bero*!' ('Witch--there is your boat!') But what was her amazement to see the shell caught up by the wind and whirled away on high till it became invisible, while a voice cried, '*Paraka*!' ('I thank you!')

"Now it came to pass some time after that the gypsy girl was on an island, where she remained some days. And when she wished to return, behold a great flood was rising, and it had washed her boat away, she could see nothing of it. But the water kept getting higher and higher, and soon there was only a little bit of the island above the flood, and the girl thought she must drown. just then she saw a white boat coming; there sat in it a woman with witch eyes; she was rowing with a broom, and a black cat sat on her shoulder. 'Jump in!' she cried to the girl, and then rowed her to the firm land.

"When she was or. the shore the woman said: 'Turn round three times to the right and look every time at the boat.' She did so, and every time she looked she saw the boat grow smaller till it was like an egg. Then the woman sang:--

"'That is the shell you threw to me,
Even a witch can grateful be.'

"Saying this she vanished, cat, broom, shell, and all.

"Now my story is fairly done,
I beg you to tell a better one."

As regards these boats which grow large or small at will we find them in the Norse ship *Skidbladner*, which certain dwarfs made and gave to Frey. It is so large that all the gods and their army can embark in it. But when not in use it may be so contracted that one may hava i pungi sino--put it in his purse or pocket. The Algonkin god Glooskap has not only the counterpart of *Skidbladnir*, but the hammer of Thor and his belt of strength. He has also the two attendant birds which bring him news, and the two wolves which mean Day and Night.

Another legend given by Dr. KRAUSS, relative to witches and eggshells is as follows:

> "By the Klek lived a rich tavern-keeper and his wife. He was thin and lean—*hager und mager*—while she was as fat as a well-fed pig.

"One day there came a gypsy woman by. She began to tell his fortune by his hand. And as she studied it seriously she became herself serious, and then said to him, 'Listen, you good-natured dolt (*moré*)! Do you know why you are so slim and your wife so stout?' 'Not I.' 'My good friend (*Latcho pral*), your wife is a witch. Every Friday when there is a new moon (*mladi petak*) she rides you up along the Klek to the devil's dance' (*Uraze kolo*). 'How can that be?' 'Simply enough. As soon as you fall asleep, she slips a magic halter over your head. Then you become a horse, and she rides you over the hills and far away over mountains and woods, cities and seas, to the witches' gathering.

> "Little you know where you have been,
> Little you think of what you have seen,

"For when you awake it is all forgotten, but the ride is hard for you, and you are wasting away, and dying. Take great care of yourself on the next Friday when there is a new moon!'

"So the gypsy went her way, and he thought it over. On the next Friday when the moon was new he went to bed early, but only pretended to sleep. Then his wife came silently as a cat to the bedside with the magic halter in her hand. As quick as lightning he jumped up, snatched it from her, and threw it over her head. Then she became, in a second, a mare. He mounted her, and away she flew through the air-over hills and dales like the wind, till they came to the witches' meeting.

"He dismounted, bound the mare to a tree, and, unseen by the company, watched them at a little distance. All the witches carried pots or jars. First they danced in a ring, then every one put her pot on the ground and danced alone round it. And these pots were egg-shells.

"While he watched, there came flying to him a witch in whom he recognized his old godmother. 'How did you come here?' she inquired. 'Well, I came here on my mare, I know not how.' 'Woe to you--begone as soon as possible. If the witches once see you it will be all up with you. Know that we are all waiting for one' (this one was his wife), 'and till she comes we cannot begin.' Then the landlord mounted his mare, cried 'Home!' and when he was there tied her up in the stable and went to bed.

"In the morning his servant-man said to him: 'There is a mare in the stable.' 'Yes,' replied the master; 'it is mine.' So he sent for a smith, and made him shoe the mare. Now, whatever is done to a witch while she is in the form of an animal remains on or in her when she resumes her natural shape.

"Then he went out and assembled a judicial or legal commission. He led the members to his house, told them all his story, led forth the mare, and took off the halter. She became a woman as before, but horse-shoes were affixed to her feet and hands. She began to weep and wail, but the judge was pitiless. He had her thrown into a pit full of quicklime, and thus she was burnt to death. And since that time people break the shells of eggs after eating their contents, lest witches should make jars or pots of them."

The following story on the same subject is from a different source:

"There was once a gypsy girl who was very clever, and whenever she heard people talk about witches she remembered it well. One day she took an egg-shell and made a small round hole in it very neatly, and are the yolk and white, but the shell she put on a heap of white sand by a stream, where it was very likely to be seen. Then she hid herself behind a bush. By and by, when it was night, there came a witch, who, seeing the shell, pronounced a word over it, when it changed to a beautiful boat, into which the witch got and sailed on the water, over the sea.

"The girl remembered the word, and soon ate another egg and turned it into a boat. Whenever she willed it went over the world to places where fruit and flowers abounded, or where people gave her much gold for such things as knives and scissors. So she grew rich and had a fine house. The boat she hid away carefully in a bush.

"There was a very envious, wicked woman, whom the girl had befriended many a time, and who hated her all the more for it. And this creature set to work, spying and sneaking, to find out the secret of the girl's prosperity. And at last she discovered the boat, and, suspecting something, hid herself in the bush hard by to watch.

"By and by the girl came with a basket full of wares for her trade, and, drawing out the boat, said, 'To Africa!'--when off it flew. The woman watched and waited. After a few hours the girl returned. Her boat was full of fine things, ostrich feathers and gold, fruit and strange flowers, all of which she carried into her house.

"Then the woman put the boat on the water, and said, 'To Africa!' But she did not know the word by means of which it was changed from an egg-shell, and which made it fly like thought. So as it went along the woman cried, 'Faster!', but it never heeded her. Then she cried again in a great rage, and at last exclaimed, 'In God's name get on with you!' Then the spell was broken, and the boat turned into an egg-shell, and the woman was drowned in the great rolling sea."

Egg-lore is inexhaustible. The eggs of Maundy Thursday (***Witten Donnertag***), says a writer in *The Queen*, protect a house against thunder and lightning, but, in fact, an egg hung up is a general protection, hence the ostrich eggs and cocoanuts of the East. Some other very interesting items in the communication referred to are as follows:

WITCHES AND EGGS

"To hang an egg laid on Ascension Day in the roof of a house," says Reginald Scot in 1584, "preserveth the same from all hurts." Probably this was written with an eye to the 'hurts' arising from witchcraft, in connection with which eggs were supposed to possess certain mysterious powers. In North Germany, if you have a desire to see the ladies of the broomstick on May Day, their festival, you must take an egg laid on Maundy Thursday, and stand where four roads meet; or else you must go into church on Good Friday, but come out before the blessing. It was formerly quite an article of domestic belief that the shells must be broken after eating eggs, lest the witches should sail out to sea in them; or, as Sir Thomas Browne declared, lest they 'should draw or prick their names therein, and veneficiously mischief' the person who had partaken of the egg. North Germans, ignoring this side of the question, say, "Break the shells or you will get the ague;" and Netherlanders advise you to secure yourself against the attacks of this disagreeable visitor by eating on Easter Day a couple of eggs which were laid on Good Friday.

SCOTTISH SUPERSTITIONS

Scotch fishers, who may be reckoned among the most superstitious of folks, believe that contrary winds and much consequent vexation of spirit will be the result of having eggs on board with them; while in the west of England it is considered very unlucky to bring birds' eggs into the house, although they may be hung up with impunity outside. Mr. Gregor, in his "***Folklore of the North-East of Scotland***," gives us some curious particulars concerning chickens, and the best methods of securing a satisfactory brood. The hen, it seems, should be set on an odd number of eggs, or the chances are that most, if not all, will be addled—a mournful prospect for the henwife; also they must be placed under the mother bird after sunset, or the chickens will be blind. If the woman who performs this office carries the eggs wrapped up in her chemise, the result will be hen birds; if she wears a man's hat, cocks. Furthermore, it is as well for her to repeat a sort of charm, 'A' in thegeethir, A oot thegeethir.'

UNLUCKY EGGS

There are many farmers' wives, even in the present day, who would never dream of allowing eggs to be brought into the house or taken out after dark—this being deemed extremely unlucky. Cuthbert Bede mentions the case of a farmer's wife in Rutland who received a setting of ducks' eggs from a neighbour at nine o'clock at night.

"I cannot imagine how she could have been so foolish," said the good woman, much distressed, and her visitor, upon inquiry, was told that ducks' eggs brought into a house after sunset would never be hatched. A Lincolnshire superstition declares that if eggs are carried over running water they will be useless for setting purposes; while in Aberdeen there is an idea prevalent among the country folks that should it thunder a short time before chickens are hatched, they will die in the shell. The same wiseacres may be credited with the notion that the year the farmer's gudewife presents him with an addition to his family is a bad season for the poultry yard. 'Bairns an' chuckens,' say they, "dinna thrive in ae year." The probable explanation being that the gudewife, taken up with the care of her bairn, has less time to attend to the rearing of the 'chuckens.'

FORTUNE-TELLING IN NORTHUMBERLAND

Besides the divination practised with the white of an egg, which certainly appears of a vague and unsatisfactory character, another species of fortune-telling with eggs is in vogue in Northumberland on the eve of St. Agnes. A maiden desirous of knowing what her future lord is like, is enjoined to boil an egg, after having spent the whole day fasting and in silence, then to extract the yolk, fill the cavity with salt, and eat the whole, including the shell. This highly unpalatable supper finished, the heroic maid must walk backwards, uttering this invocation to the saint:

"'Sweet St. Agnes, work thy fast,
If ever I be to marry man,
Or man be to marry me,
I hope him this night to sec.'"

FRIEDRICH and others assert that the saying in Luke xi. 12--"Or if he shall ask an egg shall he give him a scorpion?"—is a direct reference to ancient belief that the egg typified the good principle, and the scorpion evil, and which is certainly supported by a cloud of witnesses in the form of classic folk-lore. The egg, as a cosmogenic symbol, and indicating the origin of all things, finds a place in the mythologies of many races. These are indicated with much erudition by FRIEDRICH, "***Symbolik der Natur***," p. 686.

In Lower Alsatia it is believed that if a man will take an Easter egg into the church and look about him, if there be any witches in the congregation he may know them by their having in their hands pieces of pork instead of prayer-books, and milk-pails on their heads for bonnets;(WOLF, ***"Deutsche Mährchen und Sagen,"*** p. 270). There is also an ancient belief that an egg built into a new building will protect it against evil and witchcraft. Such eggs were found in old houses in Altenhagen and Iserlohen, while in the East there is a proverb, "the egg of the chamber" ("Hamasa" of ABU TEMMAN, v. RÜCKERT, Stuttgart, 1846), which seems to point to the same practice.

The Romans expressed a disaster by saying "Ovum ruptum est" ("The egg is smashed"). Among other egg-proverbs I find the following:

His eggs are all omelettes (*French*); *i.e.*, broken up.

Eggs in the pan give pancakes but nevermore chicks (*Low German*).

Never a chicken comes from broken eggs (*Low German*).

Bad eggs, bad chickens. Hence in America "a bad egg" for a man who is radically bad, and "a good egg" for the contrary.

Eggs not yet laid are uncertain chickens; *i.e.*, "Do not count your chickens before they are hatched."

Tread carefully among eggs (*German*).

The egg pretends to be cleverer than the hen.

He waits for the eggs and lets the hen go.

He who wants eggs must endure the clucking of the hen (*Westphalian*).

He thinks his eggs are of more account than other people's hens.

One rotten egg spoils all the pudding.

Rotten eggs and bad butter always stand by one another; or "go well together."

Old eggs, old lovers, and an old horse, Are either rotten or for the worse.

(Original:

Alte Eyer
Alte Freier
Alter Gaul
Sind meistens faul.)

"All eggs are of the same size" (Eggs are all alike), he said, and grabbed the biggest.

As like as eggs (*Old Roman*).

As sure as eggs.

His eggs all have two yolks.

If you have many eggs you can have many cakes.

He who has many eggs scatters many shells.

To throw an egg at a sparrow.

To borrow trouble for eggs not yet hatched.

Half an egg is worth more than all the shell.

A drink after an egg, and a leap after an apple.

A rotten egg in his face.

In the early mythology, the egg, as a bird was hatched from it, and as it resembled seeds, nuts, &c., from which new plants come, was regarded as the great type of production. This survives in love-charms, as when a girl in the Tyrol believes she can secure a man's love by giving him a red Easter egg. This giving red eggs at Easter is possibly derived from the ancient Parsees, who did the same at their spring festival. Among the Christians the reproductive and sexual symbolism, when retained, was applied to the resurrection of the body and the immortality of the soul. Hence Easter eggs. And as Christ by His crucifixion caused this, or originated the faith, we have the *ova de crucibus*, the origin of which has puzzled so many antiquaries; for the cross itself was, like the egg, a symbol of life, in earlier times of reproduction, and in a later age of life eternal. These eggs are made of a large size of white glass by the Armenian Christians.

CHAPTER V

Charms or Conjurations to Cure or Protect Animals

FROM the earliest ages a drum or tambourine has formed such an indispensable adjunct of Shamanic sorcery among Tartars, Lapps, Samoyedes, Eskimo, and Red Indians, that, taking it with other associations, I can hardly believe that it has not been transmitted from one to the other. In Hungary the gypsies when they wish to know if an invalid will recover, have recourse to the *cováçanescro buḍlo* (*chovihanescro bûklo*) or "witch-drum." This is a kind of rude tambourine covered with the skin of an animal, and marked with stripes which have a special meaning. On this are placed from nine to twenty-one seeds of the thorn-apple (*stramomium*).

The side of the drum is then gently struck with a little hammer, and according to the position which the seeds take on the marks, the recovery or death of the patient is predicted. The following is a picture of a gypsy drum as given by Dr. WLISLOCKI.

LAPLAND MAGIC DRUM

The wood for this is cut on Whitsunday. A is turned towards the fortuneteller; nine seeds are now thrown on the drum, and with the left hand, or with a hammer held in it, the tambourine is tapped. Should all the seeds come within the four lines all will go well, especially if three come within *a, d, e, f.* If two roll into the space between *a, i,* it is lucky for a woman, between *i* and *f* for a man. But if nearly all fall outside of *b, c, g, h,* all is unfavourable. The same divination is used to know whether animals will get well, and where stolen property is concealed. All of this corresponds exactly to the use of the same instrument by the Laplanders for the same purposes. The thorn-apple is a very poisonous plant, and the gypsies are said to have first brought it to England. This is *not* true, but it is extremely possible that they used it in stupefying, killing, and "bewitching." It is very much employed at present by the Voodoo poisoners in America.

The Turks are a Tartar race, and the drum is used among them very generally for magical purposes. I have one of these *tambouri* which, I was assured when I bought it, was made for incantations. It is of a diamond shape, has parchment on *both* sides, and is inscribed with the name Allah, in Arabic, and the well-known double triangle of Solomon, with the moon and star.

To keep domestic animals from straying or being stolen, or falling ill, they are, when a gypsy first becomes their owner, driven up before a fire by his tent. Then they are struck with a switch, which is half blacked with coal, across the back, while the following is repeated:--

"Ač tu, ač kathe!
Tu hin mange!
Te Nivasa the jiánen
Ná dikh tu ádálen!
Trin lánca bin mánge,
Me pçándáv tute:
Yeká o devlá, ávri
O Kristus, trite Maria!"

"Stay thou, stay here
Thou art mine!
And the Nivasi when they go
Thou shalt not see them!
Three chains I have,
I bind thee:
One is God, the other (beyond)
The Christ, the third, Maria!"

To charm a horse, they draw, with a coal, a ring on the left hoof and on the right a cross, and murmur

"Obles, obles te obles!
Ac tu, ac tù máy sástes
Ná th' ávehás beng tute
Devlá, devlá ač tute!
Gule devlá bishálá
E gráyeskro perá
Miseçescro dád!
Niko mánushenge áč
Káske me dáv, leske áč
Shukáres tu áč,
Voyesá te láčes áč,
Ashunen eftá Pçuvuse:
Eftá láncá hin mánge,
Ferinen ádálá
Táysá, táysá e pedá!"

"Round, round, and round
Be thou, be thou very sound
The devil shall not come to thee.
God, God shall be with thee
Sweet God drive away
From the horse's body
The Father of Evil!
Be to (go not to) any other man
To whom I give (sell) unto him
Be beautiful!
Frolicsome and good,
Seven spirits of earth hear
I have seven chains,
Protect this animal
Ever, ever!"

Then a piece of salted bread is given to the horse, and the owner spits seven times into his eyes, by which he is supposed to lose all fear for supernatural beings. According to the gypsies, horses, especially black ones, can see beings which are invisible to human eyes. I have known an old English gypsy who believed that dogs could see ghosts when men could not. The mysterious manner in which dogs and horses betray fear when there is apparently nothing to dread, the howling of the former by night, and the wild rushes of the latter, doubtless led to this opinion. The bread and salt will recall to the reader the fact that the same was given at the ancient mysteries apparently for the purpose of strengthening the neophyte so that he should not fear the supernatural beings whom he was supposed to meet. It is curious to find this peculiar form of the sacrament administered to a horse. Another protective charm is common among the Southern Hungarian gypsies. The dung of a she-goat dried and powdered is sifted on a horse's back and this spell recited:

"Miseçes prejiá,
Andrál t're perá!
Trádá čik busčákri
Miseçes perákri,--
Andral punrá, andral dumno,
Andral yákhá, andral kánná!
Nevkerádyi av ákána,
Ač tu, ač to čá mánge:
Ač tu, áč tu, áč kathe!"

"Evil be gone
From thy belly!
Drive away she-goat's dung
Evil from the belly,
From the feet, from the back,
From the eyes, from the ears
New-born be now,
Be thou, be thou only mine
Stay thou, stay thou, stay here!"

There is evidently a relation here between the dung of the she-goat and certain ancient symbols. Whatever was a sign of fruitfulness, generation, or productiveness, whether it was set forth by the generative organs, sexual passion, or even manure which fertilises, was connected with Life which is the good or vital principle opposed to death. As the goat was eminently a type of lechery, so the she-goat, owing to the great proportion of milk which she yielded, set forth abundance; hence the cornucopia of Amalthea, the prototype of the she-goat Heidrun of the Northern mythology, who yielded every day so much milk that all the Einheriar, or dwellers in Valhall, could satisfy themselves therewith. But the forms or deities indicating life were also those which shielded and protected from evil, therefore Here, the mother of life and of birth, had in Sparta a shrine where she-goats were sacrificed to her, while at Canuvium the statue of Juno Sospita (who was also Here), was covered with a she-goat's skin. It is in the ancient sense of fertility identified with protection, that the she-goat's dung is used to exorcise evil from the horse by the gypsies.

There is, in fact, in all of these char ms and exorcisms a great deal which evidently connects them with the earliest rites and religions.

In the Hungarian gypsy-tribe of the Kukuya, the following method of protecting horses is used: The animal is placed by the tent-fire and there a little hole is dug before him into which ninefold grass and some hairs from his mane and tail are put. Then his left fore-hoof is traced on the ground, and the earth within it is carefully taken out and shaken into the hole, while these lines are repeated:--

"Yeká čunul yeká bál,
Tute e bokh náñi sál,
Ko tut čorel, the merel
Sar e bálá, čunulá,
Pal e pçuv the yov ável!
Pçuvus, adalen tute,
Sástes gráy ác mánge!"

"A straw, a hair!
May you never be hungry
May he who steals you die
Like the hair and the straw,
May he go to the ground
Earth, these things to thee
May a sound horse be mine!"

If the animal be a mare and it is desired that she shall be with foal, they give her oats to eat out of an apron or a gourd, and say

"Trin kánályá, trin jiuklá,
Jiánen upre pláyá!
Cábá, pçarcs hin perá!
Trin kánályá, trin jiuklá
Jiánen tele pláyá,
É çevá ándrasaváren
Yek čumut ándre çasáren,
Tre perá sik pçáreven!"

"Three asses, three dogs,
Go up the hill!
Eat, fill thy belly with young!
Three asses, three dogs,
Go down the hill,
They close the holes,

They put the moon in (them)
Thy belly be soon fruitful!"

"The moon has here," remarks WLISLOCKI, "a phallic meaning, the mention of the ass, and the use of the gourd and apron are symbols of fertility. *Vide* DE GUBERNATIS, 'Animals in Indian Mythology,' in the chapter on the ass."

There is another formula for protecting and aiding cattle, which is practised among other races besides that of the gypsies; as, for instance, among the Slovacks of Northern Hungary. This I shall leave in the original--

"Dieser Verwahrungsmittel besteht darin, dass dem gekauften weiblichen Thiere der Mann den blanken Hintern zeigt, einem mannlichen Thiere aber eine weibliche Person. Hiebei werden die Worte gesagt:

"Sár o kár pál e punrá,
Kiyá mánge ác táysá!

Wie der Schwantz am Bein,
Sollst du stets bei mir sein!"

Or else:

"Sár e minč pal e per,
Kiyá mánge ác buter!

Wie das Loch im Leib,
Also bei mir bleib!"

To secure swine to their owner a hole is dug in the turf which is filled with salt and charcoal dust, which is covered with earth, and these words uttered:--

"Adá hin tute
Ná ává pál menge
Dáv tute, so kámáv
Pçuvusheyá, áshuná,
Čores tuna muká
Hin menge trin láncá,
Trin máy láce Urmá,
Ke ferinen men!"

"This is thine,
Come not to us
I give thee what I can
Oh Spirit of earth, hear
Let not the thief go!
We have three chains,
Three very good fairies
Who protect us."

If the swine find the hole and root it up--as they will be tolerably certain to do owing to their fondness for salt and charcoal--they will not be stolen or run away.

The *Urmen*, or Fairies, are supposed to be very favourable to cattle, therefore children who torment cows are told "*Urme tute ná bica somnakune pçábáy*"—"The fairies will not send you any golden apples!" If the English gypsies had the word *Urme* (and it may be that it exists among them even yet), this would be, "*I Urme ná bitcher tute sonnakai pábya*!"

But the mighty charm of charms to protect cattle from theft is the following: Three drops of blood are made to fall from the finger of a little child on a piece of bread which is given to the animal to eat, with these words

"Dav tute trinen rátá
Ternes te láces ávná!
Ko tut čorel, ádáleske
Hin rát te más shutyárdye!

Káná rátá te rátá
Paltire per ávná,
Yákh te yákh te báre yákh
Sikoves çál te çál
Ko kámel tut te çál!"

"I give three (drops of) blood
To become young and good;
Who steals thee to him
Shall be (is) blood and flesh dried up!

When blood and blood
Pass into thy belly,
Fire and fire and great fire

Shall devour and devour all
Who will eat thee!"

This incantation takes us back to grim old heathenism with hints of human sacrifice. When the thief was suspected or privately detected it is probable that a dose of some burning poison made good the prediction. "The word *young*," remarks Dr. WLISLOCKI, "may be here understood to mean *innocent*, since, according to ancient belief, there was a powerful magic virtue in the blood of virgins and of little children. Every new tent is therefore sprinkled by the gypsies with a few drops of a child's blood to protect it from magic or any other accident." So in prehistoric times, and through the Middle Ages, a human being was often walled up alive in the foundations of a castle to insure its durability. (*Vide* P. CASSEL, Die Symbolik des Blutes," p. 157.)

When the wandering, or tent-gypsies, find that cattle are ill and do not know the nature of the disease, they take two birds--if possible quails, called by them *bereçto* or *füryo*--one of which is killed, but the other, besprinkled with its blood, is allowed to fly away. With what remains of the blood they sprinkle some fodder, which is put before the animal, with the words:--

"So ándre tu miseç hin
Avri ává!
Káthe ker ná ávlá,
Miseçeske!
Káná rátá ná ávná,
Násvályipen ná ávná!
Miseç, tu ávri ává,
Ada ker ná láce;
Dáv rátá me káthe!"

"What in thee is evil
Come forth
Here is no home
For the evil one!
When (drops of) blood come not,
Sickness comes not,
Thou evil one, come forth!'

"Trin párne, trin kále,
Trin tçule páshlajen káthe,

Ko len hádjinel
Ač kivá mánge!"

"Three white, three black,
Three fat lie together here.
Whoever disturbs them
Remain to me! (Be mine!)"

To insure pigs thriving by a new owner, some charcoal-dust is mingled with their food and these words spoken:--

"Nivaseske ná muká,
The çál t're çábená!
Miseç yákhá tut díkhen,
The yon káthe mudáren,
Tu atunci çábá len!"

"Do not let the Nivasi
Eat thy food,
Evil eyes see thee,
And they here shall perish,
Then do thou eat them!

As a particularly powerful conjuration against thieves, the owner runs thrice, while quite naked, round the animal or object which he wishes to protect, and repeats at every turn:--

"Oh coreyá ná prejiá.
Dureder ná ává!
T're vástá, t're punrá
Avcná kirñodyá
Te ádá pedá láves!"

"Oh, thief, do not go,
Further do not come
Thy hands, thy feet
Shall decay
If thou takest this animal!"

Another "thieves' benediction" is as follows: The owner goes at midnight with the animal or object to be protected to a cross-roads, and while letting fall on the ground a few hairs of the beast, or a bit of the thing whatever it be, repeats:--

"Ada hin tute,
Ná ává pál menge,
Dav tute, so kámáv;
Pçuvuseyá áshuná!

"This home is not good,
Here I give (thee) blood!"

The gypsies call the quail the devil's bird (*Ciriclo bengeskro*), and ascribe diabolic properties to it. (***Vide CASSEL***, 6 and 162.) The daughters of the Nivasi appear as quails in the fields by day, but during the night they steal the corn. To keep them away it is held good during sowing-time to place in each of the four corners of the field, parts of a quail, or at least some of the feathers of a black hen which has never laid an egg. This superstition is also current among the Roumanian peasants of the Siebenbürgen."

The primitive meaning of the myth may perhaps be found in the Greek tradition which regarded the quail, because it was a bird of passage, as a type of revival of spring or of life. Hercules awakes from his swoon when his companion Iolaus (from the Greek ιουλος {Greek *ioulos*}, youth), holds a quail to his nose. Hercules suffered from epilepsy, for which disease the ancients thought the brain of a quail was a specific. The placing pieces of a quail, by the gypsies, in the corners of a field when corn is sown, connects the bird with spring. Artemis, a goddess of spring and life, was called by the Romans *Ortygyia*, from ορτυξ {Greek *ortuks*}, a quail. Therefore, as signifying new life, the quail became itself a cure for many diseases. And it seems to be like the Wren, also a bird of witchcraft and sorcery, or a kind of witch itself. It is a protector, because, owing to its pugnacity, it was a type of pluck, battle and victory. In Phœnicia it was sacrificed to Hercules, and the Romans were so fanatical in regard to it that AUGUSTUS punished a city-father for serving upon his table a quail which had become celebrated for its prowess. And so it has become a devil's bird among the gypsies because in the old time it was regarded as a devil of a bird for fighting.

The gypsies are hardly to be regarded as Christians, but when they wish to contend against the powers of darkness they occasionally invoke Christian influences. If a cow gives bloody milk it is thought to be caused by her eating *Wachtelkraut*, or quail weed, which is a poison. In such a case they sprinkle the milk on a field frequented by quails and repeat:--

"Dav rátá tumenge
Adá ná hin láče!
Ráyeskro Kristeskro rátá
Adá hin máy láce
Adá hin ámenge!"

"I give to you blood,
Which is not good!
The Lord Christ's blood
Is truly good,
That is ours!"

If a cow makes water while being milked, she is bewitched, and it is well in such a case to catch some of the urine, mix it with onion-peelings and the egg of a black hen. This is boiled and mixed with the cow's food while these lines are repeated:

"Ko ándré hin, avriává,
Trin Urma cingárden les,
Trin Urma tráden les
Andre yándengré ker
Beshél yov ándre ker
Hin leske máy yakhá,
Hin leske máy páña!"

"Who is within, let him come out!
Three Urme call him,
Three Urme drive him
Into the egg-shell house,
There he lives in the house
He has much fire,
He has much water!"

Then half the shell of the egg of the black hen is thrown into a running stream and the other half into a fire.

Next to the Nivasi and Pçuvuse, or spirits of earth and air, and human sorcerers or witches, the being who is most dreaded as injuring cattle is the *Chagrin* or Cagrino. These demons have the form of a hedgehog, are of yellowish colour, and are half a yard in length, and a span in breadth. "I am certain," says WLISLOCKI, "that this creature is none other than the equally demoniac being called *Harginn*, still believed in by the inhabitants of North-western India. (*Vide* LIEBRECHT, p. 112, and LEITNER, '***Results of a Tour in Dardistan***

Kashmir,' &c., vol. i. p. 13) The exact identity of the description of the two, as well as that of the name, prove that the gypsies brought the belief from their Indian home." It may here be observed that the Indian name is Harginn, and the true gypsy word is pronounced very nearly like '*Hágrin*--the *o* being an arbitrary addition. The transposition of letters in a word is extremely common among the Hindu gypsies. The *Chagrin* specially torments horses, by sitting on their backs and making water on their bodies. The next day they appear to be weary, sad, sick, and weak, bathed in sweat, with their manes tangled. When this is seen the following ceremony is resorted to: The horse is tied to a stake which has been rubbed with garlic juice, then a red thread is laid in the form of a cross on the ground, but so far from the heels of the horse that he cannot disturb it. And while laying it down the performer sings:

"Sáve miseç ač káthe,
Ác ándre lunge táve,
Andre leg páshader páñi.
De tu tire páñi
Andre çuča Cháriñeyá,
Andre tu sik mudárá!"

"All evil stay here,
Stay in the long thread,
In the next brook (water).
Give thy water,
Jump in Chagrin!
Therein perish quickly!"

Of the widely-spread and ancient belief in the magic virtues of garlic and red wool I have elsewhere spoken. That witches and goblins or imps ride horses by night and then restore them in the morning to their stalls in a wretched condition--trembling, enfeebled, and with tangled manes--is believed all the world over, and it would probably be found that the Chagrin also gallops them.

Another charm against this being consists of taking some of the hair of the animal, a little salt, and the blood of a bat, which is all mixed with meal and cooked to a bread. With this the foot of the horse is smeared, and then the empty pipkin is put into the trunk of a high tree while these words are uttered

"Ac tu čin kathe,
Čin ádá tçutes ávlá!"

"Stay so long here,
Till it shall be full!"

The blood of the bat may be derived from an Oriental belief that the bat being the most perfect of birds, because it has breasts and suckles its young, it is specially adapted to magical uses. In the Tyrol he who bears the left eye of a bat may become invisible, and in Hesse he who wears the heart of a bat bound to his arm with red thread will always win at cards. The manes of the horses which have been tangled and twisted by the Chagrin must not be cut off or disentangled unless these words are spoken:--

"Čin tu jid', cin ádá bálá jiden."

"So long live thou, long as these hairs shall live."

It is an European belief that knots of hair made by witches must not be disentangled. The belief that such knots are made intentionally by some intelligence is very natural. I have often been surprised to find how frequently knots form themselves in the cord of my eye-glass, even when pains are taken at night to lay it down so as to be free of them. *Apropos* of which I may mention that this teasing personality of the eye-glass and cord seems to have been noted by others. I was once travelling on the Nile in company with a Persian prince, who became convinced that his eye-glass was very unlucky, and therefore threw it into the river.

The Chagrin specially torments mares which have recently foaled; therefore it is held needful, soon after the birth, to put into the water which the mother drinks glowing hot coals, which are thrice taken from the fire. With these are included pieces of iron, such as nails, knives, &c., and the following words are solemnly murmured:--

"Piyá tu te ña ač sovnibnastár!"

"Drink, and do not be sleepy!"

Many readers may here observe that charcoal and iron form a real tonic, or very practical strengthening dose for the enfeebled mare. But here, as in many cases medicine makes a cure and the devil or the doctor gets the credit. The Chagrin is supposed to attack horses only while they are asleep. Its urine often causes swellings or sores. These are covered by day with a patch of red cloth, which is stuck at night into a hole in a tree, which is closed with a cork, while these words are pronounced

"Ač tu káthe
Čin áulá táv pedá
Čin pedá yek ruk
Čin ruk yek mánush
Ko mudarel tut."

"Remain thou here
Till the rag become an animal,
Till the animal, a tree,
Till the tree, a man,
Who will destroy thee!"

Dr. WLISLOCKI suggests that "the idea of the tree's becoming a man, is derived from the old gypsy belief that the first human beings were made from the leaves of trees, and refers to what he has elsewhere written on a tradition of the creation of the world, as held by Transylvanian gypsies. The following is a children's song, in which the belief may be traced:

"Amaro dád jál ándro bes
Čingerel odoy čaves,
Del dáyákri andre pádá
Yek čavoro ádá ávla."

"Our father went into a wood,
There he cut a boy,
Laid it in mother's bed,
So a boy comes."

The Greeks believed that man was made from an ash-tree, and the Norsemen probably derived it from the same source with them. In 1862 I published in *The Continental Magazine* (New York) a paper on the lore connected with the ash, in which effort was made to show that in early times in India the Banyan was specially worshipped, and that the descendants of men familiar with this cult had, after migrating to the Far West, transferred the worship and traditions of the banyan to the ash. It has been observed that the ash-tree sometimes--like the banyan--sends its shoots down to the ground, where they take root. The Algonkin Indians seem to have taken this belief of man's origin from the ash from the Norsemen, as a very large proportion of their myths correspond closely to those of the Edda. But, in brief, if the

Greeks and Norsemen were of Aryan origin, and had ever had a language in common, they probably had common myths.

The following is the remedy for the so-called *Würmer*, or worms, *i.e.*, external sores. Before sunrise wolf's milk (*Wolfsmilch, rukeskro tçud*) is collected, mixed with salt, garlic, and water, put into a pot, and boiled down to a brew. With a part of this the afflicted spot is rubbed, the rest is thrown into a brook, with the words:

"Kirmora jánen ándre tçud
Andrál tçud, andré sir
Andrál sir, andré páñi,
Panensá kiyá dádeske,
Kiyá Niváseske
Pçandel tumen shelchá
Eñávárdesh teñá!"

"Worms go in the milk,
From the milk into the garlic,
From the garlic into the water,
With the water to (your) father,
To the Nivasi,
He shall bind you with a rope,
Ninety-nine (yards long)."

A common cure of worms in swine among the Transylvanian tent-gypsies is to stand ere the sun rises before a *çadcerli*, or nettle, and while pouring on it the urine of the animal to be cured, repeat:

"Láče, láče detehárá!
Hin mánge máy bute trásha
Kirmora hin [báleceske],
Te me penáv, penáv tute!
Káles hin yon, loles, párnes,
Deisislá hin yon mulánes!"

"Good, good morrow!
I have much sorrow.
Worms are in [my swine to-day]
And I say, to you I say,
Black are they or white or red
By to-morrow be they dead!"

The nettle has its own peculiar associations. According to the gypsies it grows chiefly in places where there is a subterranean passage to the dwellings of the Pçuvus or Earth-fairies, therefore it is consecrated to them and called *Kásta Pçuvasengré*, Pcuvus-wood. Hence the gypsy children while gathering nettles for pigs sing:

"Čádcerli ná pçábuvá!
André ker me ná jiáv,
Kiyá Pçuvus ná jiáv,
Tráden, tráden kirmorá!"

"Nettle, nettle do not burn,
In your house no one shall go,
No one to the Pcuvus goes,
Drive, drive away the worms!"

"The nettle," says FRIEDRICH ("***Symbolik der Natur***," p. 324), "because it causes a burning pain is among the Hindoos a demoniac symbol, for, as they say, the great serpent poured out its poison on it. But as evil is an antidote for evil, the nettle held in the hand is q. guard against ghosts, and it is good for beer when laid upon the barrel." "From its employment as an aphrodisiac, and its use in flagellation to restore sexual power, it is regarded as sacred to Nature by the followers of a secret sect or society still existing in several countries, especially Persia" (*MS. account of certain Secret Societies*). The gypsies believe that. the Earth-fairies are the foes of every kind of worm and creeping insect with the exception of the snail, which they therefore call the "gráy Pçuvusengré," the Pçuvus-horse. *Grypuvusengree* would in English gypsy mean the earthy-horse. English gypsies, and the English peasantry, as well as gypsies, call snails "cattle, because they have horns." Snails are a type of voluptuousness, because they are hermaphrodite and exceedingly giving to sexual indulgence, so that as many as half a dozen may be found mutually giving and taking pleasure. Hence in German *Schnecke*, a snail, is a term applied to the *pudendum muliebre*. And as anything significant of fertility, generation, and sexual enjoyment was supposed to constitute a charm or amulet against witchcraft, *i.e.*, all evil influences, which are allied to sterility, chastity, and barrenness, a snail's shell forms a powerful fetish for a true believer. The reference to white, black, or red in the foregoing charm, or rather the one before it, refers, says Dr. WLISLOCKI, to the gypsy belief that there are white, black, and red Earth-fairies. A girl can win (illicit) love from a man by inducing him to carry a snail shell which she has had for some time about her person. To present a snail shell is to make a very direct but not very delicate declaration of love to any one. I have heard of a lady who caused an intense excitement in a village by collecting about a hundred large snails, gilding their shells, and then turning them loose in several gardens, where their discovery excited, as may be supposed, great excitement among the finders.

If pigs lose their appetites a brew is made of milk, charcoal dust, and their own dung, which is put before them with the words: "*Friss Hexe und verreck*!"

"In this place I must remark that the Transylvanian tent-gypsies use for *grumus merdæ* also the expression *Hirte* (*feris*)" (WLISLOCKI). To cure a cough in animals one should take from the hoofs of the first riding horse, dirt or dust, and put it into the mouth of the suffering animal with the words

"Prejiál te náñi yov ável!"

"May he go away and never return!"

To have a horse always in good spirits and lively during the waning moon his spine is rubbed with garlic, while these words are uttered:

"Miseç ándre tut,
O beng the çal but!
Lačes ándré tut
Ačel ándre tut!"

"(What is) evil in thee,
May the devil eat it much!
(What is) good in thee,
May it remain in thee!"

But it is far more effective when the garlic is put on a rag of the clothes of one who has been hanged, and the place rubbed with it: in which we have a remnant of the earliest witchcraft, before Shamanism, which had recourse to the vilest and most vulgar methods of exciting awe and belief. This is in all probability the earliest form in which magic, or the power of controlling invisible or supernatural influences manifested itself, and it is very interesting to observe that it still survives, and that the world still presents every phase of its faiths, *ab initio*.

There is a very curious belief or principle attached to the use of *songs* in conjuring witches, or in averting their own sorcery. It is that the witch is obliged, willy nilly, to listen to the end to what is in metre, an idea founded on the attraction of melody, which is much stronger among savages and children than with civilized adults. Nearly allied to this is the belief that if the witch sees interlaced or bewildering and confused patterns she must follow them out, and by means of this her thoughts are diverted or scattered. Hence the serpentine inscriptions of the Norsemen and their intertwining bands which were firmly believed to bring good luck or avert evil influence. A traveller in Persia states that the patterns of the carpets of that country are made as bewildering as possible "to avert the evil eye." And it is with this purpose that in Italian, as in all other witchcraft, so many spells and charms depend on interwoven braided cords.

"Twist ye, twine ye, even so,
Mingle threads of joy and woe."

The basis for this belief is the fascination, or instinct, which many persons, especially children, feel to trace out patterns, to thread the mazes of labryinths or to analyze and disentangle knots and "cat's cradles." Did space permit, nor inclination fail, I could point out some curious proofs that the old belief in the power of long and curling hair to fascinate was derived not only from its beauty but also because of the magic of its curves and entanglements.

The gypsies believe that the Earth-spirits are specially interested in animals. They also teach women the secrets of medicine and sorcery. There are indications of this in the negro magic. Miss MARY OWEN, an accomplished Folk-lorist of St. Joseph, Missouri, who has been deeply instructed in Voodooism, informs me that a woman to become a witch must go by night into a field and pull up a weed by the roots. From the quantity of soil which clings to it, is inferred the degree of magic power which the pupil will attain. I am not astonished to learn that when this lady was initiated, the amount of earth collected was unusually great. In such cases the *Pchuvus* (or Poovus in English gypsy), indicate their good-will by bestowing "earth," which, from meaning luck or good-fortune, has passed in popular parlance to signifying money.

"Geit suer Heidrun heitr stendr uppi a Valholl. . . . En or spenum hennar rennr moilk. . . tháer cro sva miklar at allir einheria verda fuldrucknir af." ("A ewe named Heidrun stands up in Valhalla. And from her udders runs milk; there is so much that all the heroes may drink their fill of it"). (***SNORRO STURLESON'S*** "Edda," 20th tale).

CHAPTER VI

Of Pregnancy And Charms, Or Folk-Lore Connected With It—Boar's Teeth And Charms For Preventing The Flow of Blood

LIKE all Orientals the gypsy desires intensely to have a family. Superstition comes in to increase the wish, for a barren woman in Eastern Europe is generally suspected of having had intercourse with a vampire or spirit before her marriage, and she who has done this, willingly or unconsciously, never has children. They have recourse to many magic medicines or means to promote conception; one of the most harmless it, Hungary is to eat grass from the grave in which a woman with child has been buried. While doing this the woman repeats:--

"Dui riká hin mire minč,
Dui yârá hin leskro kor,
Avnás dûi yek jelo,
Keren ákána yek jeles."

Or else the woman drinks the water in which the husband has cast hot coals, or, better still, has spit, saying:

"Káy me yákh som
Ac tu ángár,
Káy me brishind som,
Ac tu pâni!"

"Where I am flame
Be thou the coals
Where 1 am rain
Be thou the water!"

Or at times the husband takes an egg, makes a small hole at each end, and then blows the yolk and white into the mouth of his wife who swallows them.

There are innumerable ways and means to ensure pregnancy, some of which are very dangerous. Faith in the so-called "artificial propagation" is extensively spread. "Will der zigeuner einen Sohn erzielen, so gürtet er sich mit dem Halfterzaume eines männlichen Pferdes und ümgekehrt mit dem einer Stüte, will er eine Tochter erzeugen." ("Gebräuche d. Trans. Zig." Dr. H. von WLISLOCKI. "Ill. Zeitschrift. Band," 51. No. 16.)

If a gypsy woman in Transylvania wishes to know whether she be with child, she must stand for nine evenings at a cross-road with an axe or hammer, which she must wet with her own water, and then bury there. Should it be dug up on the ninth morning after, and found rusty, it is a sign that she is "in blessed circumstances."

To bring on the *menses* a gypsy woman must, while roses are in bloom, wash herself all over with rose-water, and then pour the water over a rose-bush. Or she takes an egg, pours its contents into a jug, and makes water on it. If the egg swims the next morning on the surface she is *enceinte*; if the yolk is separate from the white she will bear a son, if they are mingled a daughter. In Tuscany women wishing for children go to a priest, get a blessed apple and pronounce Over it an incantation to Santa Anna, which was probably addressed in Roman days to Lucina, who was very probably, according to the Romagna dialect, *lu S'anna*--Santa Anna herself. I have several old Roman spell, from MARCELLUS, which still exist word for word in Italian, but fitted to modern usage in this manner like old windows to new houses.

Should a woman eat fish while pregnant the child will be slow in learning to speak, but if she feed on snails it will be slow in learning to walk. The proverbs, "Dumb as a fish," and "Slow as a snail," appear here.

To protect a child against the evil eye it is hung with amulets, generally with shells (*die eine Aehnlichkeit mit der weiblichen Scham haben*). And these must be observed on all occasions, and for everything, ceremonies, of which there are literally hundreds, showing that gypsies, notwithstanding their supposed freedom from conventionalisms, are, like all superstitious people, harassed and vexed to a degree which would seem incredible to educated Europeans, with observances and rites of the most ridiculous and vexatious nature. The shells alluded to are, however, of great interest, as they indicate the transmission of the old belief that symbols typical of generation, pleasure, and reproductiveness, are repugnant to witchcraft which is allied to barrenness, destruction, negation, and every kind of pain and sterility.

Hence a necklace of shells, especially cowries or snail shells, or the brilliant and pretty *conchiglie* found in such abundance near Venice, are regarded as protecting animals or children from the evil eye, and facilitating love, luxury, and productiveness. I have read an article in which a learned writer rejects with indignation the "prurient idea" that the cowrie, which gave its name *porcellana* to porcelain, derived it from *porcella, in sensu obsceno*; *porcella* being a Roman word not only for pig but for the female organ. But every donkey-boy in Cairo could have told him that the cowrie is used in strings on asses as on children because the shell has the likeness which the writer to whom I refer rejects with indignation.

The pig, as is well known, is a common amulet, the origin thereof being that it is extremely prolific. It has within a few years been very much revived in silver as a charm for ladies, and may be found in most shops where ornaments for watch-chains are sold. The boar's tooth, as I have before mentioned, has been since time immemorial a charm; I have found them attached to chatelaines and bunches of keys, specially in Austria, from one to four or five centuries past. They are found in prehistoric graves. The tusk is properly a male emblem; a pig is sometimes placed on the base. These are still very commonly made and sold. I saw one worn by the son of a travelling basket-maker, who spoke Romany, and I purchased several in Vienna (1888), also in Copenhagen in 1889.

In Florence very large boars' tusks are set as brooches, and may be found generally in the smaller jewellers' shops and on the Ponte Vecchio. They are regarded as protective against *malocchio*—general term for evil influences--especially for women during pregnancy, and as securing plenty, *i.e.*, prosperity and increase, be it of worldly goods, honour, or prosperity.

There is in the museum at Budapest a boar's tusk, mounted or set as an amulet, which is apparently of Celtic origin, and which certainly belongs to the migration of races, or a very early period. And it is in this eastern portion of Europe that it is still most generally worn as a charm.

BOAR'S TOOTH. VIENNA.

In connection with pregnancy and childbirth there is the *profluvium* excessive flow of blood, or menses or hemorrhages, for which there exist many charms, not only among gypsies but all races. This includes the stopping any bleeding--an art in which Scott's Lady of Deloraine was an expert, and which many practised within a century.

> "Tom Potts was but a serving man,
> And yet he was a doctor good,
> He bound a handkerchief on the wound.
> And with some kind of words he staunched the blood."

What these same kind of words were among old Germans and Romans may be learned from the following: JACOB GRIMM had long been familiar with a German magic spell of the eleventh century—*stringendum sanguinem*, or stopping bleeding—but as he says, "noch nicht zu deuten vermochte," could not explain them. They were as follows:

> "Tumbo saz in berke,
> Mit tumbemo kinde in arme,
> Tumb hiez der berc
> Tumb hiez daz kint,
> Der heiligo Tumbo
> Versegne disc wunta."

"Tumbo (*i.e.*, dumm or stupid) sat in the hill
With a stupid child in arms,
Dumb (stupid) the hill was called
Dumb was called the child,
The holy Tumbo (or dumb).
Heal (bless) this wound!"

Some years after he found the following among the magic formulas, of MARCELLUS BURDIGALENSIS:

"Carmen utile profluvio mulieri:

"Stupidus in monte ibat,
Stupidus stupuit,
Adjuro te matrix
Ne hoc iracunda suscipias.

"Pari ratione scriptum ligabis."

I.e.: "A song useful for a flow of blood in woman:

"The stupid man went into the mountain,
The stupid man was amazed;
I adjure thee, oh womb,
Be not angry!

"Which shall also be bound as a writing," *i.e.*, according to a previous direction that it shall be written on virgin parchment, and bound with a linen cord about the waist of him or of her--*quæ patietur de qualibet parte corporis sanguinis fluxum*--who suffers anywhere from flow of blood.

It is possible that the Stupidus and his blessing of women has here some remotely derived reference to the reverence amounting to worship of idiots in the East, who are described as being surrounded in some parts of India by matrons seeking for their touch and benediction, and soliciting their embraces. This is effected very often in an almost public manner; that is to say, by a crowd of women closely surrounding the couple, *i.e.*, the idiot or lunatic and one of their number are joined, so that passers-by cannot see what is going on. The children born of these casual matches are not unusually themselves of weak mind, but are considered all the more holy. This recalls the allusion in the charm

"Stupid sat in the hill
With a stupid child in arms."

This obscure myth of the stupid god appears to be very ancient.

"This Tritas is called intelligent. How then does he appear sometimes stupid? The language itself supplies the explanation. In Sanskrit *bâlas* means both child and stolid, and the third brother is supposed to be stolid because, at his first appearance especially, he is a child. (Tritas is one of the three brothers or gods, *i.e.*, the trinity)." ("***Zoological Mythology***," by ANGELO DE GUBERNATIS, 1872).

I am indebted to the as yet unpublished collection of Gypsyana made by Prof. ANTON HERRMANN for the following:--

There is a superstition among our gypsies that if the shadow of a cross on a grave falls on a woman with child she will have a miscarriage, and this seems to be peculiarly appropriate to girls who have "anticipated the privileges of matrimony." The following rhyme seems to describe the hesitation of a girl who has gone to a cross to produce the result alluded to, but who is withheld by love for her unborn infant:

"Cigno trušul pal handako
Hin ada ušalinako;
The žiav me pro ušalin,
Ajt' mange lašavo na kin.

Sar e praytin kad' chasarel,
Save šilc barvâl marel,
Pal basavo te prasape,
Mre čajori mojd kâmâle."

"Cross upon a grave so small
Here I see thy shadow fall,
If it fall on me they say
All my shame will pass away.

As the autumn leaf is blown,
By the wind to die alone,
Yet in shame and misery,
My baby will be clear to me!"

There is a belief allied to this of the power of the dead in graves to work wonders, to the effect that if any one plucks a rose from a grave, he or she will soon die. In the following song a gypsy picks a rose from the grave of the one be loved, hoping that it will cause his death:

"Cignoro hrobosa
Hin sukares rosa
Mange la pchagavas,
Doi me na kâmavas.

Beš'las piranake,
Hrobas hin joy mange,
Pchgavas, choč žanav
Pal lele avava
Te me ne brinzinav.
The me počivinav."

"On her little tomb there grows
By itself a lovely rose,
All alone the rose I break,
And I do it for her sake.

I sat by her I held so dear,
Now her grave and mine are near,
I break the rose because I know
That to her I soon must go,
Grief cannot my spirit stir,
Since I know I go to her!"

M. Kounavine (contribution by Dr. A. Elysseeff, *Gypsy-Lore Journal*, July, 1890), gives the following as a Russian gypsy spell against barrenness:

"Laki, thou destroyest and dost make everything on earth; thou canst see nothing old, for death lives in thee, thou givest birth to all upon the earth for thou thyself art life. By thy might cause me to bear good fruit, I who am deprived of the joy of motherhood, and barren as a rock."

According to Dr. Elysseeff, Laki is related to the Indian goddess Lakshmi, although differing from her in character. Another incantation of the same nature is as follows:

"Thou art the mother of every living creature and the distributor of good thou doest according to thy wisdom in destroying what is useless or what has lived its destined time; by thy wisdom thou makest the earth to regenerate all that is new. . . . Thou dost not seek the death of any one, for thou art the benefactress of mankind."

CHAPTER VII

The Recovery of Stolen Property—Love-Charms—Shoes And Love-Potions, Or Philtres

WHEN a man has lost anything, or been robbed, he often has in his own mind, quite unconsciously, some suspicion or clue to it. A clever fortune-teller or gypsy who has made a life-long study of such clues, can often elicit from the loser, hints which enable the magician to surmise the truth. Many people place absolute confidence in their servants, and perhaps suspect nobody. The detective or gypsy has no such faith in man, and suspects everybody. Where positive knowledge cannot be established there is, however, another resource. The thief is often as superstitious as his victim. Hence he fears that some mysterious curse may be laid on him, which he cannot escape. In the Pacific Islands, as among negroes everywhere, a man will die if taboo or voodoo attaches to the taking of objects which have been consecrated by a certain formula. Therefore such formulas are commonly employed. Among the Hungarian gypsies to recover a stolen animal, some of its dung is taken and thrown to the East and the West with the words:

"Kay tut o kam dikhel:
Odoy ává kiyá mánge!"

"Where the sun sees thee,
Hence return to me!"

But when a horse has been stolen, they take what is left of his harness, bury it in the earth and make a fire over it, saying

"Kó tut cordyás
Nasvales th' ávlás
Leske sor ná ávlás,
Tu ná a□ kiyá leske
Avá sástes kiyá mange!
Leskro sor káthe pashlyol
Sár e tçuv avriurál!"

"Who stole thee
Sick may he be
May his strength depart
Do not thou remain by him,
Come (back) sound to me,
His strength lies here
As the smoke goes away!"

To know in which direction the stolen thing lies, they carry a sucking babe to a stream, hold it over the water and say:

"Pen mánge, oh Nivaseya
Čaveskro vástehá
Kay hin m'ro gráy,
Ujes hin čavo,
Ujes sár o kam
Ujes sár páñi
Ujes sár čumut
Ujes sar legujes?
Pen mánge, oh Niváseyá.
Cáveskro vastchá
Kay hin m'ro gráy!"

"Tell me, oh Nivaseha,
By the child's hand!
Where is my horse ?
Pure is the child
Pure as the sun,
Pure as water,
Pure as the moon,
Pure as the purest.
Tell me, oh Nivaseha,
By the child's hand!
Where is my horse?"

In this we have an illustration of the widely spread belief that an innocent child is a powerful agent in prophecy and sorcery. The oath "by the hand" is still in vogue among all gypsies. "Apo miro dadeskro vast!" ("By my father's hand!") is one of their greatest oaths in Germany, ("***Die Zigeuner***," von RICHARD LIEBICH), and I have met with an old gypsy in England who knew it.

If a man who is seeking for stolen goods finds willow twigs grown into a knot, he ties it up and says:

"Me avri pçándáv čoreskro báçht!"

"I tie up the thief's luck!"

There is also a belief among the gypsies that these knots are twined by the fairies, and that whoever undoes them undoes his own luck, or that of the person on whom he is thinking. (*Vide* ROCHOLZ, "***Alemannisches Kinderlied und Kinderspiel aus der Schweiz,***" p. 146). These willow-knots are much used in love-charms. To win the love of a maid, a man cuts one of them, puts it into his mouth, and says:

"T're báçt me çáv,
T're baçt me piyáv,
Dáv tute m're baçt,
Káná tu mánge sál."

I eat thy luck,
I drink thy luck
Give me that luck of thine,
Then thou shalt be mine."

Then the lover, if he can, secretly hides this knot in the bed of the wished-for bride. It is worth noting that these lines are so much like English Gypsy as it was once spoken that there are still men who would, in England, understand every word of it. Somewhat allied to this is another charm. The lover takes a blade of grass in his mouth, and turning to the East and the West, says:

"Kay o kám, avriável,
Kiya mánge lele beshel!
Kay o kám tel' ável,
Kiya lelákri me beshav."

"Where the sun goes up
Shall my love be by me
Where the sun goes down
There by her I'll be."

Then the blade of grass is cut up into pieces and mingled with some food which the girl must eat, and if she swallow the least bit of the grass, she will be *gewogen und treugesinnt*--moved to love, and true-hearted. On which Dr. WLISLOCKI remarks on the old custom "also known to the Hindoos," by which any one wishing to deprecate the wrath of another, or to express complete subjection, takes a blade of grass in his mouth. Of which GRIMM writes: "This custom may have sprung from the idea that the one conquered gave himself up like a domestic animal to the absolute power of another. And with this appears to be connected the ancient custom of holding out grass as a sign of surrender. The conquered man took the blade of grass in his mouth and then transferred it to his conqueror."

If a gypsy girl be in love she finds the foot-print of her "object," digs out the earth which is within its outline and buries this under a willow-tree, saying:

"Upro pçuv hin but Pçuvá;
Kás kámáv, mange th' ávlá!
Bárvol, bárvol, sálciye,
Brigá ná hin mánge!
Yov tover, me pori,
Yov kokosh, me cátrá,
Ádá, ádá me kamav!"

"Many earths on earth there be,
Whom I love my own shall be,
Grow, grow willow tree!
Sorrow none unto me!
He the axe, I the helve,
He the cock, I the hen,
This, this (be as) I will!"

Another love-charm which belongs to ancient black witchcraft, and is known far and wide, is the following: When dogs are coupling (*Wenn Hund und Hündin bei der Paarung zusammenhangen*) the lover suddenly covers them with a cloth, if possible, one which is afterwards presented to the girl whom he seeks, while he says:

"Me jiuklo, yoy jiukli,
Yoy tover, me pori,
Me kokosh, yoy cátrá,
Ádá, ádá, me kamáv!"

"I the dog, she the bitch,
I the helve, she the axe,
I the cock (and) she the hen,
That, that I desire!"

vast moors overgrown with furzes and thorns. That the dead might not pass over them barefoot, a pair of shoes was laid with them in the grave."

The shoe was of old in many countries a symbol of life, liberty, or entire personal control. In Ruth we are told that "it was the custom in Israel concerning changing, that a man plucked off his shoe and delivered it to his neighbour." So the bride, who was originally always a slave, transferred herself by the symbol of the shoe. When the Emperor Waldimir made proposals of marriage to the daughter of Ragnald, she replied scornfully that she would not take off her shoes to the son of a slave. Gregory of Tours, in speaking of wedding, says The bridegroom, having given a ring to the bride, presents her with a shoe."

As regards the Scandinavian hel-shoe, or hell-shoon, Kelley, in his "Indo-European Folk-lore," tells us that a funeral is still called a dead shoe in the Henneberg district; and the writer already cited adds that in a MS. of the Cotton Library, containing an account. of Cleveland in Yorkshire, in the reign of Queen Elizabeth, there is a passage which illustrates this curious custom. It was quoted by Sir Walter Scott in the notes to "***Minstrelsy of the Scottish Border***," and runs thus:

> "When any dieth certaine women sing a song to the dead bodie, reciting the journey that the partye deceased must goe; and they are of beliefe that once in their lives it is goode to give a pair of new shoes to a poor man; forasmuch as before this life they are to pass bare-foote through a great lande, full of thornes and furzen—excepte by the meryte of the almes aforesaid they have redeemed the forfeyte--for at the edge of the launde an oulde man shall meet them with the same shoes that were given by the partie when he was lyving, and after he hath shodde them dismisseth them to go, through thick and thin without scratch or scalle.

This must be a very agreeable reflection to all gentlemen who have bestowed their old boots on waiters, or ladies who have in like fashion gifted their maids. It is true, the legend specifies new shoes; but surely a pair of thirty-shilling boots only half worn count for as much as a new pair of half a sovereign *chaussures*. However, if one is to go "through thick and thin without scratch or scalle," it may be just as, well to be on the safe side, and give a good new extra stout pair to the gardener for Christmas. For truly these superstitions are strange things, and no one knows what may be in them.

There are one or two quaint shoe stories of the olden time which may be of value to the collector. It befell once in the beginnings of Bohemia, that, according to Schafarik ("***Slawische Alterthümer***," vol. ii. p. 422), Lïbussa, queen of that land, found herself compelled by her council to wed. And the wise men, being consulted, declared that he who was to marry the queen would be found by her favourite horse, who would lead the way till he found a man eating from an iron table, and kneel to him. So the horse went on, and unto a field where a man sat eating a peasant's dinner from a ploughshare. This was the farmer Prschemischl. So they covered him with the royal robes and led him to the queen expectant. But ere going he took his shoes of willow-wood and placed them in his bosom and kept them to remind him ever after of his low origin. It will, of course, at once strike the reader, as it has the learned, that this is a story which would naturally originate in any country where there are iron ploughshares, horses, queens, and wooden shoes: and, as Schafarik shrewdly suggests, that it was all "a put-up job;" since, of course, Prschemischl was already a lover of the queen, the horse was trained to find him and to kneel before him, and, finally, that the ploughshare and wooden shoes were the prepared properties of the little drama. The only little flaw in this evidence is the name Prschemischl, which, it must be admitted, is extremely difficult to get over.

The Seven League Boots and the shoes of Peter Schlemilil, which take one over the world at will, have a variation in a pair recorded in another tale. There was a beautiful and extremely proud damsel, who refused a young man with every conceivable aggravation of the offence, informing him that when she ran after him, and not before that, he might hope to marry her; and at the same time meeting a poor old gypsy woman who begged her for a pair of old shoes. To which the proud Princess replied:

> "Shoes here, shoes there;
> Give me a couple, I'll give thee a pair."

To which the old gypsy, who was a witch, grimly muttered, "I'll give thee a pair which ------" The rest of the expression was really too unamiable to repeat. Well, the youth and the witch met, and, going to the lady's shoemaker, "made him make" a superbly elegant pair of shoes, which were sent to the damsel as a gift. Such a gift! No sooner were they put on than off they started, carrying the Princess, *malgré elle*, over hill and dale. By and by she saw that a man—the man, of course, whom she had refused—was in advance of her. As in the song of the Cork Leg, "the shoes never stopped, but kept on the pace." And the young man led her to a lonely castle and reasoned with her. And as she had promised to marry should she ever run after him, and as she had pursued him a whole day, she kept her word. The shoes she sent to the witch filled with gold; and they were wedded, and all went as merry as a thousand grigs in a duck-pond.

The shoe, as has been shown by a Danish writer in a book chiefly devoted to the subject, is a type of life, especially as shown in productiveness and fertility. Hence old shoes and grain are thrown after a bride, as people say, for luck; but the Jews do it crying, "Peru urphu" "Increase and multiply." For this, and much more, the reader may consult that wonderful treasury of Folk-lore, "***Die Symbolik und Mythologie der Natur***," J. B. FRIEDRICH, Würzburg, 1859. To which we would add our mite by remarking as a curious confirmation of this theory, that:

> "There was an old woman who lived in a shoe,
> Who had so many children she didn't know what to do."

This passes now for a mere nursery-rhyme; but doubtless there are those who will trace it back to the early morning of mythology, and prove that it was once a Himaritic hymn, sung to some Melitta who has long passed away down the back entry of time.

For several additional Hungarian gypsy love-charms and spells, collected by Dr. Wlislocki, published in *Ethnographia*, and subsequently in *The Gipsy-Lore Journal* for June, 1890, I am greatly indebted to the kindness of Mr. D. MacRitchie:

"The gypsy girls of Transylvania believe that spells to 'know your future husband' can be best carried out on the eves of certain days, such as New Year, Easter, and Saint George. 'On New Year's Eve they throw shoes or boots on a willow tree, but are only allowed to throw them nine times.' Compare this with the throwing of the old shoe after the bride in many countries. 'If the shoe catches in the branches the girl who threw it will be married within a year.'

> "'Per de, per de prájtina,
> Varckaj hin, hász kâmav?
> Basá, párro dzsiuklo,
> Pirano dzsâl mai szigo.'

> "'Scattered leaves around I see,
> Where can my true lover be?

Ah, the white dog barks at last
And my love comes running fast!'

"If during the singing the bark of a dog should be heard, the damsel will be 'wedded and bedded and a' 'ere New Year comes again. This is virtually the same with a charm practised in Tuscany, which from other ancient witness I believe to be of Etruscan origin. Allied to this is the following: On the night of Saint George's Day (query, Saint George's Eve?) gypsy girls blindfold a white dog, then, letting it loose, place themselves quietly in several places. She to whom the dog runs first will be the first married. Blindman's buff was anciently an amorous, semi-magical, or witches' game, only that in place of the dog a man was blindfolded.

"'Or the girl pulls a hair from her head, fastens a ring to it, and dangles it in a jug. The ring vibrates or swings, and so often as it touches the side of the jug so many years will it be before she marries.' This is an ancient spell of Eastern origin. As performed according to old works the thread must be wound around the ring-finger and touch the pulse. On the edge of a bowl the letters of the alphabet, or numerals, are marked, and the ring swinging against these spells words or denotes numbers. The touching of the latter indicates the number of lovers a girl is to have.

"Early on Whitsunday morning the girls go out, and if they see clouds in the East they throw twigs in that direction, saying:

"'Predzsia, csirik leja,
Te ná tráda m're píranes.'

'Fly my bird-fly, I say,
Do not chase my love away.'

For they think that if on Whitsun-morn there are many clouds in the East few girls will be married during the coming year. This peculiar, seemingly incomprehensible, custom of the gypsies originated in an old belief, the germ of which we find in the Hindoo myth, according to which the spring morning which spreads brightness and blessings descends from the blue bird of heaven, who, on the other hand, also represents night or winter. Special preparations are made so that the predictions shall be fulfilled. On the days mentioned the girls are neither allowed to wash themselves, nor to kiss any one, nor go to church. At Easter, or on the Eve of Saint George, the girl must eat fish, in order to see the future in her dreams.

"On Easter morning the girls boil water, in the bubbles of which they try to make out the names of their future husbands.

"To find out whether the future husband is young or old the girl must take nine seeds of the thorn-apple, ploughed-up earth of nine different places, and water from as many more. With these she kneads a cake, which is laid on a cross-road on Easter or Saint George's morning. If a woman steps first on the cake her husband will be a widower or an old man, but if a man the husband will be single or young.

"To see the form of a future husband a girl must go on the night of Saint George to a cross-road. Her hair is combed backwards, and, pricking the little finger of the left hand, she must let three drops of blood fall on the ground while saying:

> "'Mro rat dav piraneszke,
> Kász dikhav, avava adaleske.'
>
> "'I give my blood to my loved one,
> Whom I shall see shall be mine own!'

"Then the form of her future husband will rise slowly out of the blood and fade as slowly away. She must then gather up the dust, or mud-blood, and throw it into a river, otherwise the Nivashi, or Water-spirits, will lick up the blood, and the girl be drowned within the Year. It is said that about twenty years ago the beautiful Roszi (Rosa), the daughter of Peter Danku, the waywode, or chief of the Kukuja tribe, was drowned during the time of her betrothal because when she performed this ceremony she had neglected to gather up the sprinkled blood.

"If a girl wishes to see the form of her future husband, and also to know what luck awaits her love, she goes on any of the fore-named nights to a cross-road, and sits down on the ground, putting before her a fried fish and a glass of brandy. Then the form of her future husband will appear and stand before her for a time, silent and immovable. Should he then take the fish the marriage will be happy, but if he begin with the brandy it will be truly wretched. But if he takes neither, one of the two will die during the year.

"That the laying of cards, the interpretation of dreams, the reading of the future in the hand, and similar divinations are constantly practised is quite natural, but it would lead us too far to enlarge on all these practices. But there are charms to win or cause love which are more interesting. Among these are the love-potions or philtres, for preparing which gypsies have always been famed.

"The simplest and least hurtful beverage which they give unknown to persons to secure love is made as follows: "On any of the nights mentioned they collect in the meadows gander-goose (Romání, *vast bengeszkero*--devil's hand; in Latin, *Orchis maculata*; German, *Knaberkraut*), the yellow roots of which they dry and crush and mix with their *menses*, and this they introduce to the food of the person whose love they wish to secure"

Of the same character is a potion which they prepare as follows: On the day of Saint John they catch a green frog and put it in a closed earthen receptacle full of small holes, and this they place in an ant-hill. The ants cat the frog and leave the skeleton. This s ground to powder, mixed with the blood of a bat and dried bath-flies and shaped into small buns, which are, as the chance occurs, put secretly into the food of the person to be charmed.

There is yet another charm connected with this which I leave in the original Latin in which it is modestly given by Dr. Wlislocki: "Qualibet supradictarum noctium occiduntur duo canes nigri, mas et femina, quorum genitalia exstirpata ad condensationem coquntur. Hujus materiæ particula consumpta quemvis invincibili amore facit exardescare in eam eamve, qui hoc medio prodigioso usus est."

It may be remarked that these abominable charms are also not only known to the Tuscan witches of the present day, but are found in Voodoo sorcery, and are indeed all over the world. To use revolting means in black sorcery may be, or perhaps certainly is, spontaneous--sporadic, but when we find the peculiar details of the processes identical, we are so much nearer to transmission or history that the burden of disproving must fall on the doubter.

"To the less revolting philtres belongs one in which the girl puts the ashes of a burnt piece of her dress which had been wet with perspiration and has, perhaps, hair adhering to it, into a man's food or drink (also Tuscan).

"To bury the foot of a badger (also Voodoo), or the eye of a crow, under one's sleeping-place is believed to excite or awaken love.

"According to gypsy belief one can spread love by transplanting blood, perspiration, or hair into the body of a person.

"By burning the hair, blood, or saliva of any one, his or her love can be extinguished.

"The following is a charm used to punish a faithless lover. The deceived maid lights a candle at midnight and pricks it several times with a needle, saying:--

"'Pchâgerâv momely
Pchâgera tre vodyi!'

"'Thrice the candle's broke by me
Thrice thy heart shall broken be!'

"If the faithless lover marries another. the girl mixes the broken shell of a crab in his food or drink, or hides one of her hairs in a bird's nest. This will make the marriage unhappy, and the husband will continually pine for his neglected sweetheart."

This last charm is allied to another current among the Slavonians, and elsewhere mentioned, by which it is believed that if a bird gets any of a man's hair and works it into a nest he will suffer terribly till it is completely decayed.

CHAPTER VIII

Roumanian And Transylvanian Sorceries And Superstititions, Connected With Those of The Gypsies

IN her very interesting account of Roumanian superstitions, Mrs. E. GERARD ("The Land Beyond the Forest"), finds three distinct sources for them firstly, the indigenous, which seems to have been formed by or adapted to the wild and picturesque scenery and character of the country; secondly, those derived from the old German customs and beliefs brought by the so-called Saxon, in reality Lower Rhenish colonists; and thirdly, the influence of the gypsies, "themselves a race of fortune-tellers and witches." All these kinds of superstition have twined and intermingled, acted and reacted upon one another so that in many cases it becomes a difficult matter to determine the exact parentage of some particular belief or custom.

It may be often difficult to ascertain in what particular country or among what people a superstition was *last* found, but there is very little trouble when we compare the great body of all such beliefs of all races and ages and thereby find the parent sources. It is not many years since philologists, having taken up some favourite language--for instance, Irish—discovering many words in many tongues almost identical with others in "Earse," boldly claimed that this tongue was the original of all the others. Now we find the roots of them all in the Aryan. So when we examine Folk-lore, it is doubtless of great importance that we should learn where a tradition last lived; but we must not stop there-we must keep on inquiring till we reach the beginning. As a rule, with little exception, when we find anywhere the grosser forms of fetish and black witchcraft, we may conclude that we have remains of the world's oldest faith, or first beginning of supernaturalism in suffering and terror, a fear of mysterious evil influences. For with all due respect to the fact that such superstitions *might* have sprung up sporadically wherever similar causes existed to create them, it is, in the first place, a very rare *chance* that they should assume exactly like forms. Secondly, we must consider that as there are even now millions of people who receive with ready faith and carefully nurse these primæval beliefs, so there has been from the beginning of time abundant opportunity for their transmission and growth. Thirdly, nothing is so quickly transmitted as Folk-lore, which in one sense includes myths and religion. If jade was in the prehistoric stone age carried from Iona or Tartary all over Europe, it is even more probable that myths went with it quite as far and fast.

It is not by loose, fanciful, and careless guess-work as to how the resemblance of Greek or Norse legends to those of the Red Indians is due to similar conditions of climate and life, that we shall arrive at *facts*; neither will the truth be ascertained by assuming that there was a certain beginning of them all in a certain country, or that they were all developed out of one mythology, be it solar or Shemitic, Hindoo or

Hebrew. What we want is *impartial* examination—comparison and analysis. On this basis we find that all the Folk-lore or magic of Europe, and especially of its Eastern portion, has a great deal which is derived from black witchcraft, or from the succeeding Shamanism. When we find that a superstition is based on fertility, the "mystery of generation," or "Phallic worship"—as, for instance, wearing boars' teeth or a little pig for a charm--we may conclude that it is very ancient, but still not older than the time when wise men had begun to reflect on the mysteries of birth and death and weave them into myths. The exorcism of diseases as devils, and the belief that they, in common with other evils, may be drummed, or smoked, or *incanted* away into animals, trees, and streams, belongs in most cases to Shamanism. In all probability the oldest sorcery of all was entirely concerned with driving out devils and injuring enemies—just as most of the play of small boys runs to fighting or the semblance of it, or as the mutual relations of most animals in the lower stages consist of devouring one another. This was the very beginning of the beginnings, and it would be really marvellous that so much of it has survived were it not that to the one who is not quite dazzled or blinded by modern enlightenment there is still existent a great outer circle of human darkness, and that this darkness may be found in thousands of intermittent varying shadows or marvellous chiaroscuro, even in the brightest sun-pictures of modern life. As I write I have before me a copy of the *Philadelphia Press*, of April 14, 1889, in which a J. C. BATFORD, M.D., advertises that if any one will send him two two-cent postage stamps—*i.e.*, twopence—"with a lock of your hair, name, age, and sex," he will send a clairvoyant diagnosis of your disease. This divining by the lock of hair is extremely ancient, and had its origin in the belief that he who could obtain one from an enemy could reach his soul and kill him. From communicating a disease by means of such a lock, and ascertaining what was the matter with a man, in the same manner, was a very obvious step forward.

Of all people living in Europe the peasantry of Italy and Sicily and the gypsies seem to have retained most of this Shamanism and witchcraft, and as the latter have been for centuries its chief priests, travelling here and there disseminating it, we may conclude that even where they did not originate it they have been active in keeping the old faith alive. In Roumania, where the gypsy is called in to conjure on all occasions, "people believe themselves to be surrounded by whole legions of devils, witches, and goblins." There is scarcely a day or hour in which these bad spirits have not power, "and a whole complicated system, about as laborious as the mastering an unknown language, is required in order to teach an unfortunate peasant to steer clear of the dangers by which he supposes himself to be beset."

On Wednesday and Friday no one should use needle or scissors, bake bread, or sow flax. No bargain should ever be concluded on a Friday, and Venus, here called Paraschiva, to whom this day is sacred, punishes all infractions of the law. There was among the Wends a flax-goddess, Pscipolnitza, and the shears as emblematic of death are naturally antipathetic to Venus, the source of life. Whether Mars has anything in common with *Mors* I know not, but in Roumania he is decidedly an evil spirit of death, whence Marti, or Tuesday, is one, when spinning is positively prohibited (here we have Venus again), and washing the hands and combing the hair are not unattended with danger. Whence it appears that the devil agrees with not a few saints in detesting neatness of the person. And as it is unlucky to wash anything on Saturday, or to spin on Thursday, or to work in the fields on Thursday between Easter and Pentecost, it will be seen that Laziness and Dirt have between them a fine field in Roumania. Add to this that, as in Russia, more than half the days in the year are Saints' days, or fast days or festivals on which it is "unlucky" to work at all, and (*illegible*) find that industry cannot be said to be much encouraged by Faith in (*illegible*) of its forms. This belief in *holy* days which bring ill-luck to those who work on them, which is still flourishing in every country in the world, goes back to time whereof the memory of man hath naught to the contrary. A distinct difference is here to be observed however between *naturally* resting from work--on certain days, which is of course an inherent instinct in all mankind, and the declaring such rest to be *obligatory*, and its infraction punishable by death, disaster, and bad luck, and still more the increasing such Sabbaths to such an extent as to interfere with industry, or the turning them into fast days or Saints' days with "observances." Here the old Shamanism comes in, if not the evil witchcraft itself which exacted penance and fasting, and ceremonies to exorcise the devils. The first belief was that evil spirits inflicted pain on man, and that man, by efforts which cost him suffering, could repel or retaliate on them. This was simple action and reaction, and the repulsion was effected with starving, enduring smoke, or using repulsive and filthy objects. Out of this in due time came penance of all kinds.

The Oriental or Greek Church is found at every turn, even more than the Catholic, interchanged, twined, and confused with ancient sorcery. THEODORE, like SAINT SIMEON and ANTHONY in Tuscany, is very much more of a goblin than a holy man. His weakness is young women, and sometimes in the shape of a beautiful youth, at others of a frightful monster, he carries off those who are found working on his day--that is the 23rd of January. THEODORE, according to the Solar mythologists personifies the sun. (DE GUBERNATIS, "***Zoological Mythology***," vol. ii. p. 296). In any case the saint who seizes girls is the Hindoo Krishna or his prototype, and therefore may have come through the gypsies. The overworked solar myth derives some support from the fact that among the Serbs on THEODORE'S day the *Sintotere,* or centaur, as the name declares-who is half horse and half man, rides over the people who fall in his power. The Centaurs were connected with the "rape of maidens," as shown in the legend of the Lapithæ, and it is very probable that Theodore himself is, in the language of the Western

Americans, "half a horse," which they regard as the greatest compliment which can be paid to a man.

"Wonderful potions and salves," says Mrs. GERARD, "composed of the fat of bears, dogs, snakes, and snails, with the oil of rain-worms, spiders, and midges, rubbed into a paste, are concocted by these Bohemians (*i.e.*, gypsies). Saxon and Roumanian mothers are often in the habit of giving a child to be nursed for nine days to some Tzigane women supposed to have power to undo the spell."

These revolting ingredients are not the result of modern invention, but relics of the primitive witchcraft or *Ur-religion*, which was founded on pain, terror, and the repulsive. Among other Roumanian-Romany traditions are the following:

Swallows here as elsewhere are luck-bringing birds, and termed *Galiniele lui Dieu*--fowls of the Lord. So in England we hear that:

"The robin and the wren
Are God Almighty's cock and hen."

There is always a treasure to be found where the first swallow is seen. Among the Romans when it was observed one ran to the nearest fountain and washed his eyes, and then during the whole year to come, dolorem omnem oculorum tuorum hirundines auferant—the swallows will carry away all your complaints of the eyes.

The skull of a horse over the gate of a courtyard, or the bones of fallen animals buried under the doorstep are preservatives against ghosts. In Roman architecture the skulls of oxen, rams, and horses continually occur as a decoration, and they are used as charms to-day in Tuscany. Black fowls are believed to be in the service of witches The skull of a ram placed at the boundary of a parish in Roumania keeps off disease from cattle; it was evidently a fetish in all ages. In Slavonian, Esthonian, and Italian tales black poultry occur as diabolical—to appease the devil a black cock must be sacrificed. But in Roumania the (black) Brahmaputra fowl is believed, curiously enough, to be the offspring of the devil and a Jewish girl—truly an insignificant result of such clever parentage.

A cow that has wandered away will be safe from witches if the owner sticks a pair of scissors or shears in the centre crossbeam of the dwelling-room. The Folk-lore of shears is extensive; FRIEDRICH derives it from the cutting of the threads of life by the Fates. Thus Juno appears on a Roman coin (ECKHEL, "***Numis. Vet.***" viii. p. 358) as holding the shears of death. The swallow is said in a Swedish fairy tale to have been the handmaid of the Virgin Mary, and to have stolen her scissors, for which reason she was turned into a bird—the swallow's tail being supposed to resemble that article. Gypsies in England use the shears in incantations.

A whirlwind denotes that the devil is dancing with a witch, and he who approaches too near it may be carried off bodily to hell (as has indeed happened to many a wicked Pike in a cyclone or blizzard in Western America), though he may escape by losing his cap.

It is very dangerous to point at a rainbow or an approaching thunderstorm. Probably the devil who here guides the whirlwind or directs the storm regards the act as impolite. He punishes those who thus indicate the rainbow by a gnawing disease. Lightning is averted by sticking a knife in a loaf of bread and spinning the two on the floor of the loft of the house while the storm lasts. The knife appears not only in many gypsy spells, but in the Etruscan-Florentine magic.

The legends of Donidaniel and the College of Sorcery in Salamanca appear in the gypsy Roumanian *Scholomance*, or school which exists somewhere far away deep in the heart of the mountains, "where the secrets of nature, the language of animals, and all magic spells are taught by the devil in person." Only ten scholars are admitted at a time, and when the course of learning has expired nine are dismissed to their homes, but the tenth is detained by the professor in payment. Henceforth, mounted on an *ismeju*, or dragon, he becomes the devil's aide-de-camp, and assists, him in preparing thunderbolts and managing storms and tempests. "A small lake, immeasurably deep, high up in the mountains, south of Hermanstadt, is supposed to be the caldron in which the dragon lies sleeping and where the thunder is brewed."

"Whoever turns three somersaults the first time he hears thunder will be free from pains in the back during the twelvemonth." Of this prescription--which reads as if it had originated with Timothy, in "Japhet in Search of a Father," when he practised as a mountebank—it may be said that it is most unlikely that any person who is capable of putting it in practice should suffer with such pains.

To be free from headache rub the forehead with a piece of iron or stone. This may be a presage of the electric cure or of that by "metallic tractors."

It is unfortunate in all Catholic countries to meet with a priest or nun, especially when he or she is the first person encountered in the morning. In Roumania this is limited to the Greek *popa*. But to be first met by a gypsy on going forth is a very fortunate omen indeed. According to a widely-spread and ancient belief it is also very lucky to meet with any woman of easy virtue--the easier the better. This is doubtless derived from the ancient worship of Venus, and the belief that any thing or person connected with celibacy and chastity, such as a nun, is unlucky. It would appear from this that the Roumanians, or their gypsy oracles, have formed an opinion that their own *popas* are strictly abstinent as regards love, while Protestant priests marry and are accordingly productive. Why the Catholic clergy are included with the latter is not at all clear. It is lucky also to meet a gypsy at any time, and doubtless this belief has been well encouraged by the Romany.

"It's kushti bak to wellán a Rom,
When tute's a pirryin pré the drom."

"When you are going along the street
It's lucky a gypsy man to meet."

Likewise, it is lucky to meet with a woman carrying a jug full of water, &c., but unlucky if it be empty. So in the New Testament the virgins whose lamps were full of oil received great honour. The lamp was an ancient symbol of life; hence it is very often found covered with aphrodisiac symbols or made in Phallic forms. It is barely possible that common old popular simile of "Not by a jug-full," meaning "not by a great deal"—is derived from this association of a full vessel with abundance.

It is a Roumanian gypsy custom to do homage to the *Wodna zena*, or "Water-woman" (Hungarian gypsy, *Nivashi*), by spilling a few drops of water on the ground after filling a jug, and it is regarded as an insult to offer drink without observing this ceremony. A Roumanian will never draw water against the current (also as in the Hungarian gypsy charms), as it would provoke the water-spirit. If water is drawn in the nighttime, whoever does so must blow three times over the brimming jug, and pour a few drops on the coals.

The mythology of the Roumanians agrees with that of the gypsies. It is sylvan, and Indian. In deep pools of water lurks the dreadful *balaur* or *Wodna muz—i.e.*, the Waterman (*Muz* is both gypsy and Slavonian)who lies in wait for victims. In every forest lives the *mama padura*, or *weshni dye*, "the forest mother," who is believed to be benevolent to human beings, especially towards children who have lost their way in the wood. But the Panusch is an amorous spirit who, like the wanton satyrs of old, haunts the silent woodland shades, and lies in wait for helpless maids. "Surely," observes Mrs. GERARD, "this is a corruption of 'great Pan,' who is not dead after all, but merely banished to the land beyond the forest." What a find this would have been for HEINE when writing "The Gods in Exile!"

"In deep forests and lonely mountain gorges there wanders about a wild huntsman of superhuman size." He appears to be of a mysterious nature, and is very seldom seen. Once he met a peasant who had shot ninety-nine bears, and warned him never to attempt to kill another. But the peasant disregarded his advice, and, missing his aim, was torn in pieces by the bear.

Very singular is the story that this Lord of the Forest once taught a hunter—that if he loaded his gun on New Year's Night with a live adder he would never miss a shot during the ensuing year. It is not probable that he was told to put a live and "wiggling" snake into his gun. The story of itself suggests the firing out the ramrod for luck. It has been observed by C. LLOYD MORGAN that if a drop of the oil of a foul tobacco pipe be placed in the mouth of a snake the muscles instantly become set in knotted lumps and the creature becomes rigid. If much is given the snake dies, but if only a small amount is employed it may be restored. This, as Mr. OAKLEY has suggested, may explain the stories of Indian snake-charmers being able to turn a snake into a stick. It is performed by spitting into the snake's mouth and then placing the hand on its head till it becomes stiffened. "The effect maybe produced by opium or some other narcotic." And it may also occur to the reader that the jugglers who performed before PHARAOH were not unacquainted with this mystery. It is probable that the hunter in the gypsy Roumanian story first gave his adder tobacco before firing it off.

The *Om ren*, or wild man, is a malevolent forest spectre, the terror of hunters and shepherds. He is usually seen in winter, and when he finds an intruder on his haunts, he tears up pine trees by the roots with which he slays the victim, or throws him over a precipice, or overwhelms him with rocks. In every detail he corresponds to a being greatly feared by the Algonkin Indians of America.

The *oameni micuti*, or "small men," are grey-bearded dwarfs, dressed like miners. They are the kobolds or Bergmännchen of Germany. They seldom harm a miner, and when one has perished in the mine they make it known to his family by three knocks on his door. They may be heard quarrelling among themselves and hitting at one another with their axes, or blowing their horns as a signal of battle. These "horns of Elf-land blowing" connect them with the *Korriagan* of Brittany, who are fairies who always carry and play on the same instrument. PRÆTORIUS devotes a long chapter to all the learning extant on the subject of these *Bergmännrigen*, or Subterraneans.

The mountain monk is the very counterpart of Friar Rush in English fairy-lore, and is also of Indian origin. He delights in kicking over water-pails, putting out lamps, and committing mischief, merry, mad, or sad. Sometimes he has been known to strangle workmen whom he dislikes, though, on the other hand, he often helps distressed miners by filling their empty lamps or guiding those who have lost their way.

But he always bids them keep it a secret, and if they tell they suffer for it.

Gana is queen of the witches, and corresponds to the Diana of the Italians. Gana is probably only a variation of the word Diana. Among the Wallachians this goddess is in fact known as *Dina* and Sina. She, like the *wilde Jüger*, rushes in headlong hunt over the heavens or through the skies followed by a throng of witches and fairies. "People show the places where she has passed, and where the grass and leaves are dry" (FRIEDRICH). She is a powerful enchantress, and is strongest in her sorcery about Easter-tide. To guard against her the Wallachians at this time carry a piece of lime-tree or linden wood. She is a beautiful but terrible enchantress, who presides over the evil spirits who meet on May eve. She was the ruler of all Transylvania (a hunting country) before Christianity prevailed there. Her beauty bewitched many, but whoever let himself he lured into drinking mead from her urus (or wild ox) drinking-horn perished. She is like the Norse Freya, a cat goddess, and seems to be allied to the Chesme, or cat, or fountain-spirit of the Turks. According to ancient Indian mythology the moon is a cat who chases the mice (stars) of night, and in the fifth book of OVID'S "Metamorphoses," when the gods fled from the giants Diana took the form of a cat:

> "*Fele* soror Phœbi, nivea Saturni a vacca
> Pisce Venus latuit."
>
> (V. 325, 332.)

"According to the Hellenic cosmogony the sun and moon created the animals-the sun creating the lion and the moon the cat" (DE GUBERNATIS, "***Zoological Mythology***," ii. 58). Gertrude, the chief sorceress or queen of the witches in old German lore, appears when dead as surrounded by mice; she is, in fact, a cat. The Turkish Chesme, or fountain-cat, inveigles youths to death like the Gana, Diana, or Lorelei, who does the same, and is also a water-sprite.

The Dschuma is a fierce virgin, or sometimes an old witch, who is incarnate disease, such as the cholera. She is supposed to suffer from cold and nakedness, and may be heard at night when disease is raging, wailing for want. Then the maidens make garments and hang them out; but it is a most effective charm when seven old women spin, weave, and sew for her a scarlet shirt all in one night without once speaking.

A curious book might be written on the efficacy of nakedness in witch-spells. In some places in Roumania there is a spirit always naked (at least appearing such), who requires a new suit of clothes every year. These are given by the inhabitants of the district haunted by such an elf, who on New Year's Night lay them out in some place supposed to be frequented by him or her.

In 1866, in a Wallachian village in the district of Bihar, to avert the cholera, six youths and maidens, all quite naked, traced with a ploughshare a furrow round their village to form a charmed circle over which the disease could not pass.

When the land is suffering from long droughts the Roumanians ascribe it to the gypsies, who by occult means make dry weather in order to favour their own trade of brickmaking. When the necessary rain cannot be obtained by beating the guilty Tziganes, the peasants resort to the Papaluga, or Rain-maiden. For this they strip a young gypsy girl stark-naked, and then cover her up in flowers and leaves, leaving only the head visible. Thus adorned the Papaluga, or Miss jack-in-the-Green, is conducted with music round the village, every person pouring water on her as she passes. When a gypsy girl cannot be had, or the Tziganes are supposed to be innocent, a Roumanian maiden may be taken. This custom is very widely spread.

Forty years ago there was a strange mania in the northern cities of the United States for "fast" girls of the most reckless kind to go out naked very late by night into the street to endeavour to run around a public square or block of houses and regain their homes without being caught by the police. I suspect that superstition suggested this strange risk. It is an old witch-charm that if a girl can, when the moon is full, go forth and run around a certain enclosure, group of trees, or dwelling, without being seen, she will marry the man whom she loves. There are also many magical ceremonies which, to ensure success, must be performed in full moonlight and when quite naked. "Among the Saxons in Transylvania when there is a very severe drought it is customary in some places for several girls, led by an old woman, and all of them absolutely naked, to go at midnight to the courtyard of some peasant and steal his harrow. With this they walk across fields to the nearest stream, where the harrow is put afloat with a burning light on each corner" (Mrs. GERARD, "***Land Beyond***," &c.). This is evidently the old Hindoo floating of lamps by maidens on the Ganges, and in all probability of gypsy importation.

She who will pronounce a certain spell, strip herself quite naked, and can steal into the room where a man is lying sound asleep and can clip from his head a lock of hair and escape without awakening him or meeting any one will obtain absolute mastery over him, or at least over his affections. The hair must be worn in a bag or ring on the person. But woe unto her who is caught, since in that case the enchantment "all goes the other way." Once a beautiful but very poor Hungarian maid gave all she had to a young gypsy girl for a charm to win the love of a certain lord, and was taught this, which proved to be a perfect success. Having clipped the lock of hair she wove it in a ring and wedded him.

After a time she died, and the gypsy being called in to dress the corpse found and kept the ring. Then the lord fell in love with the gypsy and married her. But ere long she too died, and was buried, and the ring with her. And from that day the lord seemed as if possessed to sit by her grave, and finally built a house there, and never seemed happy save when in it.

"If a Roumanian maid," says Mrs. GERARD, "desires to see her future husband's face in the water she has only to step naked at midnight into the nearest lake or river, or, if she shrink from this, let her take a stand on the more congenial dung-hill with a piece of Christmas cake in her mouth, and as the clock strikes twelve listen attentively for the first sound of a dog's bark. From whichever side it proceeds will also come the expected suitor."

A naked maid standing on a "congenial dung-hill" with a piece of Christmas cake in 'her mouth would be a subject for an artist which should be eagerly seized in these days when "excuses for the nude in art" are becoming so rare. It is worth observing that this conjuration is very much like one observed in Tuscany, in which Saint Anthony is invoked to manifest by a dog's barking at night, as by other sounds, whether the applicant, or invoker, shall obtain her desire.

At the birth of a child in Wallachia every one present takes a stone and throws it behind him, saying, "This into the jaws of the Streghoi" 1—"a custom," says Mrs. GERARD, "which would seem to suggest Saturn and the swaddled up stones." It is much more suggestive of the stones thrown by Deucalion and Pyrrha. *Strigoi* is translated as "evil spirits" it is evidently, originally at least, the *streghe*, or witches of Italy, from the Latin *strix*, the dreaded witch-bird of Ovid. "FESTUS derives the word *à stringendo* from the opinion that they strangle children." Middle Latin *strega* (Paulus Grillandus).

He or she who finds a red ribbon, tape, or even a piece of red stuff of any kind, especially if it be wool, will have luck in love. It must be picked up and carried as an amulet, and when raising it from the ground the finder must make a wish for the love of some person, or if he have no particular desire for any one, he may wish for luck in love, or a sweetheart. This is, I believe, pretty generally known in some form all over the world. A yellow ribbon or flower, especially if it be floating on water, presages gold; a white object, silver, or peace or reconciliation with enemies.

It is also lucky for love to find a key. In Tuscany there is a special formula which must be spoken while picking it up. Very old keys are valuable amulets. Those who carry them will learn secrets, penetrate mysteries, and succeed in what they undertake.

If you can get a shoe which a girl has worn you may make sad havoc with her heart if you carry it near your own. Also hang it up over your bed and put into it the leaves of rue.

During November, 1889, not a few newspaper commentators busied themselves with conjectures as to why a Scotch constable buried the boots of a murdered man. That it was done through some superstitious belief is conceded; but what the fashion of the superstition is seems unknown. It originated, beyond question, in the old Norse custom of always burying the dead in their shoes or with them. For they believed that the deceased would have, when he arrived in the other world, to traverse broad and burning plains before he could reach his destination, be it Valhalla or the dreary home of Hel; and to protect his feet from the fire his friends bound on them the "hell-shoon!' Other cares were also taken: and in the saga of Olof Tryggvasen we are told that one monarch was thoughtfully provided with a cow; while the Vikings were buried in their ships, so that they could keep on pirating "for ever and-ever."

The superstition of the burial of the boots probably survives in England. It is about seventeen years since the writer heard from an old gypsy that when another gypsy was "pûvado," or "earthed," a very good pair of boots was placed by him in the grave. The reason was not given; perhaps it was not known. These customs often survive after the cause is forgotten, simply from some feeling that good or bad luck attends their observance or the neglect of it. Many years since a writer in an article on shoes in *The English Magazine* stated that, "according to an Aryan tradition, the greater part of the way from the land of the living to that of death lay through morasses and

For much learning on this subject of the *Strix* the reader may consult DE GUBERNATIS, "***Myth of Animals***," vol. ii. p. 202.

"As long as the child is unbaptized it must be carefully watched for fear lest it be changed or stolen away." This is common to Christians, heathen, and gypsies to watch it for several days. "A piece of iron, or a broom laid beneath the pillow will keep spirits away." So in Roumania and Tuscany. QUINTUS SERENUS, however, recommends that when the *striga atra* presses the infant, garlic be used, the strong odour of which (to their credit be it said) is greatly detested by witches.

"The Romans used to cook their cæna demonum for the house-spirits, and the Hindoos prepared food for them." From them it has passed through the gypsies to Eastern Europe, and now the Roumanian, who has by a simple ceremony made a contract with the devil, receives from him an attendant spirit called a *spiridsui* or *spiridush* which will

"Serve his master faithfully
For seven long year,"

but in return expecting the first mouthful of every dish eaten by his master.

"So many differing fancies have mankind,
That they the master-sprites may spell and bind."

Nearly connected with the Roumanian we have the beliefs in magic of the Transylvanian Saxons, all of them shared with the gypsies and probably partially derived from them. Many people must have wondered what could have been the origin of the saying in reference to a very small place that "there was not room to swing a cat in it." "But I don't want to swing a cat in it," was the very natural rejoinder of a well-known American litterateur to this remark applied to his house. It is possible that we may find the origin of this odd saying in a superstition current in Transylvania, whither it in all probability was carried by the gypsies, whose specialty it is to bear the seeds of superstitions about here and there as the winds do those of plants. In this country it is said that if a cat runs away, when recovered she must be swung three times round to attach her to the dwelling.

The same is done by a stolen cat by the thief if he would retain it. Truly this seems a strange way to induce an attachment--or *pour encourager les autres*. It is evident, however, that to the professional cat-stealer the size of his room must be a matter of some importance. it is a pity that this saying and faith were unknown to MONCRIEF-MARADAN, "***The Historiogriffie of Cats***," ("Œuvres," Paris, 1794), who would assuredly have made the most of it.

As regards entering new houses in Transylvania the rule is not "Devil take the hindmost," but the foremost. The first person or being who enters the maiden mansion must die, therefore it is safe to throw in a preliminary dog or cat. The scape-cat is, however, to be preferred. I can remember once, when about six years of age, looking down into a well in Massachusetts and being told that the reflection which I saw was the face of a little boy who lived there. This made a deep impression on me, and I reflected that it was very remarkable that the dweller in the well could assume the appearance of every one who looked at him. In Transylvania it is, says Mrs. E. GERARD, "dangerous to stare down long into a well, for the well-dame who dwells at the bottom is easily offended. But children are often curious, and so, bending over the edge, they call out mockingly, 'Dame of the Well, pull me down into it!' and then run away rapidly."

Whoever has been robbed and wishes to find the thief should take a black hen, and for nine Fridays must with the hen fast strictly; the thief will then either bring back the plunder or die. This is called "taking up the black fast" against any one. It is said that a peasant of Petersdorf returned one day from Bistritz with 200 florins, which he had received for oxen. Being very tipsy he laid down to sleep, having first hidden his money in a hole in the kitchen wall. When he awoke he missed his coin, and having quite forgotten what he had done with it believed it had been stolen. So he went to an Old Wallachian, probably a gypsy, and induced him to take up the black fast against the thief. But as he himself had the money the spell worked against him and he grew weaker and pined away as it went on. By some chance at the last moment he found his money, but it was too late, and he died. Pages of black hen-lore may be gathered from the works of FRIEDRICH, DE GUBERNATIS and others; suffice it to say that Bubastis, the Egyptian moon-goddess, appears to have been the original mistress of the mysterious animal, if not the black hen as well as cat herself, and mother of all the witches.

Magic qualities are attached in Hungary as in Germany to the lime or linden tree; in some villages it is usual to plant one before a house to prevent witches from entering. From very early times the lime tree was sacred to Venus among the Greeks, as it was to Lada among the

Slavonians. This, it is said, was due to its leaves being of the shape of a heart. In a Slavonian love-song the wooer exclaims:

> "As the bee is drawn by the lime-perfume (or linden-bloom)
> My heart is drawn by thee."

This was transmitted to Christian symbolism, whence the penance laid by CHRIST On MARY MAGDALEN was that "she should have no other food save lime-tree leaves, drink naught except the dew which hung on them, and sleep on no other bed save one made of its leaves" (MENZEL, "***Christliche Symbolik***," vol. ii. p. 57) "For Magdalena had loved much, therefore her penance was by means of that which is a symbol of love."

Mrs. GERARD tells us that "a particular growth of vine leaf, whose exact definition I have not succeeded in rightly ascertaining, is eagerly sought by Saxon girls in some villages. Whoever finds it, puts it in her hair, and if she then kisses the first man she meets on her way home she will soon be married. A story is related of a girl, who having found this growth, meeting a nobleman in a carriage stopped the horses and begged leave to kiss him." To which he consented. This particular growth, unknown to Mrs. GERARD, is when the leaves or tendrils or shoots form a natural knot. Among the gypsies in Hungary, as may be elsewhere read, such knots in the willow are esteemed as of great magic efficacy in love. A knot is a symbol of true love in all countries.

> "This knot I tic, this knot I knit,
> For that true love whom I know not yet."

On Easter Monday in Transylvania the lads run about the towns and villages sprinkling with water all the girls or women whom they meet. This is supposed to cause the flax to grow well. On the following day the girls return the attention by watering the boys. "This custom, which appears to be a very old one," says Mrs. GERARD, "is also prevalent among various Slav races, such as Poles and Serbs. In Poland it used to be *de rigeur* that water be poured over a girl who was still asleep, so in every house a victim was selected who had to feign—sleep and patiently receive the cold shower-bath, which was to ensure the luck of the family during the year. The custom has now become modified to suit a more delicate age, and instead of formidable horse-buckets of water, dainty little perfume squirts have come to be used in many places." As the custom not only of sprinkling water, but also of squirting or spraying perfumes is from ancient India (as it is indeed prevalent all over the East), it is probable that the gypsies who are always foremost in all festivals may have brought this "holi" custom to Eastern Europe. Of late it has extended to London, as appears by the following extract from *The St. James's Gazette*, April, 1889.

"The newest weapon of terror in the West End is the 'scent revolver.' Its use is simple. You dine--not wisely but the other thing—and then you stroll into the Park, with your nickel-plated scent revolver in your pocket. Feeling disposed for a frolic, you walk up to a woman, present your weapon, pull the trigger, and in a moment she is drenched, not with gore but with scent, which is nearly as unpleasant if not quite so deadly. Mr. Andrew King, who amused himself in that way, has been fined 10s. at Marlborough Street. Let us hope that the 'revolver' was confiscated into the bargain."

One way of interrogating fate in love affairs is to slice an apple in two with a sharp knife; if this can be done without cutting a seed the wish of the heart will be fulfilled. Of yore, in many lands the apple was ever sacred to love, wisdom, and divination. Once in Germany a well-formed child became, through bewitchment, sorely crooked and cramped; by the advice of a monk the mother cut an apple in three pieces and made the child eat them, whereupon it became as before. In Illzach, in Alsace, there is a custom called "Andresle." On Saint Andrew's Eve a girl must take from a widow, and without returning thanks for it, an apple. As in Hungary she cuts it in two and must eat one half of it before midnight, and the other half after it; then in sleep she will see her future husband. And there is yet another love-spell of the split apple given by SCHEIBLE ("***Die gute alte Zeit***," Stuttgart, 1847, p, 297) which runs as follows:--

"On Friday early as may be,
Take the fairest apple from a tree,
Then in thy blood on paper white
Thy own name and thy true love's write,
That apple thou in two shalt cut,
And for its cure that paper put,
With two sharp pins of myrtle wood
Join the halves till it seem good,
In the oven let it dry,
And wrapped in leaves of myrtle lie,
Under the pillow of thy dear,
Yet let it be unknown to her

And if it a secret be
She soon will show her love for thee."

Similar apple sorceries were known to the Norsemen. Because the apple was so nearly connected with love and luxury—"Geschlectsliebe und Zeugungslust"—those who were initiated in the mysteries and vowed to chastity were forbidden to eat it. And for the same reason apples, hares, and Cupids, or "Amorets," were often depicted together. In Genesis, as in the Canticles of Solomon, apples, or at least the fruit from which the modern apple inherited its traditions are a symbol of sexual love. In Florence women wishing for children go to a priest and get from him a blessed apple, over which they pronounce an incantation to Santa Anna—*la San' Na*—who was the Lucina of the Latins.

Though not connected with this work, I cannot help observing that this extraordinary simile probably originated in a very common ornament used as a figurehead, or in decorations, on Mississippi steamboats, as well as ships. This is the seahorse (hippocampus), which may be often seen of large size, carved and gilt. Its fish tail might be easily confused with that of an alligator. PRÆTORIUS (1666) enumerates, among other monsters, the horse-crocodile.

SCHOTT, "***Wallachische Mährchen***," p. 297. Stuttgart, 1845.

CHAPTER IX

The Rendezvous or Meetings of Witches, Sorcerers, And Vilas—A Continuation of South Slavonian Gypsy-Lore

IN Eastern Europe witches and their kin, or kind, assemble on the eve of Saint John and of Saint George, Christmas and Easter, at cross-roads on the broad *pustas*, or prairies, and there brew their magic potions. This, as Dr. KRAUSS observes, originated in feasts held at the same time in pre-Christian times. "So it was that a thousand years ago old and young assembled in woods or on plains to bring gifts to their gods, and celebrated with dances, games, and offerings the festival of spring, or of awaking and blooming Nature. These celebrations have taken Christian names, but innumerable old heathen rites and customs are still to be found in them." It may be here observed that mingled with these are many of a purely gypsy-Oriental origin, which came from the same source and which it remains for careful ethnologists and critical Folk-lorists to disentangle and make clear. The priestesses of prehistoric times on these occasions performed ceremonies, as was natural, to protect cattle or land from evil influences. To honour their deities the "wise women" bore certain kinds of boughs and adorned animals with flowers and wreaths. The new religion declared that this was all sorcery and devil-work, but the belief in the efficacy of the rites continued. The priestesses became witches, or Vilas, the terms being often confused, but they were still feared and revered.

In all the South Slavonian. country the peasants on Saint George's. Day adorn the horns of cattle with garlands, in gypsy Indian style, to protect them from evil influences. I have observed that even in Egypt among Mahometans Saint George is regarded with great reverence, and I knew one who on this day always sacrificed a sheep. The cow or ox which is not thus decorated becomes a prey in some way to witches. The garlands are hung up at night over the stable door, where they remain all the ensuing year. If a peasant neglects to crown his cow, he not only does not receive a certain fee from its owner, but is in danger of being beaten. On the same day the shepherdess, or cow-herd, takes in one hand salt, in the other a potsherd containing live coals. In the coals roses are burned. By this means witches lose all power over the animal. Near Karlstadt the mistress of the family merely strikes it with a cross to produce the same effect.

Among the Transylvanian Hungarian gypsies there is a magical ceremony performed on Saint George's Day, traces of which may be found in England. Then the girls bake a peculiar kind of cake, in which certain herbs are mixed, and which Dr. von WLISLOCKI declares has an agreeable taste. This is divided among friends and foes, and it is believed to have the property of reconciling the bitterest enemies and of increasing the love of friends. But it is most efficient as a love-charm, especially when given by women to men. The following gypsy song commemorates a deed of this kind by a husband, who recurred to it with joy:

"Kásáve romñi ná jidel,
Ke kásávo maro the del;
Sar m're gule lele pekel
Káná Sváto Gordye ável.

"Furmuntel bute luludya
Furmuntel yoy bute charma
Andre petrel but kámábe
Ko chal robo avla bake."

No one bakes such bread as my wife, such as she baked me on St. George's Day. Many flowers and dew were kneaded into the cake with love. Whoever eats of it will be her slave."

In England I was told by an old gypsy woman named LIZZIE BUCKLAND, that in the old time gypsy girls made a peculiar kind of cake, a *Romany morriclo*, which they baked especially for their lovers, and used to throw to them over the hedge by night. To make it more acceptable, and probably to facilitate the action of the charm, they would put money into the cake. It was observed of old among the Romans that *fascinatio* began with flattery, compliments, and presents!

On the night of Saint John the witch climbs to the top of the hurdle fence which surrounds the cow-yard, and sings the following spell:

"K meni sir,
K meni maslo,
K meni puter,

K meni mleko
Avam pak kravsku kožu!"

"To me the cheese,
To me the tallow (or meat),
To me the butter,
To me the milk,
To you only the cowhide."

Or, as it may be expressed in rhyme:

"The cheese, meat, butter, and milk for me,
But only the cowhide left for thee."

Then the cow will die, the carcass be buried, and the skin sold. To prevent all this the owner goes early on St. John's Day to the meadow and gathers the morning dew in a cloak. This he carries home, and after binding the cow to a beam washes her with it. She is then milked, and it is believed that if all has gone right she will yield four bucketsful.

In the chapter on "Conjurations and Exorcisms among the Hungarian Gypsies," I have mentioned the importance which they attach to the being born a seventh or twelfth child. This is the same throughout South Slavonia, where the belief that such persons in a series of births are exceptionally gifted is shared by both gypsies, with whom it probably originated, and the peasants. What renders this almost certain is that Dr. KRAUSS mentions that the oldest information as to the subject among the Slavs dates only from 1854, while the faith is ancient among the gypsies. He refers here to the so-called *Kerstniki*, who on the eve of St. John do battle with the witches. *Krstnik* is a Greek word, meaning, literally, one who has been baptized. But the Krstnik proper is the youngest of twelve brothers, all sons of the same father. There appears to be some confusion and uncertainty among the Slavs as to whether all the twelve brothers or only the twelfth are "Krstnik"—according to the gypsy faith it would be the latter. These "twelvers" are the great protectors of the world from witchcraft. But they are in great danger on Saint John's Eve, for then the witches, having most power, assail them with sticks and stakes, or stumps of saplings, for which reason it is usual in the autumn to carefully remove everything of the kind from the ground.

A krstnik is described by Miklosič as "Človek kterega vile obijubiju," "A man who has won the love of a Vila." The Vila ladies, or a certain class of them, are extremely desirous of contracting the closest intimacy—in short, of becoming the mistresses, of superior men. The reader may find numerous anecdotes of such amours in the "***Curiosa***" of Heinrich KORNMANN, 1666, and in my "***Egyptian Sketch Book***" (Trübner &. Co., London, 1874). In the heathen days, as at present among all gypsies and Orientals, it was believed to be a wonderfully lucky thing for a man to get the love of one of these beautiful beings. What the difficulties were which kept them from finding lovers is not very clear, unless it were that the latter must be twelfth sons, or, what is far more difficult to find, young men who would not gossip about their supernatural sweethearts to other mortals, who would remain true to them, and who finally would implicitly obey all their commands and follow their advice. There is a vast array of tales, Gypsy, Arab, Provençal, Norman, German, and Scandinavian, which show that on these points the Vila, or forest-maiden, or spirit of earth or air, or fairy, was absolutely exacting and implacable, being herself probably allowed by occult laws to contract an intimacy only with men of a high order, or such as are--

"Few in a heap and very hard to find."

On the other hand, the Vila yearns intensely for men and their near company, because there is about those who have been baptized a certain perfume or odour of sanctity, and as the unfortunate nymph is not immortal herself, she likes to get even an association or sniff of it from those who are. According to the Rosicrucian Mythology, as set forth in the "***Undine***" of LA MOTTE FOUQUÉ, she may acquire a soul by marrying a man who will be faithful to her—which accounts for the fact that so few Undines live for ever. However this may be, it appears that the Krstniki are specially favoured, and frequently invited by the Vilas to step in--generally to a hollow tree—and make a call. The hollow tree proves to be a door to Fairyland, and the call a residence of seven days, which on returning home the caller finds were seven years, for:

"When we are pleasantly employed, time flies."

These spirits have one point in common with their gypsy friends--they steal children—with this difference, that the Vila only takes those which have been baptized, while the gypsy—at present, at least—is probably not particular in this respect. But I have very little doubt that originally one motive, and perhaps the only one which induced these thefts, was the desire of the gypsies, as heathens and sorcerers, to have among them, "for luck," a child which had received the initiation into that mysterious religion from which they were excluded, and which, as many of their charms and spells prove, they really regarded as a higher magic. It is on this ground only, or for this sole reason, that we can comprehend many of the child-stealings effected by gypsies; for it is absolutely true that, very often when they have large families of their own, they will, for no apparent cause whatever, neither for the sake of plunder, profit, or revenge, adopt or steal some poor child and bring it up, kindly enough after their rough fashion; and in doing this they are influenced, as I firmly believe, far more by a superstitious feeling of *bâk*, or luck, and the desire to have a *Mascot* in the tent, than any other. That children have been robbed or stolen for revenge does not in the least disprove what I believe—that in most cases the motive for the deed is simply superstition.

On the eve of Saint George old women cut thistle-twigs and bring them to the door of the stall. This is only another form of the nettle which enters so largely into the Hungarian gypsy incantations, and they also make crosses with cow dung on the doors. This is directly of Indian origin, and points to gypsy tradition. Others drive large nails into the doors—also a curious relic of a widely-spread ancient custom, of which a trace may be found in the Vienna *Stock im Eisen*, or trunk driven full of nails by wandering apprentices, which may be seen near the church of Saint Stephen. But the thistle-twigs are still held to be by far the most efficacious. In Vinica, or near it, these twigs are cut before sunset. They are laid separately in many places, but are especially placed in garlands on the necks of cattle. If a witch, in spite of these precautions, contrives to get into the stable, all will go wrong with the beasts during the coming year.

Now there was once a man who would have none of this thistle work—nay, he mocked at those who believed in it. So it came to pass that all through the year witches came every night and milked his cows. And he reflected, "I must find out who does this!" So he hid himself in the bay and kept sharp watch. All at once, about eleven o'clock, there came in a milk-pail, which moved of its own accord, and the cows began to let down their milk into it. The farmer sprang out and kicked it over. Then it changed into a tremendous toad which turned to attack him, so that in terror he took refuge in his house. That proved to be a lucky thing for him. A week after came the day of Saint George. Then he hung thistle-twigs on his stable door, and after that his cows gave milk in plenty.

Witches may be seen on Saint George's Day, and that unseen by them if a man will do as follows: He must rise before the sun, turn all his clothes inside out and then put them on. Then he must cut a green turf and place it on his head. Thus he becomes invisible, for the witches believe he is under the earth, being themselves apparently bewitched by this.

Very early on the day of Saint George, or before sunrise, the witches climb into the church belfry to get the grease from the axle on which the bell swings, and a piece of the bell-rope, for these things are essential to them. Dr. KRAUSS observes that in the MS. from which he took this, *schmierfetet* or axle-grease, is indicated by the word *svierc*, "in which one at once recognizes the German word *schwartz*, a black." It is remarkable that the Chippeway and other Algonkin Indians attach particular value to the black dye made from the grease of the axle of a grindstone.

The extraordinary pains which they took to obtain this had attracted the attention of a man in Minnesota, who told me of it. It required a whole day to obtain a very little of it. The Indians, when asked by curious white people what this was for, said it was for dyeing baskets, but, as my informant observed, the quantity obtained was utterly inadequate to any such purpose, and even better black dyes (*e.g.*, hickory bark and alum) are known to, and can be very easily obtained by, them. The real object was to use the grease in "medicine," *i.e.*, for sorcery. The eagerness of both witches in Europe and Indians in America to obtain such a singular substance is very strange. However, the idea must be a recent one among the Indians, for there were certainly no grindstones among them before the coming of the white men.

> "For all that I can tell, said he,
> Is that it is a mystery,"

Heathens though they be, many gypsies have a superstitious belief in the efficacy of the sacramental bread and wine, and there are many instances of their stealing them for magical purposes. So in the Middle Ages witches and sorcerers used these objects for the most singular purposes, Paulus Grillandus, in his "***Tractatus de Hereticis et Sortilegiis***," &c. (Lyons, 1547), assuring his readers that he had known a witch who had two holy wafers, inscribed with magical characters which she used for debauching innocent girls and betraying them to men, and that it was a belief that if a woman had the sacred oil fresh on her lips no man could refrain from kissing her. This is the union of two kinds of magic; a view which never once occurred to theological writers. And here I may appropriately mention that while the proofs of this work were passing through my hands accident threw into my way an extremely rare work, which illustrates to perfection the identity of popular and ecclesiastical sorcery. This is entitled, "***De Effectibus Magicis, ac de Nuce Maga Beneventana***," "***Six Books of Magic Effects and of the Witch Walnut-tree of Benevento***." A work necessary, joyous, and useful to Astrologists, Philosophers, Physicians, Exorcists, and Doctors, and Students of Holy Scriptures. By the Chief Physician, PETER PIPERNO. It appears to have been privately printed at Naples in 1647, and came from a conventual library. It bare, written on a fly-leaf, the word *Proibito*.

In it every kind of disorder or disease is declared to be caused by devils and witches. The author believes with DELRIO that disease entered into the world as a consequence of sin (*referenda sit ad primæ nostræ matris peccatum*)--a view held by JOHN MILTON; hence, of course, all disease is caused solely by the devil. In his volume of two hundred large and close pages, our PETER PIPERNO displays a vast erudition on the origin of devils and diseases, is bitter on the rival school of magical practitioners who use cures and incantations unlike his own, and then gives us the name and nature of all diseases, according to the different parts of the body, &c., the medical prescriptions proper for them, and what is, in his opinion, most needful of all, the *incantation* or exorcism to be pronounced. Sometimes there are several of these, as one for making up a pill, another on taking it, &c. There are also general conjurations--I mean benedictions—for the medicines altogether or in particular, such as the *Benedictio Syruporum*, "The Blessing of the Syrups," and there is a very affecting and appropriately moving one for making or taking Castor Oil, and oils of all kinds, as follows:

"BENEDICTIO OLEI.

"This begins with the *In nomine Patris*, &c., and *Adjutorium nostrum*, &c., and then:

"I exorcise you all aromatics, herbs, roots, seeds, stones, gums, and whatever is to be compounded with this oil, by God the Father, God the Son, and God the Holy Ghost, by the God triune yet one, by the holy and single Trinity, that the impure Spirit depart from you, and with it every incursion of Satan, every fraud of the Enemy, every evil of the Devil, and that mixed with oil you may free the subject from all infirmities, incantations, bindings, witchcrafts, from all diabolical fraud, art, and power, by the merits of our Lord Jesus Christ and the most beloved Virgin Mary, and of all the saints. Amen."

The curses for the devils of colds, fevers, rheumatisms, gouts, stomachaches, &c., are awful, both in number, length, and quality; enough to frighten a cowboy or "exhort an impenitent mule" into docility. There is the *Exorcismus terribilis*, or "Terrible Exorcism" of Saint Zeno, in which the disorder is addressed literally as "A dirty, false, heretical, drunken, lewd, proud, envious, deceitful, vile, swindling, stupid devil" with some twenty more epithets which, if applied in these our days to the devil himself, would ground an action for libel and bring heavy damages in any court. It is to be remarked that in many prescriptions the author adds to legitimate remedies, ingredients which are simply taken from popular necromancy, or witchcraft, as for instance, rue—fugæ dæmonum—verbena, and artemisia, all of which are still in use in Tuscany against sorcery and the evil eye.

The really magical character of these exorcisms is shown by the vast array of strange words used in them, many of which have a common source with those used by sorcerers of the Cabalistic or Agrippa school, such as *Agla, Tetragrammaton, Adonai, Fons, Origo, Serpens, Avis, Leo, Imago, Sol, Floy, Vitis, Mons, Lapis, Angularis, Ischyros, Pantheon*, all of which are old heathen terms of incantation. These are called in the exorcism "words by virtue of which"—*per virtutem istorum verborum*—the devils are invited to depart. The whole is as much a work of sorcery as any ever inscribed in a catalogue of *occulta*, and it was as a specimen of *occulta* that I bought it.

In Northern Sagas it appeared that Berserkers, or desperate warriors, frequently bound themselves together in companies of twelve. Vide the Hervor Saga, Olaf Tryggvason's and the Gautrek Saga. So there were the twelve Norse gods and the twelve apostles.

CHAPTER X

Of The Haunts, Homes, And Habits of Witches in The South Slavic Lands—Bogeys And Humbugs

THE witches in Slavonian gypsy-lore have now and then parties which meet to spin, always by full moonlight on a cross-road. But it is not advisable, says KRAUSS, to pass by on such occasions, as the least they do to the heedless wayfarer is to bewitch and sink him into a deep sleep. But they are particularly fond of assembling socially in the tops of trees, especially of the ash, walnut, and linden or lime kinds, preferring those whose branches grow in the manner here depicted.

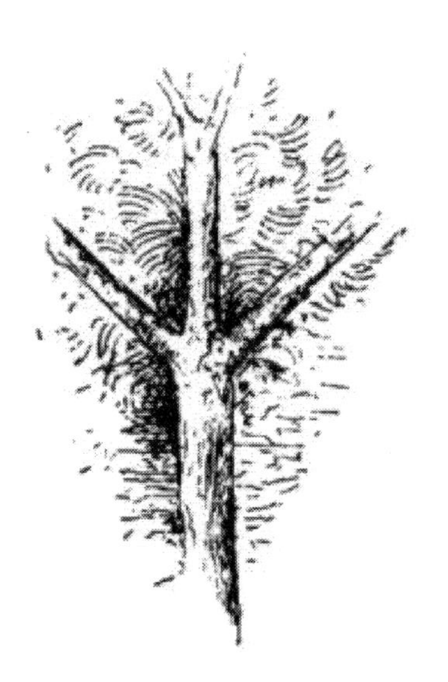

It is but a few days ago, as I write, that I observed all along the route from Padua to Florence thousands of trees supporting vines, which trees had been trained to take this form, the farmers being as much influenced by "luck" in so doing as utility; for it is not really essential that the tree shall so exactly receive this shape, to hold a vine, as is proved by the fact that there are plantations here and there where this method of training the trees is not observed. It is very suggestive of the *triçula* or trident of Siva, which originated the *trushul*, or cross of the gypsies. As regards the properties of the ash tree KRAUSS remarks that "roots with magic power grew under ash trees," and quotes a song of a maiden who, having learned that her lover is untrue, replies:

> "Ima trava u okolo Save,
> I korenja okolo jasenja,"
>
> "There are herbs by the Save,
> And roots around ash trees,"

...meaning that she can prepare a love-potion from these. There is in the Edda a passage in which we are also told that there are magic powers in the roots of trees, the reference being probably to the ash, and possibly to the *alraun*, or images made of its roots, which are sometimes misnamed mandrakes.

Other resorts of Slavonian gypsy witches are near or in deep woods and ravines, also on dung-hills, or places where ashes, lye, or rubbish is thrown, or among dense bushes. Or as soon as the sun sets they assemble in orchards of plum trees, or among ancient ruins, while on summer nights they hold their revels in barns, old hollow trees, by dark hedges or in subterranean caverns. The peasants greatly dread dung-hills after dark, for fear of cruel treatment by them. When a wild wind is blowing the witches love dearly to dance. Then they whirl about in eddying figures and capers, and when the sweat falls from them woe to the man who treads upon it!—for he will become at once dumb or lame, and may be called lucky should he escape with only an inflammation of the lungs. In fact, if a man even walks in a place where witches have been he will become bewildered or mad, and remain so till driven homeward by hunger. But such places may generally be recognized by their footprints in the sand; for witches have only four toes—the great toe being wanting. These mysterious four toe-tracks, which are indeed often seen, are supposed by unbelievers to be made by wild geese, swans, or wild ducks, but in reply to this the peasant or gypsy declares that witches often take the form of such fowl. And there is, moreover, much Rabbinical tradition which proves that the devil and his friends have feet like peacocks, which are notoriously birds of evil omen, as is set forth by a contributor to The *St. James's Gazette*, November 16, 1888:

"Again, take peacocks. Nobody who has not gone exhaustively into the subject can have any adequate idea of the amount of general inconvenience diffused by a peacock. Broken hearts, broken limbs, pecuniary reverses, and various forms of infectious disease have all been traced to the presence of a peacock, or even a peacock feather, on the premises."

The evil reputation of the peacock is due to his having been the only creature who was induced to show Satan the way into Paradise. (For a poem on this subject, *vide* "***Legends of the Birds***," by C. G. LELAND, Philadelphia, 1864).

If any one should by chance pop in—like Tam O'Shanter—to an assembly of witches, he must at once quickly cover his head, make the sign of the cross, take three steps backwards and a fourth forwards. Then the witches cannot injure him. Should a gentleman in London or Brighton abruptly intrude into a five o'clock tea, while Peel or Primrose witches are discussing some specially racy scandal, he should, however, make instantly so many steps backwards as will take him to his overcoat or cane, and then, after a turn, so many downstairs as will bring him into the street.

If any man should take in his hand from the garden fence anything which a witch has laid there, he will in the same year fall sick, and if he has played with it he must die. There be land-witches and water-witches—whoever goes to swim in a place where these latter are found will drown and his body never be recovered. Sometimes in these places the water is very deep, but perfectly clear, in others it is still and very muddy, to which no one can come within seven paces because of an abominable and stifling vapour. And, moreover, as a dead cat is generally seen swimming on the top of such pools, no one need be endangered by them.

The fact that the gypsy and South Slavonian or Hungarian Folklore is directly derived from classic or Oriental sources is evident from the fact that the Shemitic-Persian devil, who is the head and body of all witchcraft in Western Europe, very seldom appears in that of the Eastern parts. The witches there seem invariably to derive their art from one another; even in Venice they have no unusual fear of death or of a future state. A witch who has received the gift or power of sorcery cannot die till she transfers it to another, and this she often finds it difficult to do, as is illustrated by a story told me in Florence in 1886 by the same girl to whom I have already referred.

"There was a girl here in the city who became a witch against her will. And how? She was ill in a hospital, and by her in a bed was *una vecchia, ammalata gravamente, e non poteva morire*—an old woman seriously ill, yet who could not die. And the old woman groaned and cried continually, *'Oimé! muoio! A chi lasció? non diceva che.'* 'Alas! to whom shall I leave?'--but she did not say what. Then the poor girl, thinking of course she meant property, said: *'Lasciate à me--son tanto povera!'* ('Leave it to me--I am so poor!) At once the old woman died, and *'La povera giovana se é trovato in eredita della streghoneria'*--the poor girl found she had inherited witchcraft.

"Now the girl went home, where she lived with her brother and mother. And having become a witch she began to go out often by night, which the mother observing, said to her son, *'Qualche volta tu troverai tua sorella colla pancia grossa.'* ('Some day you will find your sister with child.') 'Don't think such a thing, mamma,' he replied. 'However, I will find out where it is she goes.'

"So he watched, and one night he saw his sister go out of the door, *sullo punto della mezza notte*—just at midnight. Then he caught her by the hair, and twisted it round his arm. She began to scream terribly, when--*ecco*! there came running a great number of cats—*e cominciarono a miolare, e fare un gran chiasso*--they began to mew and make a great row, and for an hour the sister struggled to escape--but in vain, for her hair was fast—and screamed while the cats screeched, till it struck one, when the cats vanished and the *sorella* was insensible. But from that time she had no witchcraft in her, and became a *buona donna*, or good girl, as she had been before—*come era prima.*'"

It is very evident that in this story there is no diabolical agency, and that the witchcraft is simply a quality which is transferred like a disease, and which may be removed. Thus in Venice—where, as is evident from the works of BERNONI, the witches are of Gypsy-Slavic-Greek origin—a witch loses all her power if made to shed even one drop of blood, or sometimes if she be defeated or found out to be a witch. In none of these countries has she received the horrible character of a mere instrument of a stupendous evil power, whose entire will and work is to damn all mankind (already full of original sin) to eternal torture. For this *ne plus ultra* of horror could only result from the Hebrew-Persian conception of perfect malignity, incarnate as an *anti*-god, and be developed by gloomy ascetics who begrudged mankind every smile and every gleam of sunlight. In India and Eastern Europe the witch and demon are simply awful powers of nature, like thunder and pestilence, darkness and malaria, they nowhere appear as aiming at destroying the *soul.* For such an idea as this it required a theology and mythology emanating from the basis of an absolutely perfect *monotheos*, which gave birth to an antithesis;

infinite good, when concentrated, naturally suggesting a shadow counterpart of evil. In Eastern Europe the witch is, indeed, still confused with the Vila, who was once, and often still is, a benevolent elementary spirit, who often punishes only the bad, and gladly favours the good. It is as curious as it is interesting to see how, under the influence of the Church, everything which was not directly connected with the current theology was made to turn sour and bitter and poisonous, and how darkness and frost stole over flowery fields which once were gay in genial sunshine. It is a necessary result that in attaining higher ideals the lesser must fade or change. Devilism, or the dread of the child and savage of the powers of darkness and mysterious evil, ends by incarnating all that is painful or terrible in evil spirits, which suggest their opposites. From Devilism results Polytheism, with one leading and good spirit, who in time becomes supreme. Then we have Monotheism. But as evil still exists, it is supposed that there are innately evil powers or spirits who oppose the good. By following the same process the leader of these becomes an anti-type, Lucifer, or Satan, or arch-devil, the result being Dualism. In this we have a spirit endowed with incredible activity and power, who is only not omnipotent, and whose malignity far transcends anything attributed to the gods or devils of Polytheism. His constant aim is to damn all mankind to all eternity, and his power is so great that to save even a small portion of mankind from this fate, God himself, or His own Son, must undergo penance as a man—an idea found in the Buddhism of India. This is all the regular and logical sequence of Fetishism and Shamanism. Witchcraft, and the tales told of it, follow in the path of the religion of the age. In the earliest time women were apparently the only physicians-that is to say magicians- and as man was in his lowest stage the magic was a vile witchcraft. Then came the Shaman--a man who taught in Animism a more refined sorcery, which was, however, as yet the only religion. But the witch still existed, and so she continued to exist, *pari passu*, through all the developments of religion. And to this day every form and phase of the magician and witch exist somewhere, it sometimes happening that traces of the earliest and most barbarous sorcery are plain and palpable in the most advanced faith. There may be changes of name and of association, but in simple truth it is all "magic" and nothing else.

Gypsy, Hungarian, Slavonian, Indian, and Italian witches, however they may differ from those of Western Europe on theological grounds, agree with them in meeting for the purposes of riotous dancing and debauchery. It has been observed that this kind of erotic dancing appears to have been cultivated in the East, and even in Europe, from the earliest times, by a class of women who, if not absolutely proved to be gypsies, had at any rate many points of resemblance with them. "The Syrian girl who haunts the taverns round," described by VIRGIL, suggests the Syrian and Egyptian dancer, who is evidently of Indo-Persian--that is to say of Nuri, or gypsy--origin. The Spanish dancing girls of remote antiquity have been conjectured to have come from this universal Hindoo Romany stock. I have seen many of the Almeh in Egypt—they all seemed to be gypsyish, and many were absolutely of the Helebi, Nauar, or Rhagarin stocks. This is indeed not *proved*, that all the deliberately cultivated profligate dancing of the world is of Indo-Persian, or gypsy origin, but there is a great deal, a very great deal, which renders it probable. And it is remarkable that it occurred to PIERRE DELANCRE that the Persian *ballerine* had much in common with witches. Now the dancers of India are said to have originated in ten thousand gypsies sent from Persia, and who were of such vagabond habits that they could not be persuaded to settle down anywhere. Of these Delancre says:

"The *Persian* girls dance at their sacrifices like witches at a Sabbat, that is naked, to the sound of an instrument. And the witches in their accursed assemblies are either entirely naked or *en chemise*, with a great cat clinging to their back, as many have at divers times confessed. The dame called *Volta* is the commonest and the most indecent. It is believed that the devil taught three kinds of dances to the witches of Ginevra, and these dances were very wild and rude, since in them they employed switches and sticks, as do those who teach animals to dance.

"And there was in this country a girl to whom the devil had given a rod of iron, which had the power to make any one dance who was touched with it. She ridiculed the judges during her trial, declaring they could not make her die, but they found a way to blunt her petulance.

"The devils danced with the most beautiful witches, in the form of a he-goat, or of any other animal, and coupled with them, so that no married woman or maid ever came back from these dances chaste as they had gone. They generally dance in a round, back to back, rarely a solo, or in pairs.

"There are three kinds of witch-dances; the first is the *trescone alla Boema*, or the Bohemian rigadoon" (perhaps the polka), "the second is like that of some of our work-people in the country, that is to say by always jumping" (this may be like the Tyrolese dances), "the third with the back turned, as in the second rigadoon, in which all are drawn up holding one another by the hand, and in a certain cadence hustling or bumping one another, *deretano contro deretano*. These dances are to the sound of a tambourine, a flute, a violin, or of another instrument which is struck with a stick. Such is the only music of the Sabbat, and all witches assert that there are in the world no concerts so well executed."

"A tambourine, a violin, a flute," with perhaps a *zimbel*, which is struck with a stick. Does not this describe to perfection gypsy music, and is not the whole a picture of the wildest gypsy dancing wherever found? Or it would apply to the Hindoo debauches, as still celebrated in honour of Sakktya, "the female principle" in India. In any case the suggestion is a very interesting one, since it leads to the query as to whether the entire sisterhood of ancient strolling, licentious dancers, whether Syrian, Spanish, or Egyptian, were not possibly of Indian-gypsy origin, and whether, in their character as fortune-tellers and sorceresses, they did not suggest the dances said to be familiar to the witches.

Mr. DAVID RITCHIE, the editor, with Mr. FRANCIS GROOME, of the *Journal of the Gypsy-Lore Society*, has mentioned (vol. i. No. 2) that KLINGSOHR, a reputed author of the "Nibelungen Lied," was described as a "*Zingar* wizard" by DIETRICH the Thuringian. Like ODIN, this KLINGSOHR rode upon a wolf--a kind of steed much affected by witches and sorcerers. There is an old English rhyming romance in which a knight is represented as disguising himself as an Ethiopian minstrel. These and other stories—as, for instance, that of Sir Estmere, not only indicate a connection between the characters of minstrel and magician, but suggest that some kind of men from the far East first suggested the identity between them. Of course there have been wild dancers and witches, and minstrel-sorcerers, or *vates*, prophet-poets, in all countries, but it may also be borne in mind that nowhere in history do we find the female erotic dancer and fortune-teller, or witch, combined in such vast numbers as in India and Persia, and that these were, and are, what may be truly called gypsies. Forming from prehistoric times a caste, or distinct class, it is very probable that they roamed from India to Spain, possibly here and there all over Europe. The extraordinary diplomatic skill, energy, and geographic knowledge displayed by the first band of gypsies who, about 1417, succeeded in rapidly obtaining permits for their people to wander in every country in Europe except England, indicate great unity of plan and purpose. That these gypsies, as supposed sorcerers, appearing in every country in Europe, should not have influenced and coloured in some way the conceptions of witchcraft seems to be incredible. If a superstitious man had never before in his life thought of witches dancing to the devil's music, it might occur to him when looking on at some of the performances of Spanish and Syrian gypsy women, and if the man had previously been informed--as everybody was in the fifteenth century or later--that these women were all witches and sorceresses, it could hardly fall to occur to him that it was after this fashion that the sisters danced at the Sabbat. Of which opinion all that can be said is, that if not proved it is extremely possible, and may be at least probed and looked into by those of the learned who are desirous of clearly establishing all the grounds and origins of ancient religious beliefs and superstitions, in which pies it may be found that witches and gypsies have had fingers to a far greater extent than grave historians have ever imagined.

The English gypsies believe in witches, among their own people, and it is very remarkable that in such cases at least as I have heard of, they do not regard them as *âmes damnées* or special limbs of Satan, but rather as some kinds of exceptionally gifted sorceresses or magicians. They are, however, feared from their supposed power to make mischief. Such a witch may be known by her hair, which is straight for three or four inches and then begins to curl--like a waterfall which comes down smoothly and then rebounds roundly on the rocks. It may be here remarked that all this gypsy conception of the witch is distinctly Hindoo and not in the least European or of Christians, with whom she is simply a human devil utterly given over to the devil's desires. And it is very remarkable that even the English gypsies do not associate such erring sisters—or any other kind—with the devil, as is done by their more cultivated associates.

The witch, in gypsy as in other lore, is a haunting terror of the night. It has not, that I am aware, ever been conjectured that the word *Humbug* is derived from the Norse *hum*, meaning night, or shadows (*tenebræ*) (JONÆO, "***Icelandic Latin glossary in Niall's Saga***"), and *bog*, or *bogey*, termed in several old editions of the Bible a bug, or "bugges." And as bogey came to mean a mere scarecrow, so the hum-bugges or nightly terrors became synonymes for feigned frights. "A humbug, a false alarm, a bug-bear" ("Dean Milles MS." HALLIWELL). The fact that *bug* is specialty applied to a nocturnal apparition, renders the reason for the addition of *hum* very evident.

There is a great deal that is curious in this word Bogey. Bug-a-boo is suggestive of the Slavonian *Bog* and *Buh*, both meaning God or a spirit. *Boo* or *bo* is a hobgoblin in Yorkshire, so called because it is said to be the first word which a ghost or one of his kind utters to a human being, to frighten him. Hence, "he cannot say *bo* to a goose." Hence boggart, bogle, boggle, bo-guest, *i.e.*, bar-geist, boll, boman, and, probably allied, bock (Devon), fear. Bull-beggar is probably a form of bu and bogey or boge, allied to boll (Northern), an apparition.

CHAPTER XI

Gypsy Witchcraft—The Magical Power Which is Innate in All Men And Women—How it May Be Cultivated And Developed—The Principles of Fortune-Telling

WOMEN excel in the manifestation of certain qualities which are associated with mystery and suggestive of occult influences or power. Perhaps the reader will pardon me if I devote a few pages to what I conceive to be, to a certain degree, an explanation of this magic; though, indeed, it may be justly said that in so doing We only pass the old boundary of "spiritual" sorcery to find ourselves in the wider wonderland of Science.

Whether it be the action of a faculty, a correlative action of physical functions, or a separate soul in us, the fact is indisputable that when our ordinary waking consciousness or *will* goes to sleep or rest, or even dozes, that instant an entirely different power takes command of the myriad forces of memory, and proceeds to make them act, wheel, evolute, and perform dramatic tricks, such as the Common Sense of our daily life would never admit. This power we call the Dream, but it is more than that. It can do more than make *Us*, or *Me*, or the Waking Will, believe that we are passing through fantastic scenes. It can remember or revive the memory of things forgotten by *us*; it can, when *he* is making no effort, solve for the geometrician problems which are far beyond his waking capacity--it sometimes teaches the musician airs such as he could not compose. That is to say, within ourself there dwells a more mysterious Me, in some respects a more gifted Self. There is not the least reason, in the present state of Science, to assume that this is—either a "spiritual" being or an action of material forces. It puzzled WIGAN as the dual action of the brain; and a great light is thrown on it by the "***Physiology***" of CARPENTER and the "***Memory***" of DAVID KAY (one of the most remarkable works of modern times), as well as in the "***Psycho Therapeutics***" of Dr. TUCKEY.

This power, therefore, knows things hidden from Me, and can do what *I* cannot. Let no one incautiously exclaim here that what this really means is, that I possess higher accomplishments which I do not use. The power often actually acts against Me—it plays at fast and loose with me—it tries to deceive me, and when it finds that in dreams I have detected a blunder in the plot of the play which it is spinning, it brings the whole abruptly to an end with the convulsion of a nightmare, or by letting the *curtain* fall with a crash, and—*scena est deserta*! am awake! And then "how the phantoms flee—how the dreams depart" as WESTWOOD writes. With what wonderful speed all is washed away clean from the blackboard! Our waking visions do not fly like this. But—be it noted, for it is positively true—the evanescence of our dreams is, in a vast majority of instances, exactly in proportion to their folly.

I am coming to my witchcraft directly, but I pray you have patience with my *proeme*. I wish to narrate a dream which I had a few years ago (September 5, 1887), which had an intensity of reality. Dreams, you know, reader, vary from rainbow mist to London fog, and so on to clouds, or mud. This one was hard as marble in comparison to most. A few days previously I had written a letter to a friend, in which I had discussed this subject of the dual-Me, and it seemed as if the Dream were called forth by it in answer.

I thought I was in my bed--a German one, for I was in Homburg vor der Höhe—yet I did not know exactly where I was. I at once perceived the anomaly, and was in great distress to know whether I was awake or in a dream. I seemed to be an invalid. I realized, or knew, that in another bed near mine was a nurse or attendant. I begged her to tell me if I were dreaming, and to awake me if I were. She tried to persuade me that I was in my ordinary life, awake. I was not at all satisfied. I arose and went into the street. There I met with two or three common men. I felt great hesitation in addressing them on such a singular subject, but told them that I was in distress because I feared that I was in a dream, and begged them to shake or squeeze my arm. I forget whether they complied, but I went on and met three gentlemen, to whom I made the same request. One at once promptly declared that he remembered me, saying that we had met before in Cincinnatti. He pressed my arm, but it had no effect. I began to believe that I was really awake. I returned to the room. I heard a child speaking or murmuring by the nurse. I asked her again to shake my hand. This she did so forcibly that I was now perfectly convinced that it was no dream. And the instant it came home to me that it was a reality, there seized me the thrill or feeling as of a coming nightmare—and I awoke!

Reviewing my dream when awake, I had the deepest feeling of having been *joué* or played with by a master-mocker. I recalled that, when I rose in my night-robe from the bed, I did not dress—and yet found myself fully dressed when in the street. Then I remembered that when I returned to America, in 1879, I was in great apprehension lest I should have trouble and delay with our sixteen trunks, because there was under my charge a lady who was dying. To my great relief and amazement, the officer whose duty it was to search claimed me as an old acquaintance, who had met me and T. BUCHANAN READ, the poet, in Cincinnatti in 1864, But what impressed me most of all, at once, was that the whole was caused by, and was a keen and subtle mockery of my comments in my letter, of the other Ego, and of its sarcastic power. For I had been led, step by step, through the extremest doubt, to a full conviction of being awake, and then dismissed, as it were, with a snap or sneer into wakefulness itself

Now this Dream Artist is, to judge by his works, a very different kind of a person from Me. We are not sympathetic, and herein lies a great and serious subject of study. "Dreams," says a writer, "are the novels which we read when we are fast asleep," and, at the risk of receiving punishment, I declare that *my* writer belongs to a school of novelists with which I have no feelings in common. If, as everybody assumes, it is always *I* who dream--only using other material—how is it that I always invariably disagree with, thwart, contradict, vex, and mock myself? I had rather be hanged and be done with it, before I would wrong my worst enemy with such pitiful, silly, degrading dreams and long-forgotten follies, as I am called on to endure. If this *alter-ego* were a lunatic, he could not be a more thoroughly uncongenial inmate of my brain than he often is. Our characters are radically different. Why has *he* a mind so utterly unlike mine? His tastes, his thoughts, dispositions, and petty peculiarities are all unlike mine. If we belonged to the same club, I should never talk with him.

Now we are coming to our Witchcraft. This *alter-ego* does not confine himself to dreams. A lunatic is a man who dreams wide-awake. He has lost his will or the controlling power resulting from the just co-relation of brain forces. Then the stored-up images stray out and blend. I have dreamed of telling or seeing things and of acting them at the same time. A fish and a watch and a man may seem to be the same thing at once in a dream, as they often are to a waking lunatic. A poet is a man who dreams wide-awake; but he can guide his dreams or imaginings to symmetrical form, and to a logical conclusion or coherence. With the painter and sculptor it is the same. When the *alter-ego* works harmoniously with the *waking* will, we call it Imagination.

But when the *alter-ego* draws decidedly on latent forces, or powers unknown to the waking Me, I am amazed, He does it often enough, *that* is certain. Then we have Mystery. And it is out of this that men have drawn the conclusion that they have two or three souls--an astral spirit, a power of prophecy, the art of leaving the body, and the entire machinery of occultism. Physiology is probably on the high road to explain it all, but as yet it is not explained.

Meanwhile it steals into our waking life in many ways. It comes in emotions, presentiments, harp tones, mystical conceptions, and minglings of images or ideas, and incomprehensible deductions, which are sometimes, of course, prophetic. It has nothing in common with common sense; therefore it is to some un-common sense, or to others non-sense. Sometimes it *is* one or the other. Agreeable sensations and their harmony become the Beautiful. These blend and produce a general æsthetic sense. It becomes mystical, and is easily worked on by the *alter-ego*. The most inspired passages of every poet on the beauty of Nature betray clearly the influence and hidden power of the Dream in waking life. SHELLEY, WORDSWORTH, KEATS, BYRON, were all waking dreamers *de la première force*.

He who has heard an Æolian harp play—and I have heard the seven of JUSTINUS KERNER in the old castle of Weibertreu when I was his guest--if he be a "tone-artist," has often caught series of chords which were almost melodies. This music has the same relation to definite composition which the dream has to waking common sense. There are two things which I do not understand. One is, why composers of music make so little use of the suggestive Æolian harp; the second is, why decorative designers never employ the *folding mirror* [1] to produce designs. The one is an exact counterpart of the other, and both are capable of revealing inexhaustible harmonies, for both are deeply in accordance with the evolving processes of Nature.

The poetic or artistic faculty is, we therefore assume, the action on the myriad cells of memory by a strange--sometimes apparently involuntary—fantastic power, which is at the same time higher and lower than common sense or waking consciousness. Every image which man has received from sensation lies stored away in a cell, and is, in fact, a memory by itself. There is a faculty of association or sympathy by which groups of these images are called up, and there is perception which receives them, more or less vividly, like a photographic plate. When awake, Will, or coherent Common Sense, regulates all this machinery. When asleep, the Images seem to steal out and blend and frisk about by themselves in quaint dances, guided apparently by a kind of power whom I have conventionally called the *alter-ego*. This power throws open brain or memory-cells, which waking Common Sense has forgotten; in their chaotic or fantastic searches and mingling they produce poetry; they may chance on prophecy, for if our waking self had at command the immense latent knowledge in which these elves revel, it would detect sequences and know to what many things would lead, now unto us all unknown.

I once knew a nobleman who inherited in Italy a palace which he had never seen. There were in it three hundred rooms, and it had belonged to a family which had for six hundred years collected and handed down to their descendants every kind of object, as if they had been magpies or ravens. The heir, as a grave, earnest man, only concerned himself with the armoury and picture gallery and principal rooms. But his young daughter Bertha ranged all over the place and made hundreds of the most singular discoveries. One day she came to me very much delighted, She had found an obscure room or garret, in which there were ranged about on shelves, "sitting up and all. looking at her," several hundred old dolls and marionettes. For two hundred years or more the family had kept its old dolls. In this case the father was the waking reason, the rooms the brain cells, and Bertha the sprite who ranges over all and knows where to find forgotten images in, store. Many of those whom we meet in dreams are like the ghosts of dolls.

This is the only true Night side of Nature, but its shadows and dusky twilight, and strangely-hued chiaroscuros and long pauses of gloom, come constantly into the sunlight of our waking life. Some lives have too much of it, some too little. Some receive it in coarse and evil forms, as lunatics, and sufferers from mania *à potu*; some canny people--happy Scotchmen, for instance--succeed in banishing it from life as nearly as is possible for a human being to do. Now to speak clearly, and to recapitulate distinctly, I set forth the following propositions:

I. We have a conscious will which, whether it be an independent incomprehensible spirit, or simply the correlative result or action of all our other brain powers, exists, and during our waking hours directs our thoughts and acts. While it is at work in the world with social influences, its general tendency is towards average common sense.

II. This conscious will sleeps when we sleep. But the collective images which form memory, each being indeed a separate memory, as an aggregate of bees' cells form a comb, are always ready to come forth, just as honey is always sweet, limpid, and fluid. There is between them all an associative faculty, or a strange and singular power, which begins to act when the will sleeps. Whether it be also an independent Self which plays capriciously while conscious will sleeps, or a result of correlated forces, it is not as yet possible to determine. What we know is, that it calls forth the images by association, and in a fantastic, capricious manner, imitates and combines what we have experienced, or read, or thought, during our waking hours.

III. Our waking will can only realize or act on such images as it has kept familiarly before it, or such as have been so often recalled that they recur spontaneously. But all the treasures of memory seem to be available to the dream ruler, and with them a loose facile power of grouping them into kaleidoscopic combinations. Thus, if one could imagine a kaleidoscope which at every turn made varied groups of human or other figures in different attitudes, with changing scenery; and then suppose this to be turned round by some simple vital or mechanical action, he would have an idea of the action of dreams. It is probable that the radical function of the dream-power is to prevent images from becoming utterly forgotten or rusty; and by exercising the faculty of facile or chance combination to keep awake in man originality and creativeness. For it is almost certain that, but for the intrusion of this faculty into our waking thoughts, man would become a mere animal, without an idea beyond the joint common appetites, instincts, and emotions of the lowest of his kind.

IV. The dream-power intrudes more or less into all waking life. Then it acts, though irregularly, yet in harmony, with conscious will. When it is powerful and has great skill in forming associations of images—and by images I mean, with Kay, "ideas" and can also submit these to waking wisdom, the result is poetry or art. In recalling strange, beautiful images, and in imagining scenes, we partly lapse into dreaming; in fact, we *do* dream, though conscious will sits by us all the time and even aids our work. And most poets and artists, and many inventors, will testify that, while imagining or inventing, they abstract the "mind" from the world and common-place events, seek calm and quiet, and try to get into a "brown study," which is a waking dream. That is to say, a condition which is in some respects analogous to sleep is necessary to stimulate the flow and combination of images. This brown study is a state of mind in which images flow and blend and form new shapes far more easily than when Will and Reason have the upper hand. For *they* act only in a conventional beaten track, and deal only with the known and familiar.

V. Magic is the production of that which is not measured by the capacity of the conscious working will. The dream spirit, or that which knows all our memories, and which combines, blends, separates, scatters. unites, confuses, intensifies, beautifies, or makes terrible all the persons, scenes, acts, events, tragedies, or comedies known to us, can, if it pleases, by instantaneous reasoning or intuition, perceive what waking common sense does not. We visit a sick man, and the dream spirit, out of the inexhaustible hoards of memory aided by association, which results in subtle, occult *reasoning*, perceives that the patient will die in a certain time, and this result is served up in a dramatic dream. The amount of miracles, mysteries, apparitions, omens, and theurgia which the action of these latent faculties cause, or seem to cause, is simply illimitable, for no man knows how much he knows. Few, indeed, are the ordinary well-educated Europeans of average experience of life, whose memories are not inexhaustible encyclopædias, and whose intellects are not infinite if all that is really in them could be wakened from slumber, "know thyself" would mean "know the universe." Now, there are people who, without being able to say *why*, are often inspired by this power which intuitively divines or guesses without revealing the process to common sense. They look into the eye of a person--something in glances and tones, gestures, mien, and address, suggests at once an assertion or a prediction which proves to be true. Considering that the dream-power has millions of experiences or images at its command, that it flits over them all like lightning, that it can combine, abstract, compare, and deduct, that it being, so to speak, more of a thaumaturgical artist than anything else, excels waking wisdom in subtle trickery, the wonder is, not that we so often hear of marvellous, magical, inexplicable wonders, but that they are not of daily or hourly occurrence. When we think of what we might be if we could master *ourselves*, and call on the vast sea of knowledge which is in the brain of every one who reads these lines, to give strict reckoning of its every wave and every drop of water, and every shell, pebble, wreck, weed, or grain of sand over which it rolls, and withal master the forces which make its tides and storms, *then* we may comprehend that all the wonder-working power attributed to all the sorcerers of olden time was nothing compared to what we really have within us.

It is awful, it is mysterious, it is terrible to learn this tremendous truth that we are indeed within ourselves magicians gifted with infinite intellectual power-which means the ability to know and do all things. In the past men surmised the existence of this infinite memory, this power of subtle research and combination, but between them and the truth in every land and. time interposed the idea of objective spiritual or *supernatural* existences whose aid or medium was necessary to attain to wisdom. Outside of us was always Somebody Else to be invoked, conciliated, met in vision or trance, united to in spiritual unity or syncope. Sometimes they hit upon some form of hypnotism or mesmerism, opiates or forced swoons and convulsions, and so extorted from the nerves and dream-power some of their secrets which were all duly attributed to the "spirits." But in the whole range of occult literature from HERMES TRISMEGISTUS down to Madame BLAVATSKY there is not a shade of a suspicion that all the absolutely authentic marvels of magic began and ended with man himself.

Least of all did any speculator yet conjecture how to set forth on the path which leads us to this wonderland. For there is a way to it, and a power to master the infinite stores of memory and render the dream-power a willing servant, if we take the pains to do it. Firstly—as may be found asserted, and I think fairly proved, in my work on "***Practical Education***," and in the "***Memory of David Kay***" (London, 1888)--every child by a very easy gradual process, simply that of learning by heart, and reviewing, can develope its memory to such a degree that all which that child reads, hears, or sees can be literally retained for life. Secondly, quickness of perception, which is allied to memory, can be taught so as to develope intuitive observation and intelligence to an equally incredible extent. Thirdly—and for this I have had abundant personal experience—every child can learn Design and the Minor Arts or develope the Constructive faculties, and by doing this alone a pupil becomes exceptionally clever in *all* studies. The proof of this is that the 200 pupils who attended an industrial or art school in Philadelphia took precedence in studies among 110,000 others in the public schools.

If all the stores of our memory were distinctly cognized by our waking will when they first came into our possession, we should have the first great element of power beyond all our present dreams of greatness. That this *can* be done has been recognized by many of the most advanced thinkers of the day. If a child be trained to exercise quickness of perception so that at last it observes and remembers everything—and experiment has proved this also—it will make the Dream Power a waking power absolutely in harmony and accordance with waking wisdom or conscious will. For the reason why the capricious, wild, strange fitful faculty has always remained foreign to us, is because in all our culture we have never sought to subdue and train the powers allied to it. Catch and tame one water-fairy, says the Red Indian legend, and you may get all her sisters. Waking quickness of perception is a wonderful ability. It can be trained to flit like lightning over illimitable fields of thought (supplied by a vast memory), and with them it spontaneously developes comparison and deduction. Now all of this is marvellously akin to the habitual action of the dream power *plus* that of reflection. And it is not possible to conceive that with waking quickness of perception, or voluntary subtlety of thought, cultivated in infancy to the highest power, its twin which sports in sleep should not feel its influence and act under it.

The result of this culture would inevitably be that the marvels, mysteries, and magic as they seem to us of the dream, or intuitive power, would be perfectly under our waking control, or to such an extent that we could secure all that is profitable in them. It is a very curious fact that while Reflection or Waking Wisdom slumbers, Quickness of Perception or Perception and Association seem to be always awake—in dreams or waking. A very extended series of observations has convinced me that the acquisition of a very great degree of Observation itself, or of Attention, is as possible as to learn French, and no harder; yet as a branch of study it literally does not exist. As a writer in the *New York Tribune* remarks: "In fact, observation is almost an atrophied faculty, and when a writer practises it for the purposes of his art, we regard the matter as in some sense wonderful." Interest, as MAUDSLEY has shown, is a natural result of Attention, and the two generate Will. Whether we can actually control the Dream-power is not as yet proved by experiment. All that we can say is that it is probable. But that this power manifests itself in waking hours when it submits to Reflection, is an established fact. It shows itself in all imagination, in all originality, brave art or "fantasy." Therefore it is no extravagant deduction to conclude that all of its action which now seems so wonderful, and which has furnished the ground-work for what we call magic, is perfectly within our grasp, and may be secured by simple methods of training which require only perseverance to perfect them.

The gypsy fortune-teller is accustomed for years to look keenly and earnestly into the eyes of those whom she *dukkers* or "fortune-tells." She is accustomed to make ignorant and credulous or imaginative girls feel that her mysterious insight penetrates "with a power and with a sign" to their very souls. As she looks into their palms, and still more keenly into their eyes, while conversing volubly with perfect self-possession, ere long she observes that she has made a hit—has chanced upon some true passage or relation to the girl's life. This emboldens her. Unconsciously the Dream Spirit, or the Alter-Ego, is awakened. It calls forth from the hidden stores of Memory strange facts and associations, and with it arises the latent and often unconscious quickness of Perception, and the gypsy actually apprehends and utters things which are "wonderful." There is no clairvoyance, illumination or witchcraft in such cases. If such powers existed as they are generally understood to do, we should for one case of curious prediction hear of twenty thousand. But the Dream-power is at best fitful, irregular and fantastic in its action; it is at all times untrustworthy, for it has never been trained unless of yore by Chaldæan priests and magi. In some wonderful way facts do, however, manifest themselves, evoked out of the unknown by "occult," though purely material, mental faculties; and the result is that wonder at the inexplicable—which makes miracles--until we are accustomed to them.

That gypsy women often do surmise or arrive at very curious and startling truths I know by my own experience, and also know that I myself when reading character in people's hands according to the laws laid down in books on chiromancy, when I have felt deeply interested, or as one may say excited or inspired, and have gone a little beyond mere description into conjecture and deduction, have been amazed at my own successes. It happened once that when in company with several ladies it was proposed after lunch to go to a gypsy camp on the Thames, and have fortunes told. Among these ladies was one of a very imaginative temperament, who had not only lived many years in the East, but had resided several winters as a guest in Arab families. As she was very much disappointed at not finding the gypsies, I offered to tell her fortune by onomancy, *i.e.*, by taking the letters of her name according to numbers, and deducing from them her past and future. This I did in a most reckless manner, freely setting down whatever came into my mind. It seems to me now that a kind of inspiration suggested what I wrote and predicted. What was my amazement to hear the lady declare that all which had been written as to her past life was literally true, and I saw that she was simply awed at my supposed power of prediction, and had the fullest faith in what I had declared as regarded the future. What I had intended for a jest or mere entertainment turned out to be serious enough. And reflecting on the evil consequences of such belief on a person who naturally attributed it all to magic, I deeply regretted what I had done, and have not since attempted any renewal of such oracle-work. It had previously occurred that I wrote out such a prediction for another lady which I did not clearly explain to her, but in which there was a regular recurrence and repetition of something unfortunate. This was shown in after years, and the troubles all came to pass as I had written. Now the more I studied this case the more I was convinced that it was based on unconscious observation, comparison, and deduction. FICHTE has said that no bird can fly beyond itself, but the mind sometimes does actually precede its own conscious reasoning and throw back facts to it.

It may be urged by those who still cling to the old-fashioned fetish of a distinction between Spirit and Matter, that this explanation of predictions, oracles, and insight, is simply materialistic and utterly destructive of all the poetry, grandeur, and beauty which is associated with mysterious divination. But for those who believe with MAUDSLEY, *et sui generis*, that all such distinctions are not seriously worth considering, and to him who can rise to the great philosophy now dawning on the world, there is perceptible in it something far more wonderful and poetical, beautiful and even awful, than ever was known to any occultist of old--for it is scientific and true. It is also true that man can now talk across the world and hear all sounds conveyed to him through the depths of ocean. He can catch these sounds and keep them for centuries. How long will it be before sights, scents, and tastes will be thus transferred, and the man sitting in London will see all things passing in Asia, or wherever it pleases him or an agent to turn a mirror on a view? It will be. Or how long before the discovery of cheap and perfect aerial navigation will change all society and annihilate national distinctions? That, too, will be. These and a thousand stranger discoveries will during the ensuing century burst upon the world, changing it utterly. We go on as of old in our little petty narrow grooves, declaring that *this* will be, and *that* will never come to pass, and that this or that kind of hop-scotch lines, and tip-cat and marbles rules, are the eternal laws of humanity, and lo! all the while in his study some man whom you regard as a dreamer or dolt is preparing that which will be felt forever.

One of these great discoveries, and that not the least, will be the development and mastery of memory and perception, attention, interest, and will in children, with the constructive faculty which stimulates the whole by means of easy gradual series of instructions. When this system shall be perfected, we shall advance to understanding, controlling, and disciplining the subtler and stranger powers of the brain, which now puzzle us as dreams, intuitions, poetic inspiration, and prophecy. But this prophecy comes not from it, nor from any vague guessing or hoping. It is based on facts and on years of careful study of a thousand children's minds, and from a conviction derived from calm observation, that the powers of the human mind are infinite and capable of being developed by science. And they will be!

There is very little knowledge among gypsies of real chiromancy, such as is set forth in the literature of occult or semi-occult science. Two centuries ago, when chiromancy was studied seriously and thoroughly by learned and wise men, the latter compared thousands of hands, and naturally enough evolved certain truths, such as you, reader, would probably evolve for yourself if you would do the same. Firstly they observed, as you may do, that the hand of a boor is not marked like that of a gentleman, nor that of an ignoramus like the palm of an artist or scholar. The line which indicates brain is on an average shorter in women than in men; in almost every instance certain signs infallibly indicate great sensuality. Others show a disposition to dreaminess, sentimentalism, the occult. Now as Love, Wisdom, Strength of Will, or Inertness, are associable with Venus, Apollo, Jupiter, or Saturn, and as astrology was then seriously believed in, it came to pass that the signs of chiromancy were distributed to the seven planets, and supposed to be under their dominion. It was an error, but after all it amounts to a mere classification. Properly considered, the names Jupiter, Saturn, Apollo, Mercury, Venus, and Mars are only synonymes of qualities, meaning masculine virtue and character, aptitude, art, cleverness, sexual passion, and .combativeness. He who would, without a trace of superstition, analyze and describe many hands compared with the characters of their owners, would adopt effectively the same arrangement.

When we remember the age in which they lived and the popular yearning for wonders and marvels which then characterized even the wisest men, the old chiromancers were singularly free from superstition. There were many among them who would have regarded with supreme contempt a DESBAROLLES, with his fortune-telling for twenty francs.

To these truly honest men, the gypsies, with their pretended chiromancy, were at first a great puzzle. The learned PRÆTORIUS, in his vast work on Chiromancy and Physiognomy, devotes seventy-five pages to this "foreign element in our midst," and comes to the conclusion that they are humbugs.

They do not know the *lines*--they know nothing. The intrusion of the latent powers of the mind had no place in the philosophy of PRÆTORIUS, therefore he did not perceive the back door by which the Romany slipped into the oracle. Yet there is abundant evidence even in his own valuable collection of the works of his predecessors, that many of them when tempted from merely describing character to straying into prophecy, were guided by something more mysterious than the laws of the lines of life, of the head, heart, the circle of Venus, the "hepatic," and *viâ lactea*. The Hungarian gypsies have a system of chiromancy of their own which the reader may find in the book "***Vom Wandernden Zigeunervolke***," by Dr. von WLISLOCKI, Hamburg, 1890, I had translated this and more of the kind for this chapter, but omitted it, thinking, firstly, that its place is supplied by more important matter; and, secondly, because it is, save as perhaps indicative of Indian origin, quite valueless, being merely of the prophetic kind.

I have more than once known gypsies to tell me things of my past life which were certainly remarkable, bewildering, or inexplicable. And for the ordinary seeker of "voonders oopon voonders" it is all-sufficient that a thing shall be beyond clear intelligence. "How do you explain *that*?" is their crucial question, and their cry of triumph when relating some case of an authentic apparition, a spiritual feat of thaumaturgy, or a dream fulfilled. In fact they would rather *not* have it explained. I well remember how Professor JOSEPH HENRY, when lecturing on natural science, narrated to us, his hearers, how when he told certain people how certain tricks of a common conjuror Were executed, they all protested that it could not be the way it was done. They did not wish to be disillusioned. Raise a man from the dead, make him fly through the air, and it is for everybody a miracle. Give them the power to do the same, and in a month's time it will be no longer miraculous, but something "in the due course of nature." And what single fact is there in the due course of nature which is not as inexplicable if we seek for a full explanation of it? Consider this thing every day till you ate penetrated with it, bear it in mind constantly, and in due time all, phenomena will be miracles. We can apparently get a little nearer to the causes and give our discoveries names, but the primal causes as constantly recede and are continually buried in deeper mystery. But with most people names pass for explanations.

"Can you tell me what a hypothesis is?" asked a young gentleman at a dinner party of a friend who passed for being well-informed. "Hush," was the reply. "Not now—*ladies present*."

"*Mon caporal*," asked a French soldier, "can you tell me what is meant by an equilateral?" "Certainly—*mais d'abord*—do you know Hebrew?" "No." "Ah, then it would be impossible to explain it to you."

"What is it that makes people's heads ache?" inquired an old lady of a youth who had just begun his medical studies. "Oh, it is only the convolution of the anomalies of the ellipsoid," replied the student. "just see now what it is to git larnin!" commented the dame. "He knows it all in a straight line?"

The one is satisfied that a hypothesis is something improper, the other that an equilateral is a matter which he *might* understand if he were as learned as his corporal, and the third is pleased to find that the mystery has at least a name. And human beings are satisfied in the same way as to the mysteries of Nature. Give them a name and assure them that the learned understand it, and they are satisfied.

It is a fundamental principle of human folly to assume that any alleged marvel is a "violation of the laws of Nature," or the work of supernatural influences, until it is proved *not* to be such. Nature cannot be violated. She is ever virgin. And "how do you account for *that*?" is always assumed to be a test question. It cannot be denied that in almost every case, the narrator assumes the *absolute* truth of *all* which he states, when, as is well known, even in the most commonplace incidents of ordinary life, such truth can very rarely be obtained. *Secondly*, he assumes that all the persons who were cognizant of the miracle, or were concerned in it, were not only *perfectly* truthful, but endowed with perfect perfections, and *absolutely* sound judgments. If there is the least shadow of a possibility that one of them could have erred in the least particular, the whole must fall to the ground as a proof or test—for we must have irrefragible and complete evidence before we adopt a faith on which all our life may depend. But, *thirdly*, by asking any one to account for a marvel, he assumes that the one thus called on knows everything short of the supernatural or Infinite, which is simply silly.

But there is a higher source of admiration and wonder than could ever be established by vulgar fetish, Animism, or supernaturalism, and this is to be found in the mysteries of Nature which man has never penetrated, and which, as soon as they are overcome, reveal others far grander or deeper. Thus as Alps rise beyond Alps, and seas of stars and solar systems spread in proportions of compound multiplication, our powers of vision increase. And it often happens to him who looks deeply into causes, that one of the myriad test cases of so-called "supernaturalism," when it has ignominiously broken down, as all do sooner or later, often reveals a deeper marvel or mystery than it was intended to support. Thus some Red Indians in North America, on being told how certain juggling tricks which they had accepted for magic were performed, calmly replied that it did not make the least difference—that a man must have been a magician (or divinely inspired) to be able to find out such tricks. And I myself knew an Indian trader named Ross, who, being once among a wild tribe, put on a mask of *papier maché*, which caused tremendous excitement and awe, which was not in the least diminished when he took it off and put it into their hands and explained its nature, for they maintained that the thing which could cause such terror indicated the existence of superior mental power, or magic, in the maker. In which there is, as it seems to me, indications of a much higher wisdom or sagacity than is to be found in the vulgar spiritualist who takes the event or thing itself for the miracle, and who, when found out in his tricks, ignominiously collapses.

The conclusion from all this is, that I have seen and heard of much in gypsy witchcraft and fortune-telling which, while it was directly allied to humbug of the shallowest kind, also rested on, or was inspired by, mental action or power which, in our present state of knowledge, must be regarded as strangely mysterious and of the deepest interest. And this is indeed *weird*, in the fullest and truest sense, since it is used for prophecy. I will now endeavour to illustrate this.

It is but natural that there should be "something in" gypsy fortune-telling. If the reader were to tell ten fortunes a day for twenty years it would be very remarkable indeed if in that time he had not learned some things which would seem wonderful to the world. He would detect at a glance the credulous, timid, hold, doubtful, refined or vulgar nature, just as a lawyer learns to detect character by cross-examination. Many experiments of late years have gone very far to establish the existence of a power of divining or reading thought; how this is *really* done I know not; perhaps the experts in it are as ignorant as I am, but it is very certain that certain minds, in some (as yet) marvellous way, betray their secrets to the master. That there are really gypsies who have a very highly cultivated faculty of reading the mind by the eye is certainly true. Sometimes they seem to be themselves uncertain, and see as through a glass darkly, and will reveal remarkable facts doubtfully. I remember a curious illustration of this. Once I was walking near Bath, and meeting a tinker asked him if there were any gypsies in the vicinity. He gave me the address of a woman who lived in a cottage at no great distance. I found it with some trouble, and was astonished on entering at the abominably miserable, reckless, squalid appearance of everything. There was a half or quarter-bred gypsy woman, ragged, dirty, and drunk, a swarm of miserable children, and a few articles of furniture misplaced or upset as if the inmates had really. no idea of how a room should be lived in. I addressed the woman civilly, but she was too vulgar and degraded to be capable of sensible or civil conversation with a superior. Such people actually exist among the worst class of vagabonds. But as I, disgusted, was about to leave, and gave her a small gratuity, she offered to tell my fortune, which I declined, whereupon she cried, "You *shall* see that I know something;" and certainly told me something which astonished me, of an event which had taken place two years before at a great distance. To test her I coolly denied it all, at which she seemed astonished and bewildered, saying, "Can I have made a mistake? You are certainly the person." All of this may be explained by causes which I shall set forth. But it cannot be too earnestly insisted on to people who habitually doubt, that because a thing can be explained in a certain way (*i.e.*, by humbug) that it necessarily follows that that is the *only* explanation of it. Yet this is at the present day actually and positively the popular method, and it obtains very largely indeed with the small critics of the "safe school." Mrs. Million has diamonds; she *may* have stolen them—a great many people have stolen diamonds—therefore she is probably a thief. The Icelandic sagas describe journeys to America; but the writers of the sagas were often mythical, exaggerative, and inaccurate--therefore all they narrate as regards America must be, of course, untrue.

Jack Stripe
Eats tripe,
It is therefore credible
That tripe is edible;
And it follows perforce,
As a matter of course,
That the devil will gripe
All who do not eat tripe.

But I do *not* insist that there is anything "miraculous" in gypsy fortune-telling. It may be merely the result of great practical experience and of a developed intuition, it may be mind or "thought-reading"—whatever that really is—or it may result from following certain regular rules. This latter method will be pronounced pure humbug, but of that I will speak anon. These rules followed by anybody, even the feeblest dilettante who has only read DESBAROLLES for drawing-room entertainment, will often astonish the dupe. They are, "in few," as follows:

1. It is safe in most cases with middle-aged men to declare that they have had a law-suit, or a great dispute as to property, which has given them a great deal of trouble. This must be impressively uttered. Emphasis and sinking the voice are of great assistance in fortune-telling. If the subject betray the least emotion, or admit it, promptly improve the occasion, express sympathy, and "work it up."

2. Declare that a great fortune, or something greatly to the advantage of the subject, or something which will gratify him, will soon come in his way, but that he must be keen to watch his opportunity and be bold and energetic.

3. He will have three great chances, or fortunes, in his life. If you *know* that he has inherited or made a fortune, or had a good appointment, you may say that he has already realized one of them. This seldom fails.

4. A lady of great wealth and beauty, who is of singularly sympathetic disposition, is in love with him, or ready to be, and it will depend on himself to secure his happiness. Or he will soon meet such a person when he shall least expect it.

5. "You had at one time great trouble with your relations (or friends). They treated you very unkindly." Or, "They were prepared to do so, but your resolute conduct daunted them."

6. "You have been three times in great danger of death." Pronounce this very impressively. Everybody, though it be a schoolboy believes, or likes to believe, that he has encountered perils. This is infallible, or at least it takes in most people. If the subject can be induced to relate his hairbreadth escapes, you may foretell future perils.

7. "You have had an enemy who has caused you great trouble. But he—or she—it is well not to specify which till you find out the sex—will ere long go too far, and his or her effort to injure you will recoil on him or her." Or, briefly, "It is written that some one, by trying to wrong you, will incur terrible retribution." Or, "You have had enemies, but they are all destined to come to grief." Or, "You had an enemy but you outlived him."

8. "You got yourself once into great trouble by doing a good act."

9. "Your passions have thrice got you into great trouble. Once your inconsiderate anger (or pursuit of pleasure) involved you in great suffering which, in the end, was to your advantage." Or else, "This will come to pass; therefore be on your guard."

10. "You will soon meet with a person who will have a great influence on your future life if you cultivate his friendship. You will ere long meet some one who will fall in love with you, if encouraged."

11. "You will find something very valuable if you keep your eyes open and watch closely. You have twice passed over a treasure and missed it, but you will have a third opportunity."

12. "You have done a great deal of good, or made the fortune or prosperity of persons who have been very ungrateful."

13. "You have been involved in several love affairs, but your conduct in all was really perfectly blameless."

14. "You have great capacity for something, and before long an occasion will present itself for you to exert it to your advantage."

By putting these points adroitly, and varying or combining them, startling cases of conviction may be made. Yet even into this deception will glide intuition, or the inexplicable insight to character, and the deceiver himself be led to marvel, so true is it that he who flies from Brama goes towards him, let him do what he will, for Truth is everywhere, and even lies lead to it.

The reader has often seen in London Italian women who have small birds, generally parrakeets, or paraquitos, which will for a penny pick out for her or for him slips of paper on which is printed a "fortune." If he will invest his pence in these he will in most instances find that they "fit his case" exactly, because they are framed on these or other rules, which are of very general application. There was, in 1882, an Italian named TORICELLI. Whether he was a descendant of the great natural philosopher of the same name who discovered the law of the vacuum I do not know, but he certainly exhibited--generally in Piccadilly--an ingenious application of it. He had a long glass cylinder, filled with water, in which there was a blown glass image of an imp. By pressing his hand on the top of the cover of the tube the *folletto* or *diavoletto* was made to rise or fall—from which the prediction was drawn. It will hardly be believed, but the unfortunate TORICELLI was actually arrested by the police and punished for "fortune-telling." After this he took to trained canaries or parrakeets, which picked out printed fortunes, for a living. Whether the stern arm of British justice descended on him for this latter form of sorcery and crime I do not know.

> "Forse fu dal demonio trasportato,
> Fiancheggiandosi del' autorita
> Di Origene o di San Girolamo."

Now it may be admitted that to form such rules (and there are many more far more ingenious and generally applicable) and to put them into practice with tact, adapting them to intuitions of character, not only as seen in the face but as heard in the voice or betrayed by gestures and dress and manner, must in the end develop a *power*. And, further still, this power by frequent practice enables its possessor to perform feats which are really marvellous and perhaps inexplicable, as yet, to men of science. I have, I think, indicated the road by which they travel to produce this result, but to what they arrived I do not know.

Nor do they all get there. What *genius* is, physiology, with all the vast flood of light spread by FRANCIS GALTON on hereditary gifts, cannot as yet explain. It is an absolute thing of itself, and a "miracle." Sometimes this wonderful power of prediction and of reading thought and quickly finding and applying rules falls into the hands of a genius. Then all our explanations of "humbug" and "trickery" and juggling fall to the ground, because he or she works what are absolutely as much miracles as if the artist had raised the dead. Such geniuses are the prophets of old; sometimes they are poets. There are as many clearly-defined and admirable predictions as to events in art and politics in the works of HEINE, which were fulfilled, as can be found anywhere.

By the constant application of such rules, promptly and aptly, or boldly, the fortune-teller acquires a very singular quickness of perception. There are very few persons living who really know what this *means* and to what apparently marvellous results constant practice in it may lead. Beginning with very simple and merely mechanical exercises ("***Practical Education***," p. 151. London: Whittaker & Co.), perception may be gradually developed until not only the eye and ear observe a thousand things which escape ordinary observation, and also many "images" at once, but finally the mind notes innumerable traits of character which would have once escaped it, combines these, and in a second draws conclusions which would amuse those who are ignorant—as indeed all men are as yet-of the extraordinary faculties latent in every man.

I beg the reader to pay special attention to this fact. There is nothing in all the annals of prophecy, divination, fortune-telling, or prediction, which is nearly so wonderful as what we may all do if we would by practice and exercise bring out of *ourselves* our own innate power of perception. This is not an assertion based on metaphysical theory; it is founded on fact, and is in strict accordance with the soundest conclusions of modern physiology. By means of it, joined to exercises in memorizing, all that there is in a child of ordinary intellect may be unerringly drawn out; and when in due time knowledge or information is gradually adduced, there is perhaps no limit to what that intellect may become. The study, therefore, of quickness of perception, as set forth or exercised in gypsy fortune-telling, is indeed curious; but to the far-reaching observer who is interested in education it is infinitely more useful, for it furnishes proof of the ability latent in every mind to perform what appear to be more than feats of intelligence or miracles, yet which often are all mere trifles compared to what man could effect if he were properly trained to it.

Sorcery! We are all sorcerers, and live in a wonderland of marvel and beauty if we did but know it. For the seed sprouting from the ground is as strange a truth as though we saw the hosts of heaven sweeping onward in glory, or could commune with fairies, or raise from his grave the master magician of song who laid a curse on all who should dig his dust. But like children who go to sleep in the grand opera, and are wild with delight at Punch, we turn aside from the endless miracle of nature to be charmed and bewildered with the petty thaumaturgy of guitars in the dark, cigarettes, and rope-tying, because it corresponds to and is miracle enough for us. Seek truth in Science and we shall be well balanced in the little as well as the great.

CHAPTER XII

Fortune-Telling (Continued)—Romance Based on Chance, or Hope, As Regards The Future-Folk—And Sorcery-Lore—Authentic Instances of Gypsy Prediction

IT would seem to all who now live that life would be really intolerably dry were it utterly deprived of mystery, marvel, or romance. This latter is the sentiment of hopeful *chance* allied to the beautiful. Youth is willing or eager to run great risks if the road to or through them passes by dark ravines, under castled rocks--

> "o'er dewy grass
> And waters wild and fleet"

...and ever has been from the beginning. Now, it is a matter of serious importance to know whether this romance is so deeply inherent in man that it can never be removed. For, rightly viewed, it means current religion, poetry, and almost all art—as art at least was once understood—and it would seem as if we had come, or are coming, to a time when science threatens to deprive us of it all. Such is the hidden fear of many a priest and poet—it may be worth while to consider whether it is all to pass away into earnest prose or assume new conditions. Has the world been hitherto a child, or a youth, were poetry and supernaturalism its toys, and has the time come when it is to put away childish things?

We can only argue from what we *are*, and what we clearly know or understand. And we know that there are in Nature, though measured by the senses alone, phenomena which awake delightful or terrible, sublime or beautiful, grave or gay feelings, or emotions, which inspire corresponding thoughts. There is for us "an elf-home glory-land," far over setting suns, mysterious beauty in night and stars in their eternal course, grandeur of God in the ocean, loveliness in woman, chiaroscuro in vapoury valleys and the spray of waterfalls by moonlight, exciting emotions which are certainly *not* within the domain of science--as yet--and which it is impossible for us, as we are at present constituted, to imagine as regarded entirely from the standpoint of chemical and physical analysis. To see in all this, as we are, *only* hydro-carbons, oxygen, silex and aluminium, atoms, molecules, and "laws"—that is to say, always the *parts* and combinations and no sense as regards man that he is, with his emotional sense of beauty, anywhere in the game or of any account, is going far too far. Setting teleology and theology entirely aside, Man, as the highest organism, has a right to claim that, as the highest faculties which have been as yet developed in him were caused by natural phenomena, therefore there is in the phenomena a certain *beauty* which is far more likely to lead to more advanced enjoyment of form, colour, or what we call the æsthetic sense, than to shrink away and disappear. And it seems to me that the most extended consideration of science leads to the result or conclusion that under its influence we shall find that the chemical and physical analyses of which I have spoken are only the dry A B C of a marvellously grand literature, or of a Romance and Poetry and Beauty—perhaps even of a wondrous "occult" philosophy, of whose beginning even we have, as yet, no idea.

But, great as it may be, those who will make it must derive their summary of facts or bases of observation from the past, and therefore I urge the importance of every man who can write doing what he can to collect *all* that illustrates Humanity as it is and as it was in by-gone ages. It hath not entered into the heart of man to conceive what a Folk-lore or ethnological society in ancient Greece, Rome, or Egypt might not have collected and preserved for the delight of every civilized human being of the present day. It is very true that the number of persons, as yet, who understand this--still less of those who take a real interest in it—is extremely limited, and they do not extend in England, America, or any other country, to more than a few hundreds. To the vast multitude, even of learned men, Folk-lore is only a "craze" for small literary *bric-à-brac*, a "fancy" which will have its run, and nothing more. To its earnest devotees it is the last great development of the art of learning and writing history, and a timely provision for future social science. It sets forth the most intimate inner life of people as they were, and the origins of our life as it is. In Folk-lore, Philology, Ethnology, and the study of Mythology or Religion find their greatest aid.

The amount of Red Indian Folk-lore which has been suffered to perish in the United States without exciting the least interest is beyond all belief. THOREAU could find in the Algonkin legends of New England nothing but matter for feeble-minded ridicule. But there are men coming, or a generation rising, to whom every record of the past will be of value, for they are beginning to perceive that while the collector is doing work of value the mere *theorist*, who generally undervalues if he does not actually oppose the collector, will with his rubbish be swept away "down the back-entry of time," to be utterly forgotten.

Gypsy sorcery-lore is of great value because all over the Aryan world gypsies have in ancient or modern times been, so to speak, the wandering priests of that form of popular religion which consists of a faith in fortune-telling. This is really a very important part in every cult; the most remarkable thing connected with it; as with charms, fetishes, incantations and protective spells, being the extraordinary success with which the more respectable *magi* have succeeded in convincing their followers that their own sorcery was not "magic" at all, and that the world-old heathen rites, which are substantially the same, are mere modern thieveries from the "established religion." Prediction and prophecy were the cornerstones of the classic mythology and of the Jewish law; they were equally dear to the Celtic races, and all men seem from the earliest times to have believed that coming events cast their shadows before. How this began and grew requires no deep study. Many disorders are prefaced by uneasy dreams or unaccountable melancholy, even as the greatest disaster which befel the gods of Valhalla was preceded by the troubled dreams of Balder. Sometimes the first symptom of gout is a previous irritability. But if diseases are believed to be caused by the literal occupation of the body by evil spirits these presages will be ascribed to occult spiritual influences. A man in excellent health feels gay--he goes hunting and has luck—of course his guardian spirit is believed to have inspired him to go. Then comes the priest or the gypsy to predict, and the hits are recorded and the misses are promptly forgotten.

The following instance has been related to me in good faith by a learned friend, whose books are well known to all Folk-lorists:

"I can quote from my own experience a strange event founded on a prediction made to me by a gypsy in 1863. This was before I had learned the language of the Romany or had begun to take any interest in them. At the time of which I speak, I met one day here, in T------, one or two gypsy women bearing as usual babies on their shoulders, when the oldest as I was passing by pointed me out to the bystanders, saying in German, '*Der Herr hat viel Kummer gehabt*' ('That gentleman has had much trouble '-or sorrow).

"This was true enough, as I was suffering greatly at the time from a previous bereavement, though I was no longer in mourning, nor was there at the instant any indication of gloom in my looks, for I was in a cheerful humour. So I stopped to ask her why she had made her remark. She replied, '*Ja, geben Sie mir die linke Hand und legen Sie drei Silbermünze darauf, wenn Sie weiteres hören wollen*' ('Yes, give me your hand, and put three silver coins on it, if you would hear more'). I did so, when she repeated her assertion as to my sorrow, and added, '*Aber eine Gräfinn steht für Ihnen*' ('But there is a countess awaiting you').

"I laughed at myself for listening to this, and for the strange feeling of interest or faith which I felt in it, and which my common sense told me was ridiculous. And yet the prediction, strangely enough, was fulfilled, though not in the sense in which I suppose most people would have taken it. Soon after I lost another relative, and was overwhelmed with that and other troubles when providence gent me a friend in that most amiable and remarkable woman the Countess B----, who, with that noble and gracious affability which distinguishes her, as well as her husband, Sir------, relieved my mind and cheered my depressed spirits.

"I add to this a marvellous story of a gypsy prediction which was uttered here in T------ and published last year in a small biography, but which is worth consideration because I have heard it apparently well authenticated by trustworthy people. A very great disgrace to our town--I am happy to say he was the only one--was a Mr. M------, of very good family. This man kept a mistress named R. M-------, who became acquainted with a young man who was employed as a clerk at the *Credit Anstalt*, and who always at night carried on his person its keys. This M------learned, and formed the following plot: The victim was to be enticed by the woman to her room, where she proposed to cut his throat, take the keys, and with the aid of M------ to rob the bank and escape. It succeeded so far as that the young man was brought to her room, but when she began to attempt to kill him he struggled, and was overpowering her when M------ entered the room and shot him dead.

"The precious pair were subsequently arrested and tried, and in the report of the proceedings there appears the following curious statement:

"'It is a singular thing (*cosa piu singolare*) that to this woman (M------'s mistress, Miss R------), a gypsy woman who pretended to palmistry predicted that she would come to a bad end (*ch'essa finirebbe assai male.*),' Which she effectually did, being condemned to fourteen years' hard labour, and would have been hung had not her "interesting state" inclined the judge to mercy.

"There is the following addition in the pamphlet to what has been quoted: "Being begged by the said Maria R------ to look more closely into the hand, the Zingara refused to do so, and went away muttering strange or foreign words.' (*Borbottanda strane parole*)."

To this my informant adds:

"I know of a more cheerful case of gypsy prediction, and of quite another kind, and which happened to a friend's friend of mine, also here in T-------. The 'subject' was a young lady, who was 'intended' or betrothed, to an Italian actor, who had gone to play at Madrid; but for two months she heard nothing from him, and, believing that he had neglected her, was in despair.

"One morning she was passing through one of the main streets, and was talking with my friend, when a dark gypsy girl going by, whispered to her in a hurried manner: '*Domani avrai una lettera e sarai felice*' ('To-morrow you will receive a letter and be happy'). Having said this and nothing more, without asking for money, she went away. The promised letter was in fact received, all went well, and the lady is now married to the gentleman. This is all simply, true. I leave the comments on the case to investigators. Can it be that gypsies are sometimes clairvoyant?"

My own comment on the case is that, admitting that the gypsy knew beforehand all the circumstances or even the "parties" in the affair, she had divined or "intuited" a result, and risked, as some might call it, or else tittered from a real conviction, her prophecy. How the mind, without any miracle--as miracles are commonly regarded--often arrives quite unconsciously to such conclusions, I have already considered in another chapter. Making every allowance for unconscious exaggeration and the accretive power of transmission, I am willing to believe that the story is actually true.

The following is also perfectly authentic: An English lady of excellent family, meeting a gypsy, was told by the latter that in six months the most important event of her life would come to pass. At the end of the time she died. On her death-bed she said, "I thought the gypsy meant a marriage, but I feel that something far more important is coming, for death is the great end of life."

The following was told me by a Hungarian gentleman of Szegedin:

"There was in Arad a lady who went to a ball. She had a necklace to which were attached four rings. During the evening she took this from her neck, and doubling it, wore it on her arm as a bracelet. In the house where she lived was a young gentleman who came to accompany her home from the ball. All at once, late at night, she missed her necklace and the rings, which were of great value.

"The next day she sent for a gypsy woman, who, being consulted, declared that the collar had been stolen by some one who was very intimate in her house. Her suspicions rested on the young man who had accompanied her home. He was arrested, but discharged far want of evidence.

"Three months after there came a *kellner*, a waiter, from some other city, to Arad. The lady, being in a *café* or some such place of resort, was waited on by this man, and saw one of her rings on his hand. He was arrested, and before the police declared that he held the ring in pledge, having advanced money upon it to a certain gentleman. This gentleman was the lady's betrothed, and he had stolen her necklace and rings. The gypsy had truly enough said that the articles had been taken by some one who was intimate in her house."

The gentleman who told me this story also said that the death of his father had been foretold by a gypsy--that is, by a lady who was of half-gypsy blood.

It should be borne in mind, though few realize its truth, that in stages of society where people *believe* earnestly in anything--for example, in witchcraft or the evil eye--there results in time a state of mind or body in which they are actually capable of being killed with a curse, or a fear of seeing what is not before them in the body, and of many nervous conditions which are absolutely impossible and incomprehensible to the world of culture at the present day. But there are still places where witchcraft may be said to exist literally, for there the professors of the art to all intents work miracles, *because* they are believed in. There is abundance of such faith extant, even in England. I have heard the names of three "white" witch doctors in as many towns in the West of England, who are paid a guinea a visit, their specialty being to "unlock," or neutralize, or defeat the evil efforts of black witches. This, as is indeed true, indicates that a rather high class of patients put faith in them. In Hungary, in the country, the majority, even of the better class, are very much influenced by gypsy-witches. Witness the following, which is interesting simply because, while there is very little indeed in it, it was related to me as a most conclusive proof of magic power:

"In a suburb of Szegedin, inhabited only by peasants, there is a school with a farm attached to it. The pay of the teacher is trifling, but he can make a comfortable living from the land. This was held by an old man, who had a young assistant. The old man died; the youth succeeded him, and as he found himself doing well, in due time he took a wife. They lived happily together for a year and had a daughter. In the spring the teacher had to work very hard, not only in school but on his farm, and so for the first time contracted the habit of going to the tavern to refresh himself, and what was worst, of concealing it from his wife under plausible tales, to which she gave no trust. She began to be very unhappy, and, naturally enough, suspected a rival.

"Of course she took advice from a gypsy woman, who heard all the story and consulted her cards. 'There is,' she said, 'no woman whatever in the way. There is no sign of one for good or evil, *na latchi na misec*, in the cards. But beware! for there is a great and unexpected misfortune coming, and more than this I cannot see.' So she took her pay and departed. Suddenly her child fell ill and died after eight days. Then the husband reformed his ways, and all went well with them. So, you see, the gypsy foretold it all, wonderfully and accurately."

It requires no sorcery to conjecture that the gypsy already knew the habits of the schoolmaster, as the Romany is generally familiar with the tavern of every town. To predict a misfortune at large is a sure card for every prophetess. What is remarkable is that a man of the world and one widely travelled, as was my informant, attached great importance to the story. It is evident that where so much of the sherris sack of faith accompanies such a small crust of miracle there must be a state of society in which miracles in their real sense are perfectly capable of being worked.

CHAPTER XIII

Proverbs Referring to Witches, Gypsies and Fairies

Of Fairies, Witches, Gypsies,
My nourrice sang to me ,
Sua Gypsies, Fairies, Witches,
I alsua synge to thee."
("Denham Tract.")

DR. KRAUSS has in his work, "***Sreca, Gluck und Schicksal im Volksglauben der Südslaven***," collected a number of sayings in reference to his subject, from which I have taken some, and added more from other sources.

Of an evil woman one says, as in all languages, "*To ie vila*"—that is, "a witch"; or it is uttered or muttered as, "*To je vila ljutica*"—that is, "a biting (or bitter) witch"; or to a woman whom one dislikes, "*Idi vilo!*"—"Begone, witch!" as in gypsy, "*Jasa tu chovihani!*"

Also, as in German, "*Ako i je baba, nje vjestica*"—"Though she is an old woman she is no witch"; while, on the other hand, we have, "*Svake baba viestica, a djed vjestac*"—"Every old woman is a witch, and every old man a wizard."

The proverb, "*Bizi ko vistica od biloga luka*"—"she runs from it like a witch from white garlic"--will be found fully explained in the chapter on "The Cure of Children," in which it is shown that from early times garlic has been a well-known witch-antidote.

Another saying is, "*Uzkostrsila se ko vistica*"—"Her hair is as tangled, or twisted, as that of a witch"; English gypsy, "*Lâkis balia shan risserdi sâr i chovihanis.*" But this has a slightly different meaning, since in the Slavonian it refers to matted, wild-looking locks, while the Romany is according to a belief that the hair of a witch is curled at the ends only.

Allied to this is the proverb, "*Izgleda kao aa su ga coprnice doniele sa Ivanjscica*"—"He looks as if the witches had done for him (or brought him away, 'fetched' him) on Saint John's Eve"; English Romany, "*Yuv dikela sá soved a lay sar a chovihani*"—"He looks as if he had lain with a witch."

"*Svaka vracara s vrazje strane*"—"Every witch belongs to the devil's gang"—that is, she has, sold her soul to him and is in his interests. This is allied to the saying, "*Kud ce vjestica do u svoj rod?*"—"Where should a witch go if not to her kin or, "Birds of a feather flock together."

"*Jasa ga vjestice*"—"The witches ride him"—refers to the ancient and world-wide belief that witches turn men into animals and ride them in sleep.

The hazel tree and nut are allied to the supernatural or witchly in many lands. For the divining rod, which—is, according to "***La Grande Bacchetta Divinatoria O Verga rivelatrice***" of the Abbate Valmont, the great instrument for all magic and marvels, must be made of "*un ramo forcuto di nocciuòlo*"—a forked branch of hazel-nut"—whence a proverb, "*Vracarice, coprnjice, kuko ljeskova!*"—"Sorceress, witch, hazel-stick." This is a reproach or taunt to a woman who pays great attention to magic and witchcraft. "This reveals a very ancient belief of the witch as a wood-spirit or fairy who dwells in the nut itself." More generally, it is the bush which, in old German ballads, is often addressed as Lady Hazel. In this, as in Lady Nightingale, we have a relic of addressing certain animals or plants as if they were intelligences or spirits. In one very old song in "Des Knaben Wunderhorn," a girl, angry at the hazel, who has reproached her for having loved too lightly or been too frail, says that her brother will come and cut the bush down. To which Lady Hazel replies:

> "Although he comes and cuts me down,
> I'll grow next spring, 'tis plain,
> But if a virgin wreath should fade,
> 'Twill never bloom again."

To keep children from picking unripe hazel-nuts in the Canton of Saint Gall they cry to them, "*S" Haselnussfràuli chumt*"—"The hazel-nut lady is coming!" Hence a rosary of hazel-nuts or a hazel rod brings luck, and they may be safely hung up in a house. The hazel-nut necklaces found in prehistoric tombs were probably amulets as well as ornaments.

Among popular sayings we may include the following from the *Gorski Vijenac*:

"A eto si udrijo vladiko,
U nekakve smućene vjetrove,
Ko u marču što udre yještice."

But behold, O Vladika,
Thou hast thrown thyself into every storm,
As witches throw or change themselves to cattle."

And with these we may include the curse, "*Izjele te viestice*"—"May the witches eat you!" which has its exact parallel in Romany. Also the Scottish saying, "Witches, warlocks, and gypsies soon ken ae the ither":

"Witches and warlocks without any bother,
Like gypsies on meeting well know one another."

I may appropriately add to these certain proverbs which are given in an extremely rare "Denham Tract," of which only fifty copies were printed by JOHN BELL RICHMOND, "*in. Com. Ebor.*" This quaint little work of only six pages is entitled, "*A Few Popular Rhymes, Proverbs, and Sayings relating to Fairies, Witches, and Gypsies*," and bears the dedication, "To every individual Fairy, Witch, and Gypsy from the day of the Witch of Endor down to that of Billy Dawson, the Wise Man of Stokesley, lately defunct, this tract is inscribed."

WITCHES

Vervain and Dill
Hinder witches from their will.

The following refers to rowan or mountain-ash wood, which is supposed to be a charm against witchcraft:

If your whipstick's made of rowan
You can ride your nag thro' any town.
Much about a pitch,
Quoth the devil to the witch.
A hairy man's a geary man,
But a hairy wife's a witch.
Woe to the lad
Without a rowan-tree god.

A witch-wife and an evil
Is three-halfpence worse than the devil.
Hey-how for Hallow-e'en!
When all the witches are to be seen,
Some in black and some in green,
Hey-how for Hallow-e'en!
Thout! tout! a tout, tout!
Throughout and about.
Cummer goe ye before, cummer goe ye,
Gif ye will not goe before, cummer let me!

"These lines are said to have been sung by witches at North Berwick in Lothian, accompanied by the music of a Jew's harp or trump, which was played by Geilles Duncan, a servant girl, before two hundred witches, who joined hands in a short daunce or reel, singing (also) these lines with one voice:

"'Witchy, witchy, I defy thee,
Four fingers round my thumb,
Let me go quietly by thee.'

"It will be seen that this is a phallic sign, and as such dreaded by witches. It is difficult to understand why these verses with the sign should have been given by witches."

The anti-witch rhyme used in Tweedesdale some sixty or seventy years ago was:

"'Black-luggie, lammer bead,
Rowan-tree and reed thread,
Put the witches to their speed.'

The meaning of 'black-luggie' I know not. 'Lammer bead' is a corruption of 'amber-bead.' They are still worn by a few old people in Scotland as a preservative against a variety of diseases, especially asthma, dropsy, and toothache. They also preserve the wearer from, the effects of witchcraft, as stated in the text. I have seen a twig of rowan-tree, witch-wood, quick-bane, wild ash, wicken-tree, wicky, wiggy, witchen, witch-bane, royne-tree, mountain-ash, whitty, wiggin, witch-hazel, roden-quicken, roden-quicken-royan, roun, or ran-tree, which had been gathered on the second of May (observe this), wound round with some dozens of yards of red thread, placed visible in the window to act as a charm in keeping witches and *Boggle-boes* from the house. So also we have:

"'Rowan-ash and reed thread
Keep the devils from their speed,"'
Ye brade o' witches, ye can do no good to yourself.
Fair they came,
Fair they go,
And always their heels behind them.
Neither so sinful as to sink, nor so godly as to swim.
Falser than Waghorn, and he was nineteen times falser than the devil.
Ingratitude is worse than witchcraft.
Ye're as mitch
As half a witch.
To milk the tether (*i.e.*, the cow-tie).

This refers to a belief that witches can carry off the milk from any one's cow by milking at the end of the tether.

Go in God's name—so you ride no witches.
"Rynt, you witch" quoth Bess Lockit to her mother.

Rynt, according to Skeat, is the original Cumberland word for aroint," *i.e.*, "aroint thee, get thee gone." Icelandic *ryma*--"to make room, to clear the way"--given, however, only as a guess. It seems to have been specially applied to witches.

"'Aroint thee, witch!' the rump-fed ronyon cried."
("Macbeth")

Halliwell gives the word as *rynt*, and devotes a column to it, without coming to any satisfactory conclusion. I think it is simply the old word *rynt* or *wrynt*, another form of writhe, meaning to twist or strangle, as if one should say, "Be thou strangled!" which was indeed a frequent malediction. Halliwell himself gives "*wreint*" as meaning "awry," and "*wreith destordre*"—"to wring or wreith" ("***Hollyband's Dictionarie***," 1593). The commonest curse of English gypsies at the present day is, "*Beng tasser tute*!" "May the devil strangle you"—literally *twist*, which is an exact translation of *wrinthe* or *rynt*.

"The gode man to hys cage can goo
And *wrythed* the pye's neck yn to."
("MS. Cantab." ap. H.)

Rynt may mean twist away, *i.e.*, begone, as they say in America, "he wriggled away."

They that burn you for a witch lose all their coals.

Never talk of witches on a Friday.

Ye're ower aude ffarand to be fraid o' witches.

Witches are most apt to confess on a Friday.

Friday is the witches' Sabbath.

To hug one as the devil hugs a witch.

As black
As cross
As ugly } as a witch.
As sinful

Four fingers and a thumb—witch, I defy thee.

In Italy, the signs are made differently. In Naples the *gettatura* consists of throwing out the fore and middle fingers, so as to imitate horns, with the thumb and fingers closed. Some say the thumb should be within the middle and third fingers. In Florence the anti-witch gesture is to *fare la fica*, or stick the thumb out between the fore and middle fingers.

You're like a witch, you say your prayers backward.

Witch-wood (ie., the mountain ash).

You're half a witch-*i.e.*, very cunning.

Buzz! buzz! buzz!

In the middle of the sixteenth century if a person waved his hat or bonnet in the air and cried 'Buzz!' three times, under the belief that by this act he could take the life of another, the old law and law-makers considered the person so saying and acting to be worthy of death, he being a murderer in intent, and having dealings with witches" ("Denham Tract"). Very doubtful, and probably founded on a well known old story.

"I wish I was as far from God as my nails are free from dirt!"

Said to have been a witch's prayer whilst she was in the act of cleaning her nails. In logical accuracy this recalls the black boy in America, who on being asked if he knew the way to a certain place, replied, "I only wish I had as many dollars as I know my way there."

A witch is afraid of her own blood.

A Pendle forest witch.

A Lancashire witch.

A witch cannot greet (ie., weep).

To be hog, or witch-ridden.

GYPSIES

So many gypsies, so many smiths.
The gypsies are all akin.
One of the Faw gang,
Worse than the Faw gang.

The Faws or Faas are a gypsy family whose head-quarters are at Yetholme. I have been among them and knew the queen of the gypsies and her son Robert, who were of this clan or name.

"It is supposed the Faws acquired this appellation from Johnnie Faw, lord and earl of Little Egypt; with whom James the Fourth and Queen Mary, sovereigns of Scotland, saw not only the propriety, but also the necessity of entering into special treaty" ("Denham Tract")

"***Francis Heron, king of the Faws***, bur. (Yarrow) xiii. Jan., 1756 (SHARP'S "Chron. Mir").

FAIRIES

Where the scythe cuts and the sock rives,
No more fairies and bee-hives.

Laugh like a pixy (*i.e.*, fairy).

Waters locked! waters locked! (A favourite cry of fairies.)

Borram! borram! borram! (The cry of the Irish fairies after mounting their steeds. Equivalent to the Scottish cry, "Horse! horse and hattock!")

To live in the land of the *Fair family.* (A Welsh fairy saying.)

God grant that the fairies may put money in your shoes and keep your house clean.
(One of the good wishes of the old time.)

Fairies comb goats' beards every Friday.

He who finds a piece of money will always find another in the same place, so long as he keeps it a secret.
(In reference to fairy gifts.)

It's going on, like Stokepitch's can.

A pixey or fairy saying, used in Devonshire. The family of Stokespitch or Sukespic resided near Topsham, and a barrel of ale in their cellars had for many years run freely without being exhausted. It was considered a valuable heirloom, and was esteemed accordingly, till an inquisitive maidservant took out the bung to ascertain the cause why it never run dry. On looking into the cask she found it full of cobwebs, but the fairies, it would seem, were offended, for on turning the cock, as usual, the ale had ceased to flow.

It was a common reply at Topsham to the inquiry how any affair went on "It's going on like Stokepitch's can," or proceeding prosperously.

To laugh like Robin Goodfellow.

To laugh like old Bogie; He caps Bogie.
(Amplified to "He caps Bogie, and Bogie capped old Nick.")

To play the Puck. (An Irish saying, equivalent to the English one, "To play the deuce or devil." KEIGHTLEY'S "***Fairy Mythology.***")

He has got into Lob's pound or pond. (That is, into the fairies' pinfold. KEIGHTLEY'S "***Fairy Mythology.***")

Pinch like a fairy. ("Pinch them, arms, legs, backs, shoulders, sides, and shins." "***Merry Wives of Windsor.***")

To be fairy-struck. (The paralysis is, or rather perhaps was, so called. KEIGHTLEY'S "***Fairy Mythology.***")

There has never been a merry world since the Phynoderee lost his ground. [A Manx fairy saying. See Train's "***Isle of Man,***" ii. p. 14.8. "***Popular Rhymes of the Isle of Man,***" pp. 16, 17.]

To be pixey-led.

Led astray by fairies or goblins. "When a man has got a wee drap ower muckle whuskey, misses his way home, and gets miles out of his direct course, he tells a tale of excuse and whiles lays the blame on the innocent pixies" (see KEIGHTLEY'S "***Fairy Mythology***"). Also recalling Feufollet, or the Will o' the Wisp, and the traveller who

> "thro' bog and bush
> Was lantern-led by Friar Rush."

Gypsies have from their out of doors life much familiarity with these "spirits" whom they call *mullo dûdia*, or *mûllo doods*, *i.e.*, dead or ghost lights. For an account of the adventure of a gypsy with them, see "***The English Gypsies and their Language,***" by C. G. LELAND. London: Trübner & Co. "Pyxie-led is to be in a maze, to be bewildered as if led out of the way by hobgoblins or puck, or one of the fairies. The cure is to turn one of your garments the inside outward; some say that is for a woman to turn her cap inside outward, and for a man to do the same with some of his clothes" (MS. "***Devon Glimpses***"—Halliwell). "Thee pixie-led in Popish piety" (CLOBERY'S ***"Divine Glimpses,***" 1659).

The fairies' lanthorn.

That is the glow-worm. In America a popular story represents an Irishman as believing that a fire-fly was a mosquito "*sakin*' his prey wid a lanthorn."

God speed you, gentlemen!

When an Irish peasant sees a cloud of dust sweeping along the road, he raises his hat and utters this blessing in behoof of y[e] company of invisible fairies who, as he believes, caused it." ("Fairy Mythology").

The Phooka have dirtied the blackberries.

Said when the fruit of the blackberry is spoiled through age or covered with dust at the end of the season. In the North of England we say "the devil has set his foot on the Bumble-Kites" ("Denham Tract").

> Fairy, fairy, bake me a bannock and roast me a collop,
> And I'll give ye a spintle off my god end.

This is spoken three times by the Clydesdale peasant when ploughing, because he believes that on getting to the end of the fourth furrow those good things will be found spread out on the grass "(CHAMBERS' "***Popular Rhymes, Scotland***," 3rd ed. p. 106).

> Turn your clokes (*i.e.*, coats),
> For fairy folkes
> Are in old oakes.

"I well remember that on more occasions than one, when a schoolboy, I have turned and worn my coat inside out in passing through a wood in order to avoid the 'good people.' On nutting days, those glorious red-letter festivals in the schoolboy's calendar, the use pretty generally prevailed. The rhymes in the text are the English formula" ("Denham Tract").

He's got Pigwiggan

Vulgarly called Peggy Wiggan. A severe fall or Somerset is so termed in the B'prick. The fairy Pigwiggan is celebrated by Drayton in his Nymphidia" ("***Denham Tract***"). To which may be added a few more from other sources.

> Do what you may, say what you can,
> No washing e'er whitens the black Zingan.
> ("Firdusi.")

For every gypsy that comes to toon,
A hen will be a-missing soon,
And for every gypsy woman old,
A maiden's fortune will be told.
Gypsy hair and devil's eyes,
Ever stealing, full of lies,
Yet always poor and never wise.

He who has never lived like a gypsy does not know how to enjoy life as a gentleman.

I never enjoyed the mere living as regards all that constitutes ordinary respectable life so keenly as I did after some weeks of great hunger, exposure, and misery, in an artillery company in 1863, at the time of the battle of Gettysburg.

Zigeuner Leben Greiner Leben. ("***Gipsy life a groaning life.***" KORTE'S "***Sprichwörter d. D.***")

Er taugt nicht zum Zigeuner. Spottisch vom Lügner gesagt weil er nicht wahr-sagt. (KORTE, "Sprichwörter.")

"He would not do for a gypsy." Said of a liar because he cannot tell the truth. In German to predict or tell fortunes also means to speak truly, *i.e.*, *wahr* = true, and *sprechen* = to speak.

Gypsy repentance for stolen hens is not worth much.
(*Old German Saying.*)

The Romany chi
And the Romany chal
Love luripen
And lutchipen
And dukkeripen
And huknipen
And every pen
But latchipen
And tatchipen.

The gypsy woman
And gypsy man
Love stealing
And lewdness
And fortune telling

And lying
And every *pen*
But shame
And truth.

Pen is the termination of all verbal nouns.

(GEORGE BORROW, Quoted from memory.)

It's a winter morning.

Meaning a bad day, or that matters look badly. In allusion to the Winters, a gypsy clan with a bad name.

As wild as a gypsy.

Puro romaneskoes. (In the old gypsy fashion.)

Sie hat 'nen Kobold. ("She has a brownie, or house-fairy.")

"Said of a girl who does everything deftly and readily. In some places the peasants believe that a fairy lives in the house, who does the work, brings water or wood, or curries the horses. Where such a fairy dwells, all succeeds if he or she is kindly treated" (KORTE'S "***German Proverbs***").

"Man siehet wohl wess Geisters Kind Sie (Er.) ist."

"One can well see what spirit was his sire." In allusion to men of singular or eccentric habits, who are believed to have been begotten by the incubus, or goblins, or fairies. There are ceremonies by which spirits may be attracted to come to people in dreams.

"There was a young man who lived near Monte Lupo, and one day he found in a place among some old ruins a statue of a *fate* (fairy or goddess) all naked. He set it up in its shrine, and admiring it greatly embraced it with love (ut semen ejus profluit super statuam). And that night and ever after the *fate* came to him in his dreams and lay with him, and told him where to find treasures, so that he became a rich man. But he lived no more among men, nor did he after that ever enter a church. And I have heard that any one who will do as he did can draw the *fate* to come to him, for they are greatly desirous to be loved and worshipped by men as they were in the Roman times."

The following are Hungarian or Transylvanian proverbs:

False as a Tzigane, ie., gypsy.

Dirty as a gypsy.

They live like gypsies (said of a quarrelsome couple).

He moans like a guilty Tzigane (said of a man given to useless lamenting).

He knows how to plow with the gypsies (said of a liar). Also: "He knows how to ride the gypsies' horse."

He knows the gypsy trade (*i.e.*, he is a thief).

Tzigane weather (*i.e.*, a showery day).

It is gypsy honey (*i.e.*, adulterated).

A gypsy duck *i.e.*, a poor sort of wild duck.

"The gypsy said his favourite bird would be the pig if it had only wings" (in allusion to the gypsy fondness for pork).

Mrs. GERARD gives a number of proverbs as current among Hungarian gypsies which appear to be borrowed by them from those of other races. Among them are:

Who would steal potatoes must not forget the sack.

The best smith cannot make more than one ring at a time.

Nothing is so bad but it is good enough for somebody.

Bacon makes bold.

"He eats his faith as the gypsies ate their church."

A Wallach proverb founded on another to the effect that the gypsy church was made of pork and the dogs ate it. I shall never forget how an old gypsy in Brighton laughed when I told her this, and how she repeated: "O Romani kangri sos kerdo bâllovas te i juckli hawde lis."

"No entertainment without gypsies."

In reference to gypsy musicians who are always on hand at every festivity.

The Hungarian wants only a glass of water and a gypsy fiddler to make him drunk.

In reference to the excitement which Hungarians experience in listening to gypsy music.

With a wet rag you can put to flight a whole village of gypsies (Hungarian).

It would not be advisable to attempt this with any gypsies in Great

Britain, where they are almost, without exception, only too ready to fight with anybody.

Every gypsy woman is a witch.

"Every woman is at heart a witch."

In the "***Materials for the Study of the Gypsies***," by M. I. KOUNAVINE, which I have not yet seen, there are, according to A. B. Elysseeff (*Gypsy-Lore Journal*, July, 1890), three or four score of gypsy proverbial sayings and maxims. These refer to Slavonian or far Eastern Russian Romanis. I may here state in this connection that all who are interested in this subject, or aught relating to it, will find much to interest them in this journal of the Gypsy-Lore Society, printed by T. & A. Constable, Edinburgh. The price of subscription, including membership of the society, is £1 a year--Address: David Mac Ritchie, 4, Archibald Place, Edinburgh.

CHAPTER XIV

A Gypsy Magic Spell—HOKKANI BÂSO—LELLIN DUDIKABIN, Or The Great Secret—Children's Rhymes And Incantations—Ten Little Indian Boys And Ten Little Acorn Girls of Marcellus Burdigalensis

THERE is a meaningless rhyme very common among children. It is repeated while "counting off "—or "out"—those who are taking part in a game, and allotting to each a place. There are many versions of it, but the following is exactly word for word what I learned when a boy in Philadelphia:

Ekkeri (or ickery), akkery, u-kéry an,
Fillisi', follasy, Nicholas John,
Queebee—quabee—Irishman (or, Irish Mary),
Stingle 'em—stangle 'em—buck!

With a very little alteration in sounds, and not more than children make of these verses in different places, this may be read as follows:

Ek-keri (yekori) akairi, you kair an,
Fillissin, follasy, Nákelas jân
Kivi, kávi—Irishman,
Stini, stani—buck!

This is, of course, nonsense, but it is Romany or gypsy nonsense, and it may be thus translated very accurately

First--here--you begin!
Castle, gloves. You don't play!
Go on !
Kivi—a kettle. How are you?
Stáni, buck.

The common version of the rhyme begins with:

"One—ery--two—ery, ickery an."

But one-ery is an *exact* translation of *ek-keri*; *ek*, or *yek*, meaning one in gypsy. (*Ek-orus*, or *yek-korus*, means once). And it is remarkable that in-

"*Hickory* dickory dock,
The rat ran up the clock,
The clock struck one,
And down he run,
Hickory dickory dock."

We have *hickory*, or *ek-keri*, again followed by a significant one. It may be observed that while my first quotation abounds in what are unmistakably Romany words, I can find no trace of any in any other child-rhymes of the kind. I lay stress on this, for if I were a great Celtic scholar I should not have the least difficulty in proving that cvcry word in every rhyme, down to "Tommy, make room for your uncle," was all old Irish or Gaelic.

Word for word every person who understands Romany will admit the following:

Ek, or *yek*, means one. *Yekorus*, *ekorus*, or *yeckori*, or *ekkeri*, once.

U-kair-an. *You kair an*, or begin. *Kair* is to make or do, *ânkair* to begin. "Do you begin?"

Fillissin is a castle, or gentleman's country scat (H. SMITH).

Follasi, or *follasy*, is a lady's glove.

Nâkelas. I learned this word from an old gypsy. It is used as equivalent to *don't*, but also means *ná* (*kélas*), you don't play. From *kel-ava*, I play,

Ján, *Já-an*, Go on. From *jâva*, I go. Hindu, *jána*, and *jáo*.

Kivi, or *keevy*. No meaning.

Kavi, a kettle, from *kekâvi*, commonly given as *kâvi*. Greek, κεκκάβοσ {Greek *kekkábos*}. Hindu, *kal*, a box.

Stini. No meaning that I know.

Stáni. A buck.

Of the last line it may be remarked that if we take from *ingle 'em* (*angle 'em*), which is probably added for mere jingle, there remains *stán*, or *stáni*, "a buck," followed by the very same word in English.

With the mournful examples of Mr. BELLENDEN KERR'S efforts to show that all our old proverbs, saws, sayings, and tavern signs are Dutch, and Sir WILLIAM BETHAM's Etruscan-Irish, and the works of an army of "philologists," who consider mere chance resemblance to be a proof of identical origin, I should be justly regarded as one of the seekers for mystery in moonshine if I declared that I positively believed this to be Romany. But it certainly contains words which, without any stretching or fitting, are simply gypsy, and I think it not improbable that it was some sham charm used by some Romany fortune-teller to bewilder Gorgios. Let the reader imagine the burnt-sienna, wild-cat-eyed old sorceress performing before a credulous farm-wife and her children, the great ceremony of *hâkkni pánki*—which Mr. BORROW calls *hokkani bâro*, but for which there is a far deeper name--that of the great secret"--which even my best Romany friends tried to conceal from me. This is to *lel dûdikabin*—to "take lightment." In the oldest English canting, *lightment* occurs as an equivalent for theft—whether it came from Romany, or Romany from it, I cannot tell.

This feat-which is described by almost every writer on Gypsies—is performed by inducing some woman of largely magnified faith to believe that there is hidden in her house a magic treasure, which can only be made "to come to hand" by depositing in the cellar another treasure, to which it will come by natural affinity and attraction. "For gold, as you sees, draws gold, my deari, and so if you ties up all your money in a pocket-handkercher, an' leaves it, you'll find it doubled. An' wasn't there the Squire's lady—you know Mrs. Trefarlo, of course—and didn't she draw two hundred old gold guineas out of the ground where they'd laid in an old grave-and only one guinea she gave me for all my trouble; an' I hope you'll do better than that for the poor old gypsy, my deari."

The gold and the spoons are all tied up-for, as the enchantress sagely observes, "there may be silver too"—and she solemnly repeats over it magical rhymes, while the children, standing around in awe, listen to every word. It is a good subject for a picture. Sometimes the windows are closed, and candles lighted--to add to the effect. The bundle is left or buried in a certain place. The next day the gypsy comes and sees how the charm is working. Could any one look under her cloak, he might find another bundle precisely resembling the one containing the treasure. She looks at the precious deposit, repeats her rhyme again solemnly and departs, after carefully charging the house-wife that the bundle must not be touched, looked at, or spoken of for three weeks. "Every word you tell about it, my deari, will be a guinea gone away." Sometimes she exacts an oath on the Bible, when she *chivs o manzin apré lâtti*, that nothing shall be said.

Back to the farmer's house never again. After three weeks another Extraordinary Instance of Gross Credulity appears in the country paper, and is perhaps repeated in a colossal London daily, with a reference to the absence of the schoolmaster. There is wailing and shame in the house, perhaps great suffering, for it may be that the savings of years, and bequeathed tankards, and marriage rings, and inherited jewellery, and mother's souvenirs have been swept away. The charm has worked.

"How *can* people be such fools!" Yea—how *can* they? How can fully ninety-nine out of one hundred, and I fear me nine hundred and ninety-nine out of a thousand, be capable of what amounts to precisely the same thing—paying out their cash in the hopes that the Invisible Influences in the Inscrutable Cellar or Celestial Garret will pay it back to them, cent. per cent.? Oh, reader, if you be of middle age (for there are perhaps some young agnostics beginning to appear to whom the cap does not fit), and can swear on your hat that you never in your life have been taken in by a *dûdikabin* in any form-- send me your name and I will award you for an epitaph that glorious one given in the *Nugæ Venales*:

"Hic jacet ille qui unus fuit inter mille!"

The charm has worked. But the little sharp-eared children remember it, and sing it over, and the more meaningless it sounds in their ears, the more mysterious does it become. And they never talk about the bundle--which when opened was found to contain only stones, sticks, and rags--without repeating it. So it goes from mouth to mouth, until, all mutilated, it passes current for even worse nonsense than it was at first. It may be observed, however, and the remark will be fully substantiated by any one who knows the gypsy language, that there is a Romany turn to even the roughest corners of these rhymes. *Kivi, stingli, stangli*, are all gypsyish. But, as I have already intimated, this does not appear in any other nonsense verses of the kind. There is nothing of it in:

"Intery, mintery, cutery corn,"

...or in anything else in "Mother Goose." It is alone in its sounds and sense--or nonsense. But there is not a wanderer on the roads in England who on hearing it would not exclaim, "There's a great deal of Romanes in that ere!" And if any one doubts it let him try it on any gypsy who has an average knowledge of Romany.

I should say that the word *Na-Kelas*, which means literally "Do not play," or, "You do not play," was explained to me by a gypsy as signifying not speaking, or keeping quiet. Nicholas John has really no meaning, but "You don't play—go on," fits exactly into a counting-out game.

The mystery of mysteries in the Romany tongue--of which I have spoken--is this: The *hokkani bâro*, or *huckeny boro*, or great trick, consists of three parts. Firstly, the getting into a house or into the confidence of its owner, which is effected in England by offering small wares for sale, or by begging for food, but chiefly by fortune-telling, the latter being the usual pretence in America. If the gypsy woman be at all prepared, she will have learned enough to amaze "the lady of the house," who is thereby made ready to believe anything. The second part of the trick is the conveying away the property, which is, as I have said, to *lel dûdikabin*, or "take lightning," possibly connected with the old canting term for conveyance of *bien lightment*. There is evidently a confusion of words here. And third is to "*chiv o manzin apré lâti*" to put the oath upon her, the victim, by which she binds herself not to speak of the affair for some weeks. When the deceived are all under oath not to utter a word about the trick, the gypsy mother has a safe thing of it.

The *hâkkani boro*, or great trick, or *dûdikabin*, was brought by the gypsies from the East. It has been practised by them all over the world, and is still played every day somewhere. And I have read in the Press of Philadelphia that a Mrs. BROWN--whom I sadly and reluctantly believe is the wife of an acquaintance of mine who walks before the world in other names--was arrested for the same old game of fortune-telling, and persuading a simple dame that there was treasure in the house, and all the rest of the "grand deception." And Mrs. BROWN—"good old Mrs. Brown"—went to prison, where she doubtless lingered until a bribed alderman, or a purchased pardon, or some one of the numerous devices by which justice is easily evaded in Pennsylvania, delivered her.

Yet it is not a good country on the whole for *hâkkani boro*, since the people, especially in the rural districts, have a rough and ready way of inflicting justice, which sadly interferes with the profits of aldermen and other politicians. Some years ago, in Tennessee, a gypsy woman robbed a farmer of all he was worth. Now it is no slander to say that the rural folk of Tennessee resemble Indians in several respects, and when l saw thousands of them during the Civil War, mustered out in Nashville, I often thought, as I studied these dark brown faces, high cheek-bones, and long, straight, wiry hair, that the American is indeed reverting to the aboriginal type. The Tennessee farmer and his friends reverted to it at any rate with a vengeance, for they turned out altogether, hunted the gypsies down, and having secured the sorceress, burned her alive at the stake. Which has been, as I believe, "an almighty warning" to the Romany in that sad section of the world. And thus in a single crime, and its consequence, we have curiously combined a world-old Oriental offence, an European Middle Age penalty for witchcraft, and the fierce torture of the Red Indian.

In the United States there is often to be found in a gypsy camp a negro or two a few years ago a coloured sorcerer appeared in Philadelphia, who, as I was assured, "persuaded half the in Lombard Street to dig up their cellars to find treasure--and carried off all the treasures they had." He had been, like MATTHEW ARNOLD'S scholar, among the tents of the Romany, and had learned their peculiar wisdom, and turned it to profit.

In Germany the Great Sorcery is practised with variations, and indeed in England or America or anywhere it is modified in many ways to suit the victims. The following methods are described by Dr. RICHARD LIEBICH, in "***Die Zigeuner in ihrem Wesen und in ihrer Sprache***" (Leipzig, 1863):

"When a gypsy has found some old peasant who has the reputation of being rich or very well-to-do he sets himself to work with utmost care to learn the disposition of the man with every possible detail as to his house and habits." (It is easy and congenial work to people who pass their lives in learning all they can of other folks' affairs to aid in fortune-telling, to find out the soft spots, as *Sam Slick* calls the peculiarities by which a man may be influenced.) "And so some day, when all the rest of the family are in the fields, the gypsy—man or woman—comes, and entering into a conversation, leads it to the subject of the house, remarking that it is a belief among his people that in it a treasure lies buried. He offers, if he may have permission to take it away, to give one-fourth, a third, or a half its value. This all seems fair enough, but the peasant is greedy and wants more. The gypsy, on his side, also assumes suspicion and distrust. He proves that he is a conjuror by performing some strange tricks--thus he takes an egg from under a hen, breaks it, and apparently brings out a small human skull or some strange object, and finally persuades the peasant to collect all his coin and other valuables in notes, gold, or silver, into a bundle, cautioning him to hold them fast. He must go to bed and put the packet under his pillow, while he, the conjuror, finds the treasure. This done—probably in a darkened room—he takes a bundle of similar appearance which he has quickly prepared, and under pretence of facilitating the operation and putting the man into a proper position, takes the original package and substitutes another. Then the victim is cautioned that it is of the utmost importance for him to lie perfectly still;"

> Nor move his hand nor blink his 'ee
> If ever he hoped the goud to see
> For aye aboot on ilka limb,
> The fairies had their 'een on him."

The gypsy is over the hills and far far away ere the shades of evening fall, and the family returning from their fields find the father in bed refusing to speak a word; for he has been urgently impressed with the assertion that the longer he holds his tongue and keeps the affair a secret the more money he will make. And the extreme superstition of the German peasant is such that when obliged to tell the truth he often believes that all his loss is due to a premature forced revelation of what he has done--for the gypsy in many cases has the cheek to caution the victim that if he speaks too soon the contents of the package will be turned to sand or rags—accordingly as he has prepared it.

Another and more impudent manner of playing this pretended sorcery, is to persuade the peasant that he must have a thick cloth tied around his head, and if any one addresses him to reply only by what in German is called *brummen*—uttering a kind of growl. This he does, when the. entire party proceed to carry off everything portable:

> "Chairs and tables knives and forks,
> Tankards and bottles and cups and corks,
> Beds and dishes and boots and kegs,
> Bacon and puddings and milk and eggs,
> The carpet lying on the floor,
> And the hams hung up for the winter store,

Every pillow and sheet and bed,
The dough in the trough and the baken bread,
Every bit of provant or pelf;
All that they left was the house itself."

One may imagine what the scene is like when the rest return and find the house plundered, the paterfamilias sitting in the ruins with his head tied up, answering all frantic queries with *brum--brum--brum*! It may recall the well-known poem, I think it is by PETER PINDAR WOLCOTT, of the man who was persuaded by a bet to make the motion of a pendulum, saying, "Here she goes—there she goes!" while the instigator "cleared out the house and then cleared out himself." I have little doubt that this poem was drawn from a Romany original.

Or yet, again, the gypsy having obtained the plunder and substituted the dummy packet, persuades the true believer to bury it in the barn, garden, field, or a forest, performs magic ceremonies and repeats incantations over it, and cautions him to dig it up again, perhaps six months later on a certain day, it may be his saint's or birth day, and to keep silence till then. The gypsy makes it an absolute condition--nay, he insists very earnestly on it--that the treasure shall not be dug up unless he himself is on the spot to share the spoil. But as he may possibly be prevented from coming, he tells the peasant how to proceed: he leaves with him several pieces of paper inscribed with cabalistic characters which are to be burnt when the money is removed, and teaches him what he is to repeat while doing it. With sequence as before.

It *might* be urged by the gypsy that the taking a man's money from him under the conditions that he shall get it all back with immense interest six months after, does not differ materially from persuading him to give his property to Brahmins, or even priests, with the understanding that he is to be amply rewarded for it in a future state. I n both cases the temptation to take the money down is indeed great—as befel a certain very excellently honest but extremely cautious Scotch clergyman, to whom there once came a very wicked and wealthy old reprobate who asked him "If I gie a thousand puns till the kirk d'ye think it wad save my soul?" "I'm na preparit to *preceesely* answer that question," said the shrewd dominie, "but I would vara urgently advise ye *to try it*."

Oh thou who persuadest man that for money down great good shall result to him from any kind of spiritual incantation—twist and turn it as ye will—*mutato nomine, de te fabula narratur*.

"With but a single change of name,
The story fits thee quite the same."

And few and far between are the Romanys—or even the Romans—who would not "vara earnestly advise ye to try it."

Since I wrote that last line I have met, in the *Journal of American Folk-Lore*, with a very interesting article on the Counting-out Rhymes of Children, in which the writer, H. CARRINGTON BOLTON, avows his belief that these doggerel verses or rhymes are the survivals of sortileges or divination by lot, and that it was practised among the ancient heathen nations as well as the Israelites:--

"The use of the lot at first received divine sanction, as in the story of Achan related by Joshua, but after this was withheld the practice fell into the hands of sorcerers--which very name signifies lot-taker. The doggerels themselves I regard as a survival of the spoken charms used by sorcerers in ancient times in conjunction with their mystic incantations. There are numerous examples of these charms, such as-

"'Huat Hanat Huat ista pista sista domiabo damnaustra.'
(CATO, 235 B.C.)

"And—"'Irriori, ririori essere rhuder fere.'

"And—"'Meu, treu, mor, phor
Teux, za, zor
Phe, lou, chri,
Ge, ze, on.'
(ALEXANDER OF TRALLES.)

"TYLOR in his '***Primitive Culture***' holds that things which occupy an important place in the life-history of grown men in a savage state become the playthings of children in a period of civilization; thus the sling and the bow and arrow, which formed the weapons of mankind in an early stage of its existence, and ate still the reliance of savage tribes, have become toys in the hands of all civilized children at the present day. Many games current in Europe and America are known to be sportive imitations of customs which formerly had a significant and serious aspect.

"Adopting this theory, I hold that counting-out is a survival of the practice of the sorcerer, using this word in its restricted and etymological meaning, and that the spoken and written charms originally used to enforce priestly power have become adjuncts to these puerile games, and the basis of the counting-out doggrels under consideration.

"The idea that European and American children engaged in 'counting-out' for games, are repeating in innocent ignorance the practices and language of a sorcerer of a dark age, is perhaps startling, but can be shown to have a high degree of probability. The leader in 'counting out' performs an incantation, but the children grouped round him are free from that awe and superstitious reverence which characterized the procedure in its earlier state. Many circumstances make this view plausible, and clothe the doggrels with a new and fascinating interest."

Mr. BOLTON remarks, however, that "in only one instance have I been able to directly connect a child's counting-out rhyme with a magic spell. According to LELAND the rhyme beginning with

'One-cry, two-ery, ickery, Ann,'

is a gypsy magic spell in the Romany language."

It occurred to me long, long ago, or before ever the name "Folk-lore" existed, that children's rhymes were a survival of incantations, and that those which are the same backward and forward were specially adapted to produce marvellous effects in lots. But there was one form of counting-out which was common as it was terrible. This was used when after a victory it was usual to put every tenth captive to death—whence the greatly abused word to "decimate"—or any other number selected. When there was a firm belief in the virtues of numbers as set forth by PYTHAGORAS, and PLATO in the *Timæus*, and of cabalistic names inspired by the "Intelligences," it is not remarkable that the diviners or priests or sorcerers or distributors of *sortes* and sortileges should endeavour to prove that life and death lay bound up in mystic syllables. That there were curious and occult arithmetical means of counting-out and saving elected persons is shown in certain mystic problems still existent in Boys Own Books, and other handbooks of juvenile sports. It was the one on whom the fatal word of life or death fell who was saved or condemned, so that it was no wonder that *the word* was believed to be a subtle, mysterious existence: an essence or principle, yea, a spirit or all in one—*diversi aspetti in un, confuse e misti.* He who knew the name of Names which, as the Chaldæan oracles of old declared, "rushes into the infinite worlds," knew all things and had all power; even in lesser words there lingered the fragrance of God and some re-echo of the

Bath Kol—the Daughter of the Voice who was herself the last echo of the divine utterance. So it went down through the ages-coming, like Caesar's clay, to base uses—till we now find the sacred divination by words a child's play: only that and nothing more.

Truly Mr. BOLTON spoke well when he said that such reflection clothes these doggerels with a new and fascinating interest. Now and then some little thing awakens us to the days of old, the rosy, early morning of mankind, when the stars of magic were still twinkling in the sky, and the dreamer, hardly awake, still thought himself communing with God. So I was struck the other day when a gypsy, a deep and firm believer in the power of the *amulet*, and who had long sought, yet never found, his ideal, was deeply moved when I showed him the shell on which NAV, or the Name, was mystically inscribed by Nature. Through the occult and broken traditions of his tribe there had come to him also, perhaps from Indian or Chaldæan sources, some knowledge of the ancient faith in its power.

I think that I can add to the instance of a child's counting-out game based on a magic spell, yet another. Everybody knows the song of John Brown who had

Ten little, nine little, eight little, seven little,
Six little Indian boys;
Five little, four little, three little, two little,
One little Indian boy,

And of the fate which overtook them all, one by one, inevitable as the decrees of Nemesis. This song is in action a game. I have heard it in Romany from a gypsy, and have received from a gypsy scholar another version of it, though I am sure that both were versions from the English. But in Romany, as in all languages, there have existed what may be called additional and subtractive magic songs, based on some primæval Pythagorean principle of the virtues of numbers, and, as regards form, quite like that of the ten little Indians. In the charms of MARCELLUS BURDIGALENSIS (third century), it appears as a cure for pains or disorders in the jaws (*remedium valde certum et utile faucium doloribus*), in the Song of the Seven Acorn Sisters, which the Latin-Gaul doctor describes as *carmen mirum*, in which opinion the lover of Folk-lore will heartily concur.

"CARMEN MIRUM AD GLANDULAS.

Glandulas mane carminabis, si dies minuetur, si nox ad vesperam, et digito medicinali ac pollice continens eas dices—

> Novem glandulæ sorores,
> Octo glandulæ sorores,
> Septem glandulæ sorores,
> Sex glandulæ sorores,
> Quinque glandulæ sorores,
> Quatuor glandulæ sorores,
> Tres glandulæ sorores,
> Duæ glandulæ sorores,
> Una glandula soror!

> Novem fiunt glandulæ,
> Octo fiunt glandulæ,
> Septem fiunt glandulæ,
> Sex fiunt glandulæ,
> Quinque fiunt glandulæ,
> Quattuor fiunt glandulæ,
> Tres fiunt glandulæ,
> Duæ fiunt glandulæ,
> Una fit glandula,
> Nulla fit glandula!"

> (*I.e.*, "Nine little acorn sisters (or girls),
> Eight little acorn sisters," &c.)

This is simply the same count, forwards and backwards.

It rises before us as we read—a chorus of rosy little Auluses and Marcellas, Clodias, and Manliuses, screaming in chorus—

> "Ten little, nine little, eight little, seven little,
> Six little acorn girls!"

Until it was reduced to *una glandula et nulla fit*--then there was none., They too had heard their elders repeat it as a c arm against the Jaw-ache--and can any man in his senses doubt that they applied it in turn to the divine witchcraft of fun and the sublime sorcery of sport, which are just as magical and wonderful in their way as anything in all theurgia or occultism, especially when the latter is used only to excite marvels and the amazement which is only a synonym for amusement. But it is not credible that such a palpable "leaving out" song as that of the Ten Little Acorn Girls should not having been utilized by such intelligent children as grew up into being the conquerors of the world—"knowing Latin at that."

There is yet another old Roman "wonderful song to the Acorns," apparently for the same disorder, given by the same author.

> "Albula glandula,
> Nec doleas nec noceas,
> Nec paniculas facias,
> Sed liquescas tanquam salis (mica) in aqua!

"Hoc ter novies dicens spues ad terram et glandulas ipsas pollice et digito medicinali perduces, dum carmen dices, sedante solis ortum et post occasum facies id, prout dies aut nox minuetur."

There appears in these formulas to be either a confusion or affinity as regards *glandulas*, the tonsils, and the same word signifying small acorns. As is very often the case, the similarity of name caused an opinion that there must be sympathetic curative qualities. Perhaps acorns were also used in this ceremony. In a comment on this GRIMM remarks: "*Die Glandula wird angeredet, die Glandulæ gelten für Schwestern, wie wenn das alt hoch-deutsch druos glandula (GRAFF 5, 263) personification aukündigte? Alt Nordisch ist drôs, femina.*"

There is another child's rhyme which is self-evidently drawn from an exorcism, that is to say an incantation. All my readers know the nursery song:

> "Snail, snail, come out of your hole,
> Or else I'll beat you as black as a coal
> Snail, snail, put out your head,
> Or else I'll beat you till you are dead!"

It is very remarkable that in Folk-lore the mole and the snail are identified, and, as DE GUBERNATIS states, both are the same with the grey mouse, or, as he might more accurately have declared with the mouse in general. A critic objects to this simply because it occurs in the work of DIE GUBERNATIS, among his "fanciful theories," but it need not follow that every citation or opinion in his book is false. FRIEDRICH, who certainly is not a fanciful theorist, asserted nearly thirty years ago that the mouse, owing to its living underground and in dark places as well as to its gnawing and destroying everything, is a *chthonisches Thier*, one of the animals of darkness and evil. Also "the mole, because it is of subterranean life, has received a chthonic, demoniac, misanthropic reputation."

In support of these statements he cites a great array of authorities. The connection between the mole and mouse is evident enough, that between both and the snail is also clear: firstly, from the fact that "the snail of popular superstition is demoniacal," or evil; and secondly, from the rhyme which I now quote, which is applied to both moles and snails. According to DU CANGE it was usual in the Middle Ages for children to go about carrying poles, on the ends of which was straw, which they lighted, and going round the gardens and under the trees shouted:

"Taupes et mulots,
Sortez de vas clos,
Sinon je vous brulerai la bathe et les os!"

But in Germany there are two and in Italy five versions of the same song addressed to *snails*. It is evidently a Roman Catholic formula, based on some early heathen incantation. Thus in Tuscany they sing

"Chiocciola marinella
Tira fuori le tue cornelle,
E se tu non le tirerai
Calcie pugni tu buscherai."

Both the snail and mole and mouse were, as I have said, *chthonic*, that is diabolical or of darkness. The horns of the former were supposed to connect it with the devil. "In Tuscany it is believed that in the month of April the snail makes love with serpents."

There is another nursery counting-out rhyme whose antiquity and connection with sorcery is very evident. It is as follows:

"One, two, three, four, five,
I caught a hare all alive.
Six, seven, eight, nine ten,
I let her go again."

The following from the medical spells and charms Of MARCELLUS BURDIGALENSIS manifestly explains it:

"Lepori vivo alum abstrahes, pilósque ejus de subventre tolles atque ipsum *vivum dimittes*. De illis pilis, vel lana filum validum facies et ex eo talum leporis conligabis corpusque laborantis præcinges; miro remedio subvenies. Efficacius tamen erit remedium, ita ut incredibile sit, si casu os ipsum, id est talum leporis in stercore lupi inveneris, quod ita custodire debes, ne aut terram tangat aut a muliere contingatur, sed nec filum illud de lana leporis debet mulier ulla contigere. Hoc autem remedium cum uni profuerit ad alias translatum cum volueris, et quotiens volueris proderit. Filum quoque, quod ex lana vel pilis, quos de ventre leporis tuleris, solus purus et nitidus facies, quod si ita ventri laborantis subligaveris plurimum proderit, ut sublata lana leporem vivum dimmittas, et dicas ei dum dimittis eum:

"'Fuge, fuge, lepuscule, et tecum auter coli dolorem!'"

That is to say, you must "first catch your hare," then pluck from it the fur needed *ad dolorem coli*, then "let it go again," bidding it carry the disorder with it. In which the hare appears as a scapegoat. It may be observed that all this ceremony of catching the hare, letting it go and bidding it run and carry away the disorder, is still in familiar use in Tuscany.

It has been observed to me that "any nursery rhyme may be used as a charm." To this we may reply that any conceivable human utterance may be taken for the same purpose, but this is an unfair special pleading not connected with the main issue. Mr. CARRINGTON BOLTON admits that he has only found one instance of coincidence between nursery rhymes and spells, and I have compared hundreds of both with not much more result than what I have here given. But those who are practically familiar with such formulas recognize this affinity. On asking the Florentine fortune-teller if she knew any children's counting-out rhymes which deemed to her to be the same with incantations, she at once replied

"In witchcraft you sometimes call on people one by one by name to bewitch them. And the little girls have a song which seems to be like it." Then she sang to a very pretty tune

"Ecco l'imbasciatore,
Col tra le vi la lera,
Ecco l'imbasciatrice,
Col tra la li ra la!
Cosa volete col tua la li la,
Col tra le li va la,
Voglio Giuseppina,
Col tra le li va le va.

Voglio la Cesarina,
Col tra le li ra le ra.
Voglio la Armida, &c,
Voglio la Gesualda,
Voglio la Barbera,
Voglio la Bianca,
Voglio la Fortunata,
Voglio la Uliva,
Voglio la Filomena,
Voglio la Maddalena,
Voglio la Pia,
Voglio la Gemma,
Voglio la Ida,
Voglio la Lorenzina,
Voglio la Carolina,
Voglio la Annunciatina,
Voglio la Margo," &c.

There is one thing of which those who deny the identity of any counting-out rhymes with spells are not aware. These incantations are very much in vogue with the Italian peasantry, as with the gypsies. They are repeated on all occasions for every disorder, for every trifle lost, for every want. Every child has heard them, and their jingle and even their obscurity make them attractive. They are just what children would be likely to remember and to sing over, and the applying them to games and to "counting-out" would follow as a matter of course. In a country where every peasant, servant-girl and child knows at least a few spells, the wonder would be if some of these were *not* thus popularized or perverted. It is one thing to sit in one's library and demonstrate that this or that *ought* not to be, because it is founded on a "theory" or "idea," and quite another to live among people where these ideas are in active operation. WASHINGTON IRVING has recorded that one of the Dutch governors of New York achieved a vast reputation for wisdom by shrugging his shoulders, at everything and saying, "I have my doubts as to that." And truly the race Of WOUTER VAN TWILLER is not extinct as yet by any means among modern critics.

It is worth noting in this connection that in Mrs. VALENTINE'S Nursery Rhymes (Camden edition) there are fifteen charms given which are all of a magical nature.

Since the foregoing chapter was written I have obtained in Florence several additional instances of children's rhymes which were spells.

Nearly allied to this subject of sorcery in the nursery is The Game of the Child-stealing Witch, which, as W. Wells Newell has shown in a very interesting and valuable contribution to the *American Folk-Lore Journal*, vol. iii., April, 1890, is found in many languages and lands.

In connection with divination, deceit, and robbery, it may be observed that gypsies in Eastern Europe, as in India, often tell fortunes or answer questions by taking a goblet or glass, tapping it, and pretending to hear a voice in the ring which speaks to them. This method of divination is one of the few which may have occurred sporadically, or independently in different places, as there is so much in a ringing, vibrating sound which resembles a voice. The custom is very ancient and almost universal; so Joseph (Genesis xliv. 5) says ("Vulgate"), "*Scyphus quam furati estis, ipse est, in quo bibit Dominus meus, et in quo augurari solet.*" "The goblet which ye have stolen, is it not this wherein my lord drinketh and in which he is wont to *divine*?" Joseph says again (ver. 15), "Know ye not that such a man as I can certainly divine." A great number of very orthodox scholars have endeavoured to show that "divine" here means merely "to conjecture wisely," or "to see into," in order to clear Joseph from the accusation of fortune-telling: but the cup and his interpretation of dreams tell another story. In those days in the East, as now, clever men made their way very often by fortune-telling and *theurgia* in different forms in great families, just as ladies and gentlemen are "invited out" in London and Paris to please the company with palmistry.

This divining by goblets is still common in the East. In NORDEN'S "Reise nach Egypten," &c., we are told that a native said to the travellers that he had interrogated his coffee-cup, and it had replied that the travellers were those of whom the Prophet had predicted they would come as spies and lead the way for a great immigration of Franks. In an Arabic commentary of the twelfth century the replies which the goblet gave to Joseph when it tapped on it are given in full. As coffee-drinking is very ancient it is probable that divination by means of the grounds grew out of foretelling with the cup.

Horst ("***Dæmonomagie***," vol. ii.) remarks that "prediction by means of drinking or coffee-cups," &c., is called in magic, *Scyphomancy*, and that the reader may judge how common it was in Germany in the first half of the eighteenth century by consulting the famous humorous poem of the "***Renomist***," Song iii. ver. 47. Certain goblets of thin glass will give out quite a loud ring if only blown upon, and by blowing or breathing in a peculiar way the sound may be greatly increased or modified, so as to sound like the human voice. This was shown me by an old *custode* in the museum at the Hague. It is a curious trick worth trying—especially by those who would pass for magicians!

There is yet another kind of magic cup known only by tradition, the secret of which, I believe, I was the first to re-discover. It is said that the Chinese knew of old how to make bottles, &c., which appeared to be perfectly plain, but on which, when filled with wine, inscriptions or figures appeared, and which were used in divination as to answer questions. In the winter of 1886-87, Sir HENRY AUSTIN LAYARD went with me through his glass factory at Venice. As we were standing by the furnace watching the workmen it flashed upon me quite in a second how the mysterious old goblets of the Chinese could be made. This would be by blowing a bottle, &c., of thin white glass and putting on the interior in all parts *except the pattern*, a coating of glass half an inch in thickness. The outside should then be lightly ground, to conceal tho heavy portion. If red wine or any dark fluid should then be poured into the bottle the pattern would appear of the same colour. Sir Austin Layard at once sent for his very intelligent foreman, Signor CASTELLANI, who said that he had indeed read of such goblets, but that he regarded it as a fable. But when I explained to him what had occurred to me, he said that it was perfectly possible, but that the great expense of making such objects would probably make the manufacture practically impossible. Apropos of which I may mention that those who would investigate the curiosities of glass, especially the art of making it malleable, may find a great deal in A. Nevi, "***De Arte Vitraria***" (Amsterdam), and its German translation of 1678 (which contains a chapter, "Wie die Malleabilitat dem Glase beygebracht werden konne").

It is probable that the celebrated cup of Djemschid, in Persian story, which showed on its surface all that passed in the world, owed its origin to these Chinese bottles.

CHAPTER XV

Gypsy Amulets

**"Knew many an amulet and charm
Which would do neither good nor harm,
In Rosicrucian lore as learned
As he that veré adeptus earned."—HUDIBRAS.**

WITH pleasant plausibility HEINE has traced the origin of one kind of fairy-lore to the associations and feelings which we form for familiar objects. A coin, a penknife, a pebble, which has long been carried in the pocket or worn by any one, seems to become imbued with his or her personality. If it could speak, we should expect to hear from it an echo of the familiar voice of the wearer; as happened, indeed, in Thuringia in the year 1562, when a fair maid, Adelhait von Helbach, was carried into captivity by certain ill-mannered persons. "Now her friends, pursuing, knew not whither to go, when they heard her voice, albeit very small and feeble, calling to them; and, seeking, they found in the bush by the road a silver image of the Virgin, which she had worn: and this image told them which road to take. Following the direction, they recovered her; the Raubritter who bore her away being broken on the wheel, and the image hung up for the glory of the Virgin, who had spoken by it, in the Church of our Lady of Kalbrunn." Again, these objects have such strange ways of remaining with one that we end by suspecting that they have a will of their own. With certain persons these small familiar friends become at last fetishes, which bring luck, giving to those who firmly believe in them great comfort and endurance in adversity.

Who has not been amazed at the persistency with which some button or pebble picked up, or placed perchance in the pocket, remains in all the migrations of keys and pencils and coins, faithful to the charge? How some card or counter will lurk in our pocket-book (misnamed "purse") or porte-monnaie, until it becomes clear as daylight that it has a reasonable intelligence, and stays with us because it wants to. As soon as this is recognized—especially by some person who is accustomed to feel mystery in everything, and who doubts nothing—the object becomes something which knows, possibly, a great deal which we do not. Therefore it is to be treated with care and respect, and in due time it becomes a kind of god, or at least the shrine of a small respectable genius, or fairy. I have heard of a gentleman in the Western United States who had a cane in which, as he seriously believed, a spirit had taken up its abode, and he reverenced it accordingly. The very ancient and widely-spread belief in the efficiency of magic wands probably came from an early faith in such implements as had been warranted to have magic virtues as weapons, or to aid a pedestrian in walking. Hence it happened that swords which had been enchanted, or which had taken lives, were supposed to have some indwelling intelligence. Hence also the names given to swords, and indeed to all weapons, by the Norsemen. It was believed that the sword of an executioner, after it had beheaded a certain number of men, pined for more victims, and manifested its desire by unearthly rattling or ringing. *Apropos* of which I have in my possession such a gruesome implement, which if experience in death could give it life, or make it ring in the silent watches of the night, would be a ghastly, noisy guest indeed. I once told the story in "***The Gypsies***" (Boston; 1881)—now I have something to add to it. I had met in London with an Indian gypsy named NANO, who informed me that in India he had belonged to a wandering tribe or race who called themselves Rom, or Romani, who spoke Romani *jib*, and who were the Gypsies of the Gypsies. I have in my possession a strange Hindu knife with an enormously broad blade, six inches across towards the end, with a long handle richly mounted in bronze with a little silver. I never could ascertain till I knew NANO what it had been used for. Even the old king of Oude, when he examined it, went wrong and was uncertain. Not so the gypsy. When he was in my library, and his keen black eyes rested on it, he studied it for a moment, and then said: "I know well enough that knife. I have seen it before; it is very old, and it was long in use—it was the knife used by the public executioner in Bhotan. It is Bhotanî."

NANO had volunteered the explanation, and whatever his moral character might be, he was not given to romantic invention. Time passed, I went to America, stayed there four years, and returned. In 1888 I became a member of the National Association for the Advancement of Art, and was on the Central Committee. One day we had a meeting at the house of a distinguished architect. When it was over, my host showed me his many treasures of art or archæology. While examining these, my attention was attracted by an Indian knife. It was precisely like mine, but smaller. I asked what it was, and learned that it had long been used in some place in the East for the express purpose of sacrificing young girls. And in all respects It was what we might call the feminine counterpart of my knife. And if I ever had any lingering doubt as to the accuracy of NANO's account, it disappeared when I saw the one whose history was perfectly authentic. A few years ago in Heidelburg there were sold at auction a great number of executioners' swords, some of which had been used for centuries. A gentleman who had a special fondness for this kind of *bric-à-brac*, had for many years collected them.

It may be here observed that the *knife* forms a special feature in all witch-lore, and occurs frequently among the Hungarian and Italian gypsy charms, or spells. It is sometimes stuck into a table, while a spell is muttered, protesting that it is not the *wood* which one wishes to hurt; but the heart of an enemy. Here the knife is supposed in reality to have an indwelling spirit which will pass to the heart or health of the one hated. In Tam O'Shanter there is a knife on the witches' table, and in Transylvania, as in Tuscany, a new knife, not an old one, is used in divers ceremonies. Sometimes an old and curious knife becomes an amulet and is supposed to bring luck, although the current belief is that any pointed gift causes a quarrel.

But to return to the fetish or pocket-deity which is worn in so many forms, be they written scrolls, crosses, medals or relics—*cést tout un*. Continental gypsies are notable believers in amulets. Being in a camp of very wild Cigany in Hungary a few years ago, I asked them what they wore for *bakt*, or luck; whereupon they all produced small seashells, which I was assured were potent against ordinary misfortunes. But for a babe which was really ill they had provided an "appreciable" dose in the form of three Maria Theresa silver dollars, which were hung round its neck, but hidden under its clothes. And I may here remark that all through many lands, even into the heart of

Africa, this particular dollar is held in high esteem for magical purposes. From one to another the notion has been transferred, and travellers and traders are often puzzled to know why the savages will have no coin save this. From Russia to the Cape it is the same story, and one to be specially studied by those ethnologists who do not believe in transmission, and hold that myths and legends are of local growth and accounted for by similar local conditions.

The gypsies were very desirous to know what my charm was. Fortunately I had in my pocket a very fine fossil shark's tooth which I had purchased in Whitby, and this was greatly admired by the learned of the tribe. Mindful of good example, I obtained for myself specimens of the mystic shells, foreseeing that they would answer as passes and signs among the fraternity in Germany and elsewhere. Which, indeed, came to pass a few days ago in the town of Homburg, when looking from my window in the Schwedenpfad I saw two very honest-looking gypsies go by. Walking forth, I joined them, and led them into a garden, where over beer and cigars we discussed "the affairs of Egypt." These Romanys were from the Tyrol, and had the frank bold manner of the mountain-men blended with the natural politeness of the better class of gypsy. I had taken with me in my pocket, foreseeing its use, a small bag or purse, containing an assortment of objects such as would have puzzled anybody except a Red Indian, a negro, or any believer in *medaolin* or Voodoo, or my new acquaintance; and after a conversation on *dúrkepen* (in Anglo-gypsy, *dukkerin*) or fortune-telling, I asked the men what they wore. They wished to see my amulets first. So I produced the shells; which were at once recognized and greatly admired, especially one, which is something of a curiosity, since in its natural markings is the word NAV very plainly inscribed: *Nav*, in gypsy, meaning "the name." The elder gypsy said he had no charm; he had long been seeking a good one, but had not as yet met with the correct article. And then he begged me-gracious powers, how he *did* beg!—to bestow on him one of my shells. I resolved to do so--but at another time.

The younger gypsy, who was a *pasche-paskero*, a musician, and had with him a rare old violin in a wonderfully carved wooden case at least two centuries old, was "all right" on the fetish question. He had his shell, sewn up in a black leather bag, which he wore by a cord round his neck. Then I exhibited my small museum. Every object in it was carefully and seriously examined. My shark's tooth was declared to be a very good fetish, a black pebble almost equal to the shell, and an American Indian arrow-head of quartz passed muster as of possible though somewhat doubtful virtue. But an English sixpence with a hole in it was rejected as a very petty and contemptible object. I offered it in vain as a present to my friends: they would not accept it. Neither did they want money: my dross might perish with me. It was the shell--the precious beautiful little shell on which the Romany in search of a fetish had set his heart; the shell which would bring him luck, and cause him to be envied, and ensure him admiration in the tents of the wanderers from Paris to Constantinople. He admitted that it was the very shell of shells--*a baro seréskeri sharkûni*, or famous sea-snail. I believe the gypsies would have given me their fine old Stainer violin and the carved case for it. Failing to get the shell, he implored me to give him the black pebble. I resolved to give him both in free gift the next time we met, or as a parting souvenir. Alas for the Romany chal!—we never met again. The police allow no gypsies in Homburg, and so they had to move on. I sought them that night and I sought them next day; but they were over the hills and far away. But I have no doubt that the fame of the shell on which Nature has written the Name--the very *logos* of magic itself—spread ere the summer was past even to the Carpathians. Something tells me that it is not played out yet, and that I shall hear anon something regarding it.

The cult of the shell is widely spread. One day in a public-house, in the West End of London, I, while taking my glass of bitter, entered into conversation with a rather tall, decently-attired brunette Alsatian girl, who spoke French and German, and who knew a few words of Romany, which she said she had picked up by, at least she professed not to be gypsy, and to know no more. Being minded to test the truth of this, I casually exhibited one of my shells and said it was a Hungarian gypsy amulet for *la bonne fortune*. She began to beg earnestly for it, without getting it. On several occasions at long intervals, when I met her in the street, she again implored me for the treasure, saying that she believed "if she had it, her luck would turn to good." And, being convinced of her gypsyism, I said, "It will do you no good unless you have *faith*." To which she replied, in a tone which indicated truth itself: "But I *have* faith--absolute, entire faith in it." Which seeing, and finding that she was a true convert to the power of the holy shell, I gave it to her with my blessing, knowing that it would be a joy and comfort to her in all the trial, of life.

This reminds me that I have seen, and indeed possess, a pearl-shell bearing the image of Saint Francis of Assisi, such as is sold by thousands at his shrine, and which are supposed to possess certain miraculous innate or intrinsic virtues. Thus, if worn by children, they are a cure for croup. Ah—but *that* is a *very* different thing, you know."

An idol is an object, generally an image, worshipped for its *own* sake, being supposed to not only represent a god, but to have some immanent sanctity. The Catholic priest, and for that matter all Brahmins or bonzes, assure us that *their* sacred images are "only symbols, not regarded as really dwelling-places of divinity." They are not, so to speak, magnified amulets. Yet how is it that, if this he true, so many images and pictures are regarded and represented by priests as being able *of themselves* by the touch to cure tooth-ache, and all other ills which flesh and bones are heirs to. Why is *one* image especially good for tooth-ache, while *another* of the same person cures cramp? Why, if they are all only "symbols," is one more healing or holy than another? How can our Lady of Embrun be of greater aid than our Lady of Paris? The instant we ascribe to an image or a shell real power to act, we make of it an inspired being in itself, and all the sophistry in the world as to its being a means of faith, or a symbol, or causing a higher power to act on the suppliant, is rubbish. The devotee believes *tout bonnement* that the *image* works the cure, and if he did not, any other image of the Virgin or Saint would answer the same purpose. This chaff has been thrashed out a thousand times, or many tens of thousand times in vain, as vain so far as effects go as is the remarkably plain First Commandment. And it will last, while one fetish endures, that the hierophant will call it a mere "symbol," and the ignorant worshipper, absolutely unable to comprehend him, *will* worship the symbol as the thing itself—as he is really expected to do.

According to J. B. FRIEDRICH, "***Symbolik der Natur***," the seashell, on account of its being a product of the sea, or of the all-generating moisture; and much more probably from its shape, is an emblem of woman herself. Therefore as 'Venus, Love's goddess, was born of the sea," shells are dedicated to her. ("***Museo Bourbonico***," Vol. vi. p. 10. KUGLER, "***Handbuch Geschichte der Malerei***," Berlin, 1837, Vol. iv. p. 311. Also translated by Sir H. AUSTIN LAYARD). Being one of the great emblems of productive Nature, or of life and light, and opposed to barrenness, absence of pleasure, darkness, or negation, it was of course a charm against witchcraft or evil. That the gypsies have retained it as a powerful agent for "luck," is extremely interesting, showing to what a degree they are still influenced by the early symbolism which effectively formed not one but many mythologies. Among the Hungarian gypsies the virtue or magical power of a shell is in proportion to the degree of resemblance above mentioned, which it possesses, as Wlislocki expressly declares.

This association of shells, with the mysterious and magical, is to be found among gypsies in the East, as is shown by the following: from my work entitled "The Gypsies." It describes something which I saw many times in Cairo—

"Beyond the door which, when opened, gave this sight, was a dark, ancient archway, twenty yards long, which opened on the glaring, dusty street, where camels with their drivers, and screaming *saïs* or carriage-runners and donkey-boys and crying venders kept up the wonted Oriental din. But in the archway, in its duskiest corner, there sat in silence and immovable, a living picture-a dark, handsome woman, of thirty years, who was unveiled. She had before her on the gateway floor, a square of cloth and a few shells. Sometimes an Egyptian of the lower class stopped, and there would be a grave consultation. She was a fortune-teller, and from the positions which the shells assumed when thrown she predicted what would come to pass. And then there would be a solemn conference and a thoughtful stroking of the beard, if the applicant was a man, and then the usual payment to the oracle, and a departure. And it was all world-old primæval Egyptian, as it was Chaldæan, for the woman was a Rhagarin, or gypsy, and as she sat so sat the diviners of ancient days by the wayside, casting shells for auspices, even as arrows were cast of old, to be cursed by Israel.

"It is not remarkable that among the myriad *manteias* of olden days there should have been one by shells. The sound of the sea when heard in a nautilus or conch is marvellously—like that of ocean surges murmuring far."

> "Shake me and it awakens--then apply
> Its polished lips to your attentive ear,
> And it remembers its august abodes
> And murmurs as the ocean murmurs there."

All of this is very strange to children and not less so to all unsophisticated folk, and I can remember how in boyhood I was told and listened with perfect faith to the distant roaring, and marvelled at the mystery of the ocean song being thus for ever kept alive inland. The next step to this is to hear in the sea-murmuring something like voices, and this is as curious as it is true—that if the mind be earnestly given to it, and the process be continued for a long time during several days, many persons, and probably all in time, will come to distinguish or hear human utterances and eventually words. There is no special faith required here; the mind even of the most sceptical or unimaginative will often turn back on itself, and by dint of mere perseverance produce such effects. An old pitcher or jug of a peculiar shape is also declared to be admirably adapted for this purpose, and I have one of Elizabeth's time which was trawled up from the sea near Lowestoft which would fulfil every requisition.

In 1886 I was by moonlight in a camp of gypsies in the old Roman amphitheatre near Budapest. It was a very picturesque sight, what with the blazing fire, the strangely-dressed men, the wild shrieking, singing, and dancing women. And when, as I have before mentioned, they showed me the shells which they carried for amulets, they exhibited one much larger o conch-like form, the tip of which had been removed and to which there was attached a flexible tube. This was used in a very remarkable trick. The shell, or one like it, is put into the hands of the person consulting the oracle, who is directed to listen to the voice of the Nivashi, or spirit of the air. Then he is blindfolded, the tube applied, and through it the gypsy speaks in a trained soft voice. Thus, in *conchomanteia*, the oracles still live and devotees still hear the fairies talk.

Now, be it observed that hearing is the most deceptive of the senses, as the reader may have seen exemplified by a lecturer, when the audience were persuaded that he was fiddling on one cane with another, or blowing a flute tune on one, when the music was made by a confederate behind a screen. I myself, a few days since, when in the Köppern Thal, verily believed I heard the murmur and music of children's voices, when lo! it proved to be the babbling brook. Some years ago, I forget where it happened in England, but I guarantee the truth of what I tell--it was found that the children in a certain village were in the habit of going to an ancient tomb in which there was a round hole, putting their ears to it, and, as they said, of listening to what the dead people were saying. It is facile enough to understand that among them there would be some whose unconscious creative faculty would lead them to literally hearing words or songs. There is another ancient and beautiful mystical association with shells. The conch when pierced formed a trumpet, whose notes seemed to be allied to the murmuring of the wind and waves heard in the shell when applied to the ear. The sea-god Triton blew upon a shell, "meaning thereby the roaring of the waves." "And in analogous wise a shell is represented on the Tower of the Winds in Athens, to represent Boreas, the north-east wind, and the roaring of the storm"

(MILLIN, "***Gallerie Mythologique***"). The resemblance of wind to the human voice has probably occurred to every human being, and has furnished similes for every poet. That these voices should be those of spirits is a natural following. So the last Hebrew oracle, the Bath Kol, or Daughter of the Voice, survives in shells and lives in gypsy-lore. And so we find in rags and patches on the garments of Egyptian fellahin the edges of Pharaoh's garment, which in olden time it was an honour for kings to kiss.

Deception of this kind by means of voices, apparently supernatural, is of great antiquity. The high priest Savan the Asmunian, of Egypt, is said to have used acoustic tubes for this purpose, and it is very evident that the long corridors or passages in the stone temples must have suggested it as well as whispering galleries. The Hebrew Cabalists are believed to have made one form of the mysterious Teraphim by taking the head of a child and so preparing it by magic ceremonies that when interrogated it would reply. These ceremonies consisted in fact of skilfully adjusting a phonetic tube to the head. It is very probable that the widely-spread report of this oracle gave rise to the belief that the Jews slaughtered and sacrificed children. "Eliphaz Levi," or the Abbé Constant, a writer of no weight whatever as an authority, but not devoid of erudition, and with occasional shrewd insights, gives it as his belief that the terrible murders of hundreds of children by Gilles de Retz—the absurdly so-called original of Blue-beard--were suggested by a recipe for sanguinary sorcery, drawn from some Hebrew Cabalistical book. ***Nicephorus*** (Lib. 7 c. 33) and **Cedrenus**, as cited by Grosius in his "**Magica**" (1597), tell us that when Constantine was ill a number of children were collected to be slain that the emperor might bathe in their blood (*in quo si se Imperator ablueret, certo recuperaret*), and that because he was moved by the tears of their mothers to spare their lives, was restored to health by the saints. It seems to have escaped the attention of writers that at the very time during the Middle Ages when the Jews were being most bitterly persecuted for offering children at the Passover, it was really a common thing among Christians to sacrifice children, maids, or grown-up people, by burying them alive under the foundations of castles, &c., to insure their stability--a ghastly sacrifice, which in after-times took the form of walling-up a cock and finally an egg. But from an impartial and common-sense standpoint: there could be no difference between the sacrifice of a child by a Cabalist and the torturing and burning witches and heretics by ecclesiastics, unless, indeed, that the latter was the wickeder of the two, since the babes were simply promptly killed, while the Inquisitors put their victims to death with every refinement of mental and physical torture. Both Cabalist and priest were simply engaged in different forms of one and the same fetish-work which had been handed down from the days of witchcraft. Nor did Calvin, when he burnt Servetus, differ in anything from a Voodoo sacrificing "a goat without horns."

Punishing a heretic to please or placate the Deity differs in nothing from killing any victim to get luck. Other sentiments may be mingled with this "conjuring," but the true foundation of black witchcraft (and all witchcraft is black which calls for blood, suffering, starvation, and the sacrifice of natural instincts), is the mortar of the fear of punishment, and the stones of the hope of reward, the bulk of the latter being immeasurably greater than that of the former, which is a mere *Bindemittel*, or means of connection.

It is remarkable that nowhere, not even in England, do the gypsies regard the witch as utterly horrible, diabolical, and damnable. She is with them simply a woman who has gained supernatural power, which she uses for good or misuses for evil according to her disposition. The witch of the Church—Catholic or Protestant—when closely examined is a very childish conception. She sets forth personal annoyance without any regard whatever as to whether it is really good in disguise or a natural result of our own follies. Thus witches caused thunderstorms, which, because they were terrifying and more or less destructive, were seriously treated by the Church as unmitigated evils, therefore as phenomena directly due to the devil and his servants. Theology the omniscient did not know that storms cleared the air. Witches were responsible for all pestilences, and very often for all disorders of any kind--as it was very convenient for the ignorant leech to attribute to sorcery or moral delinquency or to God a disease which he could not cure. For "***Theology, the science of sciences***," had not as yet ascertained that plagues and black deaths, and most of the ills of man are the results of neglect of cleanliness, temperance, and other sanitary laws. It is only a few years since a very eminent clergyman and president of a college in America attributed to "Divine dispensation" the deaths of a number of students, which were directly due to palpable neglect of proper sanitary arrangements by the reverend gentleman himself, and his colleagues. But, admitting the "divine dispensation," according to the mediæval theory, the president, as the agent, must have been a "wizard"—or conjuror—a delusion which the most superficial examination of his works would at once dissipate. But to return—there can be no denial whatever that according to what is admitted to be absolutely true to-day by everybody, be he orthodox or liberal, witches, had they existed, must have been agents of God, busied in preventing plagues instead of causing them--by raising storms which cleared the air. Even the Algonkin Indians knew more than the Church in this respect, for they have a strange old legend to the effect that when the god of Storms, *Wuch-ow-sen*, the giant eagle, was hindered by a magician from his accustomed work, the sea and air grew stagnant, and people died. The witch was simply another form of the Hebrew Azrael, God's Angel of Death.

Which may all lead to the question: If a belief in witches as utterly evil servants of the devil could be held as an immutable dogma of the Church and a matter of eternal truth for eternal belief-to prove which there is no end of ingenious argument and an appalling array of ecclesiastical authority cited in the black-letter "***Liber de Sortilegiis***" Of PAULUS GRILLANDUS, now lying before me (Lyons, 1547), as well as in the works of SPRENGER, BODINUS, DELRIO, and the Witch-bull of Pope Innocent—and if this belief be now exploded even among the priests, what proof have we that any of the dogmas which went with it are *absolutely* and for ever true? This is the question of *dogmatik*, *versus* development or evolution, and witchcraft is its greatest solvent. For when people believe, or make believe, in a thing so very much as to torture like devils and put to death hundreds of thousands of fellow-beings, mostly helpless and poor old women, not to mention many children, it becomes a matter of very serious import to all humanity to determine once for all whether the system or code according to which this was done was absolutely *right for ever*, or not. For if it was true, these executions and the old theory of witchcraft were all *quite* right, as the Roman Church still declares, since the Pope has sanctioned of late years several very entertaining works in which modern spiritualists, banjo-twangers, table-turners, &c., are declared to be really wizards, who perform their stupendous and appalling miracles directly by the aid of devils. And, by the way, somebody might make an interesting work not only on the works in the *Index Librum Prohibitorum*, which it entails seventy-six distinct kinds of damnation to read, but also on those which the Pope *sanctions*—I believe, blesses. Among the later of the latter is one which pretends to prove that Jews do really still continue to sacrifice Christian children at the Passover feast--and, for aught I know, to eat them, fried in oil, or "buttered with goose-grease"—apropos of which, I marvel that the Hebrews, instead of tamely denying it, do not boldly retort on the Christians the charge of torturing their own women and children to death as witches, which was a thousand times wickeder than simply bleeding them with a pen-knife, as young Hugh of Lincoln was said to have been disposed of by the Jew's daughter.

But people all say now--that was the *age*, and the Church was still under the influence of barbarism, and so on. Exactly; but that admission plainly knocks down and utterly destroys the whole platform of dogmatism and the immutable and eternal truth of any dogma whatever, for it admits evolution--and to seize on its temporary fleeting forms and proclaim that they are immutable, is to mistake the temporal for the eternal, the infinitesimal fraction for the whole. This is not worshipping GOD, the illimitable, unknown tremendous Source of Life, but His minor temporary forms, "essences," or "angels," as the Cabalists termed the successive off-castings of His manifestations.

> In Being's flood, in action's storm,
> I work and weave--above, beneath,
> Work and weave in endless motion
> The fire of the living.
> 'Tis thus at the roaring loom of Time I ply
> And weave for God the garment thou seest Him by.

Now there are infinite numbers of these garments, but none of them are GOD, though the Church declared that what they had of them were truly Divine. So Oriental princes sent their old clothes to distant provinces to be worshipped, as GESSLER sent his hat: it is an old, old story, and one which will be long repeated in many lands.

I have, not far back, mentioned a work on witchcraft by PAULUS GRILLANDUS. Its full title is "Tractatus de Hereticis et sortilegiis, omnifariam Coitio eorumque penis. Item de Questionibus et Tortura ac de Relaxatione Carceratorum"--that is, in brief, a work on Heretics, Witches breakers of the Seventh Commandment of all kinds, Examination by Torture, and Imprisonment. It was a leading *vade mecum*, or standard guide, in its time for lawyers and the clergy, especially the latter, and reads as if it had come from the library of hell, and been written by a devil, though composed, according to the preface, to promote the dignity and glory of the Christian Church. I can well believe that a sensitive humane person could be really maddened by a perusal and full comprehension of all the diabolical horrors which this book reveals, and the glimpses which it gives of what must have been endured literally by millions of heretics and "witches," and all men or women merely *accused* by anybody of any kind of "immorality," especially of "heresy." I say suspected or accused--for either was sufficient to subject a victim to horrible agonies until he or she confessed. What is most revolting is the calm, icy-cold-blooded manner in which the most awful, infernal cruelties are carefully discussed—as, for instance, if one has already had any limbs amputated for punishment whether further tortures may then be inflicted? It is absolutely a relief to find that among the six kinds of persons legally exempted from the rack, &c.—there are *only six* and these do not include invalids—are pregnant women. But such touches of common humanity are rare indeed in it. I do not exaggerate in the least when I say that the whole spirit of this work—which faithfully reflects the whole spirit of the "justice" of the Middle Ages--inclines in a ferocious, wolfish manner to *extend* and multiply punishment of the most horrible kinds to every small offence against the Church—to manufacture and increase crime as if it were capital for business, and enlarge the sphere of torture so as to create power and awe.

Nous avons changé tout cela, say the descendants of those fiends in human form. But if it was wrong *then* why did you do it if you were *infallible* inspired judges? And if you now believe that to be *atrocious* which was once holy, and a vast portion of your whole system, how can you say that the Church does not follow the laws of evolution and progress--and if so, where will it stop? It is a curious reflection that if the Pope and Cardinals of 1890 had lived four hundred years ago they would (with the exception, perhaps, of the Spaniards) have all been burned alive for heresy. Which is literally true.

Within a minute's walk from where I sit and indeed visible from my window in this town of Homburg vor der Höhe, are two round towers of other days--grim and picturesque relics of the early Middle Ages. One is called the *Hexenthurm* or Witches' Tower. In it gypsies, witches, and heretics were confined—it was the hotel specially reserved for them when they visited Homburg, and in its cells which are of the smallest between walls of the thickest, I or you, reader, Might be confined to-day, but for one MARTIN LUTHER and certain laws of evolution or progress of which Paulus Grillandus did not dream.

As I was sketching the tower, an old woman told me that there were many strange tales about it. That I can well believe but I dare say they are all summed up in the following ballad from the German of HEINE

"THE WITCH"

"FOLKS said when my granny Eliza bewitched,
She must die for her horrid transgression;
Much ink from his pen the old magistrate pitched,
But he could not extort a confession.

And when in the kettle my granny was thrown
She yelled 'Death' and 'Murder!' while dying.
And when the black smoke all around us was blown.
As a raven she rose and went flying.

Little black grandmother, feathered so well,
Oh, come to the tower where I'm sitting
Bring cakes and bring cheese to me here in the cell,
Through the iron-barred window flitting.

Little black grandmother, feathered and wise,
Just give my aunt a warning,
Lest she should come flying and pick out my eyes
When I merrily swing in the morning."

HORST in his "***Dæmonomagie,***" a History of the Belief in Magic, Demoniac marvels, Witchcraft, &c., gives the picture of a Witch-tower, at Lindheim in the Wetterau, with all its terrible history, extracted from the town archives. It is a horrible history of torturing and burning at the stake of innumerable women of all ages, the predominant feature being that any accusation by anybody whatever, or any rumour set afloat in any way, amply sufficed to bring an enemy to death, or to rob a person who had money. Hysterical women and perverse or eccentric children frequently originated these accusations merely to bring themselves into notice.

There was till within a few years a Witches' Tower in Heidelberg. It was a very picturesque structure in an out-of-the-way part of the town, in nobody's way, and was therefore of course pulled down by the good Philistine citizens, who have the same mania in Heidelberg as "their ignorant-like" in London, Philadelphia, or any other town, for removing all relics of the olden time.

In connection with sorcery and gypsies, it is worth observing that ill 1834 the latter, in Swabia, or South Germany, frequently went about among the country-people, with puppet-shows, very much of the Punch kind, and that they had a rude drama of Faust, the great wizard, which had nothing to do with that of Goethe. It was derived from the early sources, and had been little by little gypsified into a melodrama peculiar to the performers. August Zoller, in his "***Bilder aus Schwaben***" (Stuttgard, 1834), gives the following description of it. The book has a place in all Faust libraries, and has been kept alive by this single passage:

"There is a blast of a trumpet, and the voice of a man proclaims behind the scenes that the play is to begin. The curtain is drawn, and Faust leaning against the background—which represents a city-soliloquizes!

"'I am the cleverest doctor in the world, but all my cleverness does not help me to make the beautiful princess love me, I will call up Saran front the under-world to aid me in my plans to win her. Devil--I call thee!'

"Meanwhile Faust's servant--the funny man--has entered and amused the public with comical gestures. The appearance of the devil is announced by a firework (Sprühteufel) fizzing and cracking. He descends from the air, there being no arrangements for his coming up. The servant bursts into a peal of laughter, and the devil asks:

"'Faust thou hast called me; now, what is thy wish?'

"'I love the lovely princess—canst thou make her love me?'

"'Nothing is easier. Cut thy finger and sign to me thy life; then all my devilish art will be at thy service till thou hast committed four murders.'

"Faust and the devil fly forth, the servant making sarcastic remarks as to the folly of his master, and the curtain falls.

"In the second act the fair princess enters--she is three times as large as Faust, but bewails his absence in a plaintive voice and departs. Faust enters and calls for a *Furio* who shall carry him to Mantua. Enter three *Furios* (witches) who boast their power. 'I can carry you as swiftly as a moor-cock flies,' says one. This is not swift enough for Faust. 'I fly as fast as bullet from a gun,' says the second. The master answers:

"'A right good pace, but not enough for Faust.' To the third: 'How fast art *thou*?'

"'As quick as Thought.'

"'That will suffice—there's naught so swift as Thought. Bear me to Mantua, to her I love, the princess of my heart!'

"The Furio takes Faust on her back, and they fly through the air. The servant makes, as before, critical and sarcastic remarks on what has passed, and the curtain falls.

"In the third act the devil persuades Faust to murder his father, so as to inherit his treasures, 'for the old man has a tough life.' In the fourth, maddened by jealousy, he stabs the Princess and her supposed lover. The small sarcastic servant takes the murdered pair by the legs, and drags them about, cracking jokes, and giving the corpses cuff's on their ears to bring them again to life.

"In the fifth act, the clock strikes eleven. Faust has now filled to the brim the measure of his iniquity. The devil appears, proves to him that it is time to depart; it strikes twelve; the smoke of a fizzling squib and several diabolical fire-crackers fills the air, and Faust is carried away, while the small servant, as satanical and self-possessed as ever, makes his jokes on the folly of Faust—and the curtain falls."

This is the true Faust drama of the Middle Ages, with the ante-Shakespearian blending of tragedy and ribald fun. But this same mixture is found to perfection in the early Indian drama--for instance, in "Sakuntala"—and it would be indeed a very curious thing should it be discovered that the gypsies, who were in all ages small actors and showmen of small plays, had brought from the East some rude drama of a sorcerer, who is in the end cheated by his fiend. Such is, in a measure, the plot of the *Baital Pachisi* or *Vikram and the Vampire*, which is borrowed from or founded on old traditions, and the gypsies, from their familiarity with magic, and as practical actors, would, in all probability, have a Faust play of some kind, according to the laws of cause and effect. In any case the suggestion may be of value to some investigator.

Gypsies in England—that is those "of the old sort"—regard a shoestring as a kind of amulet or protection. Many think it is unlucky to have one's taken but no harm can come of it if the one who receives the picture gives the subject a shoe-string or a pair of laces.

Dr. F. S. KRAUSS in his curious work, "***Sreća, or Fortune and Fate in the popular belief of the South Slavonians***" (Vienna, 1886), draws a line of distinction between the fetish and amulet. "The fetish," he declares, "has virtue from being the dwelling of a protecting spirit. The amulet, however, is only a symbol of a higher power," that is of a power whose attention is drawn by or through it to the believer or wearer. This, however, like the distinction between idolatry and worshipping images as symbols of higher beings, becomes in the minds of the multitude (and for that matter, in all minds), a distinction without a dot of difference. The amulet may "rest upon a higher range of ideas, while the fetish stands on its own feet," but if both are regarded as *bringing luck*, and if, for instance, one rosary or image of the same person is believed to bring more luck than another, it is a fetish and nothing else. An amulet may pretend to be a genteeler kind of fetish, but they are all of the same family.

The gypsies prepare among the Bosniacs, "on the high plains of Malwan," a fetish in the form of a cradle made of nine kinds of wood, to bring luck to the child who sleeps in it. But Dr. KRAUSS falls, I presume, into a very great error, when he attributes to her Majesty the Queen of England a belief in fetish, on the strength of the following remarkable pas sage from the *Wiener Allgemeine Zeitung*:

"By command of Queen VICTORIA, Mr. MARTIN, Director of the Institute for the Blind, has attended to the making a cradle for the newly-born child of the Princess of Battenberg. The cradle is to be made entirely by blind men and women. The Queen firmly believes that objects made by blind people bring luck."

Truly, if anything could bring luck it ought to be something ordered with a kind and charitable view from poor and suffering people, but it is rather hard to promptly conclude that her Majesty believes in fetish because she benevolently ordered a cradle from the blind, and that she had no higher motive than to get something which would bring luck to her grandchild.

It may be observed in connection with this superstition that among the Hungarian gypsies several spells depend on using different kinds of wood, and that four are said to have been taken for the true cross.

Gypsies, in common with the rest of the "fetishioners" of all the world, believe in the virtue of a child's caul. Dr. KRAUSS found in Kobaš on the Save an amulet which contained such a caul with garlic and four-leaved clover. This must have been a very strong charm indeed, particularly if the garlic was fresh.

Another very great magic protector in every country among gypsies as well as Gentiles, is the thunderbolt, known in Germany as the *Donneraxt*, *Donnerstein*, *Donnerkeil*, *Albschoss*, *Strahlstein*, and *Teufelsfinger*. It was called by the Greeks *Astropelákia*, by the Latins *Gemma ceraunia*, by the Spaniards *Piedras de rayo*, by the dwellers in the French High Alps *Peyras del tron* (*pierres de tonerre*), by the Birmans *Mogio* (the child of lightning), by the Chinese *Ra-fu-seki* (the battle-axe of Tengu, the guardian of Heaven), by the Hindoos *Swayamphu*, or "the self-originated." Dr. KRAUSS, from whom I have taken these remarks, adds that in America and Australia it is also regarded as a charm protective and luck-bringing. But here there is a confusion of objects. The thunderbolt described by Dr. KRAUSS is, I believe, a petrified shell, a kind of *mucro* or belemnite. The thunderbolt of the Red Indians really resembles it, but is entirely different in its nature. The latter results from lightning entering the sand fusing it. It sometimes makes in this way a very long tube or rod, with a point. People, finding these, naturally believed that they were thunderbolts. I knew an old Penobscot Indian who, seeing the lightning strike the earth, searched and found such a thunderbolt, which he greatly prized. In process of time people who found *mucrones* in rocks believed them to be the same as the glass-like points of fused sand which they so much resembled.

The so-called thunderbolt is confused with the prehistoric stone axe, both bearing the same name in many lands. As this axe is often also a hammer it is evident that it may have been sacred to Thor. "The South Slavonian"—or gypsy—"does not distinguish," says Dr. KRAUSS, "between the thunderbolt and prehistoric axe. He calls both *strelica*. The possession of one brings luck and prosperity in all business, but it must be constantly carried on the person. Among the "thirties" there lived in Gaj in Slavonia a poor Jewish peddler named DAVID. Once he found a *strelica*. He always carried it about with him. The peasants envied him greatly its possession. They came to him in the market place and cried, "*Al si sretan, Davide*!" ("Ha, how lucky thou art, David!") The Slavonian Jews called him, for a joke, "*Strelica*."

The prehistoric axe was probably regarded as gifted with fetish power, even in the earliest age, especially when it was made of certain rare materials. Thus among the Red Indians of Massachusetts stone "tomahawks" of veined, petrified wood were specially consecrated to burial-places, while in Europe axe-heads of jade were the most coveted of possessions. A. B. MEYER has written a large work, "***Jade und Nephrit Objecte aus dem Ethriographische Museum zu Dresden, America und Europe***" (Leipzig, 1882). It has always been supposed that the objects of true jade came only from Tartary, and I believe that I was the first person to discover that it existed in quantities in Western Europe. The history of this "finding" is not without interest.

It has been usual—it is said for a thousand years—for pilgrims to Iona to bring away with them as souvenirs a few green pebbles of a peculiar kind, and to this day, as every tourist will remember, the children who come to the steamboat offer handsful of them for sale. When I was there many years ago, in Iona, I also went away with perhaps twenty of them. One evening, after returning to London, there were at my home three Chinese gentlemen attached to the Legation. The conversation turned on Buddhist pilgrimages and Fusang, and the question, founded on passages in the Chinese annals, as to whether certain monks had really passed from the Celestial Kingdom to Mexico in the fifth century and returned. This reminded me of Iona, and I produced my green pebbles, and told what I knew about them.

My visitors regarded the stones with great interest and held an animated conversation over them in Chinese, which I did not understand. Observing this I made them presents of the pebbles, and was thanked with an earnestness which seemed to me to be out of all proportion to the value of the gifts. Thinking this over the next day, I wrote to the clergyman at Iona asking him to be so kind as to send me some of the pebbles, and offering to pay for them. He did so, sending me by mail a box of the stones. Two or three were very pretty, one especially. It is of a dark green colour and slightly transparent.

Two years after, when in Philadelphia, meeting with an old friend, Dr. JOSEPH LEIDY, well known as a man of science, and, *inter alia*, as a mineralogist. I showed him my pebble and asked him what it was. He replied, "It is jade." To my query whether it might not be nephrite he answered no, that it was true jade of fine quality.

Jade is in China a talismanic stone, many occult virtues and luck-bringing qualities being ascribed to it. It is very curious, and possibly something more than a mere chance coincidence, that the green pebbles of Iona were also carried as charms. It would be remarkable if even in prehistoric times, or in the stone age, Iona and Tartary had been connected by superstition and tradition.

Among the gypsies as well as Christians in Servia, *nuts*, especially those which are heart-shaped (*i.e.*, double), are carried as fetishes or amulets. In very early times a nut, as containing like a seed the principle of germination and self-reproduction, was typical of life. Being enclosed in a shell it seemed to be in a casket or box which was of itself a mystical symbol. Hence nuts are often found in ancient graves. There are many stories accordingly in all countries in which a nut or egg is represented as being connected with the life of some particular being or person. The ogre in several tales can live until a certain egg is broken. In the Graubunden or Grisons there is the following legend:

"Once there lived near *Fideriseau* a rich peasant. To him came a poor beggar, who asked for alms in vain. Then the man replied, 'If thou wilt give me nothing yet will I give thee something. Thou shalt keep thy treasure and also thy daughter after thee; yea, and for years after she is dead her spirit shall know no rest for taking care of it. But I give thee this nut. Plant it by yonder great stone, thou stony-hearted fool. From the nut will grow a tree, and from the tree twigs from which a cradle will be made in which a child will be rocked who will redeem thy daughter from her penance.' And after the girl died, a spirit of a pale woman with dark hair was seen flying nightly near Fideris, and that for many years, for it takes a long time for an acorn to grow up into an oak. But as she is no longer seen it is believed that the cradle has been made and the child born who became the deliverer."

A. B. Elysseeff, in his very interesting article based on Kounavine's "***Materials for the Study of the Gypsies***," gives the representation of four gypsy amulets, also "a cabalistic token" that brings good luck to its wearer.

"The amulets," writes M. Elysseeff, "are made of wrought iron and belong to M. Kounavine. The cabalistic sign is designed" (copied?) "by ourselves, thanks to the amiability of a gypsy *djecmas* (sorcerer) of the province of Novogorod. The amulet A was found by M. Kounavine among the gypsies who roam with their camps in the Ural neighbourhood; some Bessarabian gypsies supplied B; C was obtained from a gypsy sorcerer of the Persian frontier, and D formed a part of some ornaments placed with their dead by gypsies of Southern Russia.

"The cabalistic sign" (*vide* illustration at head of chapter) "represents roughly a serpent, the symbol of Auromori, the evil principle in gypsy mythology. The figure of an arch surrounded with stars is, according to M. Kounavine, held by the gypsies as symbolizing the earth, the meaning of the triangle A is not known. The moon and stars which surround the earth and which are, so to speak, enclosed in the serpent's coils, symbolize the world lying in evil. This sign is engraved by gypsies upon the plates of the harness of the horses, of garments, and as designed ornaments."

It may be here remarked that the symbolism of M. Kounavine, while it may be quite accurate, must be taken with great reserve. If the "arch" he simply a horse-shoe, all these ornaments, except the serpent, may be commonly found on the trappings of London dray-horses.

"Amulet A, which also represents the sun, the moon, the stars, earth, and a serpent, can equally serve as a symbol of the universe. According to M. Kounavine, Ononi" (the Ammon of the Egyptians) "and Auromori, are symbolized upon this amulet. Amulet B represents a man surrounded by a halo, aided by the moon and the stars, and armed with a sword and arrows. Beneath is represented the horse; the serpent symbolizes Auromori. As a whole this amulet represents the conflict between the good and evil principle, Jandra (Indra) against Auromori.

"Amulet C represents a gleaming star and the serpent, and is called Baramy (Brama), symbolizing, according to M. Kounavine, the gypsy proto-divinity.

"Or amulet D, which represents a flaming pyre and some hieroglyphics, may also symbolize the prayer addressed to the divinity of the fire."

If these explanations were given by gypsy sorcerers the amulets are indeed very curious. But, abstractly, the serpent, arrows, stars, the moon, an archer, a fox, and a plant, occur, all the world over., on coins or in popular art, with or without symbolism, and I confess that I should have expected something very different as illustrating such a remarkable mythology as that given by M. Kounavine. However, the art of a nation—as, for instance, that of the Algonkin, Indians—may be very far indeed behind its myths and mental conceptions.

See the "***Algonkin Legends of New England***," by Charles G. Leland.

CHAPTER XVI

Gypsies, Toads And Toad-Lore

"I went to the toad that lies under the wall,
I charmed him out, and he came at my call."
Masque, of Queens," BEN JONSON.)

THE toad plays a prominent part in gypsy (as in other) witchcraft, which it may well do, since in most Romany dialects there is the same word for a toad or frog, and the devil. PASPATI declares that the toad suggested Satan, but I incline to think that there is some as yet undiscovered Aryan word, such as *beng*, for the devil, and that the German *Bengel*, a rascal, is a descendant from it. However, gypsies and toads are "near allied and that not wide" from one another, and sometimes their children have them for pets, which recals the statements made in the celebrated witch trials in Sweden, where it was said by those who professed to have been at the Blockula, or *Sabbat*, that the little witch children were set to play at being shepherds, their flocks being of toads.

I have been informed by gypsies that toads do really form unaccountable predilections for persons and places. The following is accurately related as it was told me in Romany fourteen years ago, in Epping Forest, by a girl. "You know, sir, that people who live out of doors all the time, as we do, see and know a great deal about such creatures. One day we went to a farmhouse, and found the wife almost dying because she thought she was bewitched by a woman who came every day in the form of a great toad to her door and looked in. And, sure enough, while she was talking the toad came, and the woman was taken in such a way with fright that I thought she'd have died. But I had a laugh to myself; for I knew that toads have such ways, and can not only be tamed, but will almost tame themselves. So we gypsies talked together in Romany, and then said we could remove the spell if she would get us a pair of shears and a cup of salt. Then we caught the toad, and tied the shears so as to make a cross—you see!—and with it threw the toad into the fire, and poured the salt on it. So the witchcraft was ended, and the lady gave us a good meal and ten shillings." (For a Romany poem on this incident *vide* "***English Gypsy Songs***," Trübner and Co., 1875). And there is a terrible tale told by R. H. Stoddard, in a poem, that one day a gentleman accidentally trod on a toad and killed it. Hearing a scream at that instant in the woods at a little distance, followed by an outcry, he went to see what was the matter, and found a gypsy camp where they were lamenting the sudden death of a child. On looking at the corpse he was horrified to observe that it presented every appearance of having been trampled to death, its wounds being the same as those he had inflicted on the toad. This story being told by me to the gypsy girl, she in no wise doubted its truth, being in fact greatly horrified at it; but was amazed at the child *chovihani*, or witch, being in two places at once.

In the Spanish Association of Witches in the year 1610 (*vide* Lorent, "***Histoire de l'Inquisition***") the toad played a great part. One who had taken his degrees in this Order testified that, on admission, a mark like a toad was stamped on his eyelid, and that a real toad was given to him which had the power to make its master invisible, to transport him to distant places, and change him to the form of many kinds of animals. There is a German interjection or curse "*Kroten-düvel!*" or "toad-devil," which is supposed to have originated as follows: When the Emperor Charlemagne came into the country of the East Saxons and asked them whom they worshipped they replied, "Krodo is our god;" to which the Emperor replied "Krodo is all the same as Kroten-düvel!" "And he made them pay bitterly by the sword and the rope for the crime of calling God, according to their language, by a name different from that which he used; for he put many thousands of them to death, like King Olof of Norway, to show that his faith was one of meekness and mercy."

It is bad to have one's looks against one. The personal appearance of the toad is such as to have giver it a bad place in the mythology of all races. The Algonkin Indians—who, like Napoleon and Slawkenbergius, were great admirers of men with fine bold noses—after having studied the plane physiognomy of the toad, decided that it indicated all the vices, and made of the creature the mother of all the witches. Nothing could have been more condemnatory; since in their religion—as in that of the Accadians, Laps, and Eskimo—a dark and horrible sorcery, in which witches conciliated evil spirits, was believed to have preceded their own nobler Shamanism, by which these enemies of mankind were forced or conquered by magic. Once the Great Toad had, as she thought, succeeded in organizing a conspiracy by which Glooskap, the Shamanic god of Nature, was to be destroyed. Then he passed his hand over her face and that of her fellow-conspirator the Porcupine; and from that time forth their noses were flat, to the great scorn of all honest well-beaked Indians.

The old Persians made the toad the symbol and pet of Ahriman, the foe of light, and declared that his *Charfester*, or attendant demons, took that form when they persecuted Ormuzd. Among the Tyrolese it is a type of envy; whence the proverb, "Envious as a toad." In the Middle

Ages, among artists and in many Church legends, it appears as Greed or Avarice: there is even to this day, in some mysterious place on the right bank of the Rhine between Laufenberg and Binzgau, a pile of coals on which sits a toad. That is to say, coals they seem to the world. But the pile is all pure gold, and the toad is a devil who guards it; and he who knows how can pronounce a spell which shall ban the grim guardian. And there is a story told by Menzel ("***Christliche Symbolik***," vol. i. p. 530), that long ago there lived in Cologne a wicked miser, who when old repented and wished to leave his money to the poor. But when he opened his great iron chest, he found that every coin in it had turned to a horrible toad with sharp teeth. This story being told to his confessor, the priest saw in it divine retribution, and told him that God would have none of his money--nay, that it would go hard with him to save his soul. And he, being willing to do anything to be free of sin, was locked up in the chest with the toads; and lo! the next day when it was opened the creatures had eaten him up. Only his clean-picked bones remained.

But in the Tyrol it is believed that the toads are themselves poor sinners, undergoing penance as Hoetschen or Hoppinen--as they are locally called--for deeds done in human form. Therefore, they are regarded with pity and sympathy by all good Christians. And it is well known that in the Church of Saint Michael in Schwatz, on the evening before the great festivals, but when no one is present, an immense toad comes crawling before the altar, where it kneels and prays, weeping bitterly. The general belief is that toads are for the most part people who made vows to go on pilgrimages, and died with the vows unfulfilled. So the poor creatures go hopping about astray, bewildered and perplexed, striving to find their way to shrines which have perchance long since ceased to exist. Once there was a toad who took seven years to go from Leifers to Weissenstein; and when the creature reached the church it suddenly changed to a resplendent white dove, which, flying up to heaven, vanished before the eyes of a large company there assembled, who bore witness to the miracle. And one day as a wagoner was going from Innsbruck to Seefeld, as he paused by the wayside a toad came hopping up and seemed to be desirous of getting into the wagon; which he, being a benevolent man, helped it to do, and gave it a place on the seat beside him. There it sat like any other respectable passenger, until they came to the side-path which leads to the church of Seefield; when, wonderful to relate! the toad suddenly turned to a maiden of angelic beauty clad in white, who, thanking the wagoner for his kindness to her when she was but a poor reptile, told him that she had once been a young lady who had vowed a pilgrimage to the church of Seefield.

In common with the frog, the toad is an emblem of productiveness, and ranks among creatures which are types of erotic passion. I have in my possession a necklace of rudely made silver toads, of Arab workmanship, intended to be worn by women who wish to become mothers. Therefore the creature, in the Old World as well as in the New, appears as a being earnestly seeking the companionship of men. Thus it happened to a youth of Aramsach, near Kattenberg, that, being one day in a lonely place by a lake, there looked up at him from the water a being somewhat like a maid but more like a hideous toad, with whom he entered into conversation; which became at last friendly and agreeable, for the strange creature talked exceeding well. Then she, thinking he might be hungry, asked him if he would fain have anything in particular to eat. He mentioned in jest a kind of cakes; whereupon, diving into the lake, she brought some up, which he ate. So he met her many times; and whenever he wished for anything, no matter what, she got it for him from the waters: the end of it all being that, despite her appalling ugliness, the youth fell in love with her and offered marriage, to which she joyfully consented. But no sooner had the ceremony been performed than she changed to a lady of wonderful beauty; and, taking him by the hand, she conducted him to the lake, into which she led him, and "in this life they were seen never more." This legend evidently belongs to frog-lore. According to one version, the toad after marriage goes to a lake, washes away her ugliness, and returns as a beauty with the bridegroom to his castle, where they live in perfect happiness.

I have also a very old silver ring, in which there is set a toad rudely yet artistically carved in hæmatite, or blood-stone. These were famous amulets until within two or three hundred years.

If you are a gypsy and have a tame toad it is a great assistance in telling fortunes, and brings luck—that commodity which, as CALLOT observed, the gypsies are always selling to everybody while they protest they themselves have none. As I tested with the last old gypsy woman whom I met: "*What bâk the divvus*?"—"What luck to-day?" "*Kekker rya*"—"None, sir," was the reply, as usual, "I never have any luck." So like a mirror they reflect all things save themselves, and show you what they know not.

> "I've seen you where you never were
> And where you never will be
> And yet within that very place
> You can be seen by me.
> For to tell what they do not know
> Is the art of the Romany."

SLEEP WELL.

Made in the USA
Middletown, DE
19 April 2017